ENOUGH!

A Critique of Capitalist Democracy and a Guide to Understanding the New Normal

by Jerome D. Belanger

Countryside Publications Ltd.
145 Industrial Dr.
Medford WI 54451
www.countrysidemag.com

Copyright © 2012 by

ISBN #0-9729661-4-5

D1469011

Table of Contents

Introduction

These are treacherous times. The economy is in a
shambles, government is a mess, society is adrift, and
leadership is powerless to fix any of it. Civilization is at a
crossroads; the planet itself is imperiled.

Americans are discouraged and upset because they
expected, and in many cases had already become accustomed
to, something much better: the American Dream.

What happened? What's happening now? And what's
going to happen?

The world of George Washington in 1789 was far different
from the world of John Kennedy in 1961 and that was nothing
like the world of Barrack Obama in 2009. What has changed is
everything: technology, communications, transportation,
wealth and our concept of it, society, the use and availability
of natural resources. Even the climate is changing, along with
our perceptions of all of these.

And yet, people go on living as if nothing has shifted
except their standard of living. They cling to the dreams of
Washington and Kennedy, and now that the dream has
tarnished in the "Great Recession," they await the return of
"normality."

They're waiting in vain. We live in a different world. It's
time — and past time — to wake up and check reality, which
is the New Normal.

Our producer-consumer society

Of all the changes in recent history, both dramatic and
subtle, one that stands out is how so many "wants" have
become "needs," with dire consequences. Humans have
become robots whose chief purpose is to produce and
consume in the service of the democratic capitalist System that
controls our lives. Capitalism and democracy no longer serve
the people or foster the American Dream: the people are now
in the thrall of the System.

By ignoring this simple fact, by going about our daily business and living our lives as if the American Dream were still a laudable (or even possible) goal, we imperil the future even more. Our producer-consumer mindset determines our education and careers, diets and health, recreation and housing; it controls every aspect of our lives. Our continued mindless addiction to it further numbs our higher nature, while endangering the planet.

And there is no escape until we are freed from the chains that shackle us.

There is never "enough"

The problem isn't capitalism, or the System. As we carefully deconstruct the current state of the world we find that the root of the problem is that we have too much "stuff," but not "enough" to satisfy either ourselves or the capitalist-democracy System. We cannot make wise use of more (is it enriching, or detracting from, our humanness?), the Earth cannot keep up with our constant demands for more, and yet we continue to produce and consume, calling it "progress."

Unemployment is a huge concern today. But what should these idle people make or do, if we already have too much?

No one looks at it from this angle, of course. Instead, we hear that unemployed people don't have money to buy even necessities, let alone the homes and luxury goods most of them demand (and feel entitled to) today. Their removal from the System constrains business enterprises, compelling employers to eliminate still more jobs, creating a downward cycle.

Unemployed people don't pay taxes; governments on all levels are forced to reduce or eliminate services and/or to accumulate still more debt. The spiral continues.

Many people think government can and should create more jobs. Nonsense! No government can create meaningful employment, and strictly speaking, neither can capitalism. Jobs are created only when somebody produces something that can be sold or traded, which means that someone else must want to acquire and consume that good or service, and they must have the means of doing so. Creating a true job out of thin air is impossible. Jobs arise from wants and needs. When essential needs and wants are satisfied, it's time for humans to shun work and turn to more important activities.

If the median human inhabitant of the planet already has more than enough to satisfy the basic requirements for survival, and more than enough extra to sate all but the most depraved greed for luxury, how can the System provide more? That would require amping up the greed, but if the planet is staggering under the environmental and ecological demands greed has already burdened it with, both in the consumption of natural resources and environmental destruction, how can it be expected to increase such production? Infinite growth on a finite planet is physically impossible.

Creating more jobs is not the answer. That would simply compound the problem. We need a better solution.

"Greed is good."

Most people take abundance, and even super-abundance, for granted: far from being associated with greed, it's considered a part of American exceptionalism, a God-given right that comes with citizenship. Some go so far as to proclaim "greed is good." For the capitalist democracy System, perhaps; it thrives on greed. For the long-term welfare of humanity and the Earth, not so much: greed degrades both.

In any event, the American Dream, by whatever name, in whatever country, is dead. The System worked as it was supposed to, for the purpose it was meant to fulfill, for as long as it could. Like a cancer, it has grown until it is killing the host it survives on, and therefore itself.

To guess at what might replace it and how that might come about requires understanding the root causes of our problems as well as their interrelated connections. Like the poetic description of the butterfly flapping its wings in Africa causing a tornado in Texas, tiny events and conditions can have huge and widespread consequences, often unforeseeable. The webs that connect everything to everything else are complex.

Making matters worse, many will say we are powerless to take corrective action because the System is enmeshed in human nature, and human nature is immutable. Perhaps. However, *cultures* can and do change, practically overnight. Witness the Americanization of most of the world via Coke and McDonald's. Every marketer dreams of spawning a hula-hoop or Beanie Baby craze, but these are not created by marketing alone: they depend on the time, the place, the mood of the people, and the circumstances; in brief, the culture. These same forces might well apply to any or all of the various problems facing humanity today, not for commerce, but for the greater good of the species.

Food is essential, but flexible

Food cultures are especially flexible, and relevant to our discussion. (We'll be talking a great deal about food as one of the basic necessities.) While some people gag at the sight of bugs and worms, or at the thought of eating dogs or horses, others think they're delicious. With a changing world — perhaps due to the collapse of unsustainable industrial agribusiness or the failure of some aspect of capitalism or global warming — food cultures could easily and quickly adapt to new conditions. Not because of laws or corporate planning and marketing. Necessity, and survival, would be terrific motivators. There are others.

This can be seen in some respects, to some small degree, in areas such as transportation and housing and interest in organic foods even now. No one plans or dictates such changes (and when overzealous bureaucracies attempt to do so they generally fail). Change results naturally, from circumstances, the tenor of the people, the availability of resources, from education and challenges and opportunities but with little or no input from "leaders" in business, industry or government.

This naturally ordered change is what we can expect. It cannot be planned or controlled, but it will certainly be challenged, and is already being challenged, by those most stubbornly embedded in the System. Their defense of the old normal is greed of the worst kind and should be seen as a threat to the survival of civilization.

A word about homesteading

Homesteading is the concept of providing for as many of your own needs as possible (food, shelter, entertainment, security, etc.), with minimal impact on the Earth, all in the interest of securing just "enough" for well-being, satisfaction and contentment: no homesteader aspires to be the richest cadaver in the cemetery.

This philosophy is at the very heart of *ENOUGH!*

I don't press it upon anyone: I merely present it as a possible and reasonable solution... and a sane way to live in any age, under any circumstances.

Chapter 1: How the O'Briens found The American Dream

The American Dream inspired millions of people to leave their homes to begin new lives in a distant and young country. It inspired heroic achievements, monumental commercial empires, and created a nation unlike any ever seen before. It changed the face of the entire planet.

Then it died.

It took with it a certain aspect of the American character, something in the national psyche that led to pride and confidence and a can-do attitude; qualities that arose from the dream itself, while at the same time nourishing and strengthening it.

While some forms of the dream persist, they're shadows of what once was. For some the dream is to win the lottery or to become a dot-com billionaire, but even more struggle to survive, which is a far cry from planning for success. America lives on, but not as it once did. What was considered normal now barely exists; today we must deal with a *new* normal.

A new beginning in a new land

The American Dream fully blossomed in the middle of the 20th century, but our story begins a hundred years earlier when the bloom was a mere bud. Some of the main protagonists in our tale arrived in America in the mid-1800s, coming from Ireland, Germany, Holland and Poland. This particular influx of immigrants came not to till the land or to labor in factories, but to dig canals; not with backhoes and bulldozers but with picks, shovels, wheelbarrows and strong backs.

For much of the country at that time, waterways were the most important means of transportation for both people and goods. While the task of digging a canal by hand might seem prodigious, it was nothing compared to building a road or railroad through the wilderness: canals were merely short ditches between long stretches of existing rivers and lakes. Canals such as the Erie, which connected the Great Lakes with the port of New York in 1825, were not only engineering marvels, but the basis of the national transportation system and economy.

One such road of water was formed by the Fox and Wisconsin Rivers. Long used by Indians, and in 1673 by Marquette and Joliet, it remained one of the principal routes between the Great Lakes and the Mississippi River until the completion of the Illinois and Michigan Canal (later evolved into the Chicago Sanitary and Ship Canal) in 1848. Travelers from the East entered the Fox River at Green Bay and paddled upstream, through Lake Winnebago, and continued on the Upper Fox to Portage, some 160 miles from and 170 feet higher than Green Bay. There, it was necessary to portage to the Wisconsin River — until the Portage Canal was constructed. After going 116 miles downstream on the Wisconsin the travelers reached the Mississippi, and ultimately, New Orleans and the Gulf of Mexico. This represented a major achievement in the opening of the interior of the young United States of America.

Capitalist entrepreneur Morgan Martin (among others), prompted by the success of the Erie Canal and steamboats on the Great Lakes, proposed to extend that waterway to the Mississippi River via the Fox and Wisconsin Rivers, beginning with a lock and canal at Portage, Wisconsin, in 1829. Cheap labor was essential. They found it by advertising among the poorest, most oppressed people of Europe, including Ireland. That was how Patrick O'Brien arrived with other countrymen to form an Irish community in Wisconsin. They were among the nearly one million who arrived in America during the "Famine Immigration."

In 1847, 115,000 "proper Bostonians" (many who could trace their lineage back to 1620 and the Mayflower) watched aghast as 37,000 Irish Catholics swamped their city in just the first year of the immigration. By 1850, immigration records showed that the Irish represented 43 percent of the foreign-born population of the entire United States. Unlike most other nationalities that came to America to farm the wide open spaces, the Irish tended to congregate in cities, notably Boston and New York. Being the poorest of the poor, living conditions in the slums were deplorable. Moreover, the Irish were despised not only because of their nationality and poverty, but their religion. Life was so miserable that even meager wages for hard labor in what was basically a frontier wilderness was an attractive option.

The Fox-Wisconsin waterway was completed in 1850 with the construction of locks at Menasha and Little Chute. By then Martin's company had folded and the state of Wisconsin had taken over, but the project was never financially successful for many reasons, both natural and man-made. Shifting sandbars on the Wisconsin River made navigation difficult, and the completion of the canal at Chicago, and the arrival of railroads, effectively eliminated demand for the Wisconsin route.

However, many jobs were created by the paper mills that were established along the lower Fox River from Lake Winnebago to Green Bay, jobs open to the men who had come to build canals, and then railroads, or to harvest the virgin pine that built such cities as Chicago. Thus O'Brien went from being a starving youth in Ireland, to a starving slum dweller in Boston, to a low-paid ditch digger, to a railroad laborer, to a respectable job in a factory in Menasha, Wisconsin. He met and married an Irish girl named Molly, they raised a family, and the American Dream was within their grasp.

The Dream flourishes

By the 1940s their descendents, still in the Fox Valley and still working in the paper mills, had only dim memories of O'Brien's life, kept alive by family lore that faded a bit more with each generation. Patrick and Molly's children included a son who married a woman whose parents had emigrated from Germany; they in turn had a son whose wife was part French and part Menomonie; the next generation was of German, Dutch and Polish extraction. Jim O'Brien, born in 1935, considered himself Irish in name only. He could just as easily have been an Andruszkiewicz, his mother's maiden name. He was an American, and living the American Dream.

It was an idyllic life, one fit for a storybook: a father, mother, two children and a dog lived happily in a small house with a well-maintained shady yard on a quiet elm-lined street of a small town in mid-America. The father went to work in the paper mill; the mother made the house a home, the kitchen a bakery and the yard a garden; and the children walked to school and played in the yard, or their friends' yards, or for games like baseball or kick the can, in the street, occasionally withdrawing to one side or the other to patiently wait for the rare auto to pass.

In the 1940s there was a milkman with a horse-drawn wagon, making early morning deliveries; a bread man, a mail man, and an ice man — mechanical refrigeration was rare — likewise making daily home deliveries, and perhaps a rag man, also with a horse-drawn wagon, collecting rags for the mill that made high-grade paper from them. The coal man was as fascinating for his coal-dust-black face with startlingly white teeth and eyes as for his delivery vehicle: not just a gasoline-powered truck, but a *dump* truck. It would not have been unusual to see a knife and scissors sharpener, a tinker, several meter readers (water, electricity, and gas), or door-to-door salesmen selling Fuller brushes or Watkins products. To the children, all seemed wonderfully mysterious and somehow worldly, even urbane, and they were greeted with reverence and awe. Of particular importance were the mailman and the policeman with his crisp white shirt and shiny black leather. An exception was the street sweeper, an elderly man with a droopy white mustache that resembled his large broom and a 50-gallon metal drum mounted on a steel-wheeled cart, who performed a mundane task they were intimately familiar with, and who never spoke to them anyway.

The dog greeted everyone equally with a happily wagging tail. There was no concern on anyone's part about the children walking to St. Patrick's school, playing outside, or even trick-or-treating after dark on Halloween when the rich aroma of smoldering leaves, burning in the gutters along the streets, wafted on the chilly night air. The distant chugging of a Soo Line steam engine and the mournful wail of its whistle in the night was not discordant; on the contrary, it added comforting sound to the tranquil visual scene.

There were no airplanes, and few people had automobiles, but the trolleys still ran. From Menasha you could ride the streetcar north to Appleton and beyond, and all the way to Oshkosh in the south. General Motors would put them out of business in the National City Lines Streetcar conspiracy from 1936-1950 but here, for now, that was of little concern.

While the Great Depression was for the most part over by the time Jim was born, frugality was still a way of life, later reinforced by World War II with its rationing and shortages. Echoing the observations of slightly older people who better recalled the Depression, Jim could say, "We were poor but we didn't know it because everybody else was poor too." The neighborhood had enough kids for two baseball teams, but only one bat and ball. There were basketballs at school, but none of the kids had ever touched a football. Soccer — and pizza — were unheard of.

Both Jim's mother and father came from large families, and family was important. There were too many birthdays to celebrate communally but holidays, major anniversaries, and all Sundays were occasions for large family gatherings, most often at Grandma and Grandpa's house not far from the Menasha canal great-great-great-grandfather O'Brien had helped construct a hundred years earlier. Not having a car, Jim and his family walked. Crossing the bridge that spanned the canal, he often stood at the rail to study the water below. Not once did he envision his ancestor laboring in the ditch; no one spoke of it.

Their house of just over 900 square feet was modest but comfortable and close to the average. The sparse furniture and amenities were also average. The ice box eventually gave way to an electric refrigerator, and the coal-fired water heater (used only on laundry day) was replaced by an electric one, the coal furnace by an oil burner, and the claw-foot bathtub by one with a shower (although Saturday night "baths" were still the norm and daily showers would have been considered extravagant).

Jim's mother was raised on a farm and many of her relatives still farmed. Jim loved visiting them on summer vacations when he could join his cousins in climbing trees and exploring tangled fencerows in search of berries and apples. Sometimes they were required to work in the garden, which wasn't quite as much fun, but afterwards there was the swimming hole and sometimes, homemade ice cream, to compensate.

The rocky farm was worked with horses: there were no engines, nor even electricity, and not even a windmill to pump water, although there was a magneto party-line telephone. Obviously, there was no indoor plumbing. Milk from the 12 cows, milked by hand by the older boys, by lantern light when necessary, was cooled in large cans in the spring house. The milk was hauled by horse-drawn wagon to the cheese factory. A few dozen chickens provided eggs for the large family and some to sell, and an occasional chicken dinner. The pig had a litter of piglets, some for home butchering and some for sale, and there were several geese and ducks, plus a huge garden. Produce was canned on the massive wood-burning stove in the spacious farmhouse kitchen, which not only cooked the meals and heated the domestic water but also warmed the house in both summer and winter. Wood was cut by hand. Jim envied his country cousins, even when watching from a distance as they butchered a cow. He was going to be a farmer.

That life seemed much more interesting than any in town: the mill workers, the tradesmen who made their rounds, and those who worked in the business section were dull by comparison. Groceries came from the Stier Tea Company, a small shop whose most fascinating aspects were the huge, aromatic, hand-cranked coffee grinder and the long pole Mr. Stier used to grab goods from the upper shelves when filling orders for housewives standing at his counter, shopping lists in hand. Meat was available only at the meat market, where New York dressed chickens (feet and heads still attached) hung in the display window along with honey-colored twisted strips of sticky fly paper, and sawdust absorbed blood on the wooden floor. There was a drug store, which surely made more money from the soda fountain and large glass cigar case than from drugs. The doctor, who of course made house calls, seldom prescribed anything requiring an actual *prescription.*

The movie theatre was popular on Saturday afternoons (especially after installing the new novelty, air conditioning) and the municipal swimming pool was crowded on hot summer days. Even the bakery was an interesting "destination," especially after installing a machine that sliced bread, a machine that had been unavailable during the war. The barber, cobbler, dry goods store and bank rounded out the business community. All were within easy walking distance.

Like many men of that period, Jim's father didn't graduate from high school, starting to work at an early age. Jim not only finished high school, but went on to college, the first in his family to do so. By then the effects of WWII on Middle America were wearing off, and progress and prosperity were evident everywhere.

Candlestick phones that had replaced crank magneto wall phones were in turn replaced by dial phones; large numbers of young ladies were no longer employed as operators. The massive steam engines with their proudly exposed pistons and connecting rods, hissing steam boxes, sweaty kerchiefed men shoveling coal into forge-like boilers, belching smokestacks and other observable working parts, were replaced by sleek diesels whose source of throbbing power was shrouded by dull steel panels. The Stier Tea Company was replaced by the Great Atlantic & Pacific Tea Company, or simply A&P, which also replaced the corner meat market; instead of standing at the counter while their orders were filled, housewives pushed shopping carts through the seemingly endless aisles, serving themselves.

Nearly everyone had a car, doctors no longer made house calls, and seemingly overnight, television became commonplace. Fears of nuclear holocaust had dimmed, Dr. Jonas Salk had conquered polio, and the American Dream was off and running.

It was still the age of Horatio Alger, when young men and even boys were expected to work and contribute to society, although new rules limited opportunities in certain fields, usually to workers less than 16 years old. Jim delivered newspapers, mowed lawns, set pins in a bowling alley, and did odd jobs. During summer vacations as a college student he worked in a paper mill, operating a beater, a huge mixer that combined heavy wads of wood pulp shipped from Canada with water to form a slurry that was piped to the machine that made the paper, or in this case, Kotex. Back on campus he washed and put up (and took down in spring) storm windows, raked leaves, washed dishes… anything he could find to pay the $35 monthly rent and $5 weekly food bill, his contribution to the five-man apartment he lived in. Only one of the students had a car, but hitch-hiking the hundred miles home was considered routine.

He graduated without a cent — in his pocket, or in debt. He easily found a job. He was on his way.

Not every American lived such a storybook life; many had different goals and aspirations; some had more ability and motivation, some had less, but for nearly all, the American Dream was real and alive.

The Golden Age arrives

The farming life Jim O'Brien had considered no longer appealed to him: by the 1950s farming had changed drastically with farms becoming much larger (and fewer and more expensive), more mechanized, and more specialized, none of which fit his vision of the American Dream. Nor did he want a desk job, or a position in a large corporation: he had no desire to become wealthy, but he craved satisfaction and freedom. Any job where he would wear a suit and tie would make his mother proud; to his father, not carrying a lunch bucket was a sign of success.

His job in the sales and marketing division of the paper company wasn't his ideal, but it was much better than working in the mill, and he enjoyed it. Their motto was, "The people who make the product don't make any money until somebody sells the product."

However, when he and a co-worker noticed a niche market their corporate employer did not serve and had no interest in serving, they explored the possibility of starting their own business to fill the gap. Beginning slowly and part-time, the effort grew into a successful full-time enterprise, eventually with a dozen employees.

By then Jim had married Jennifer, they bought a house and had two children. The business grew, although not without some tough times. In one such period his partner lost interest and went back to the security of the corporation. Jim bought him out and was amply rewarded: the business grew even more.

They bought a second home, a place in the country, a "hobby farm" based on memories of his uncle's place that was now as extinct as the magneto telephone.

When he was young his parents didn't own a car; he and Jennifer had two. The house was large enough for the children to have their own rooms. They had all the comforts modern technology offered. Life was good.

Reaching retirement age, Jim sold the company — and became a millionaire. Not that it made any difference. Their lifestyle didn't change, and the neighbors didn't consider them "rich." Their home was average, they didn't drive luxury cars, take exotic vacations, or flaunt their success.

In reality, the bulk of their wealth stemmed from their frugality, a concept many people would find puzzling. Others like them were referred to as "the millionaires next door." They had "enough."

Every generation of O'Briens born in America had been marginally better off than the previous. There were no silver spoons in this family. Anything one generation left to the next was token: a gold watch, a prized dish, some faded photographs or a Bible. Each new generation started out basically penniless. Jim and Jennifer's parents were the first to have wills, and inheritances. They died in the 1990s, leaving several thousand dollars to be divided up among the children. Until that point, there was little or no material wealth to pass on. The O'Brien heritage was less tangible but more valuable: a solid upbringing, hope, and opportunity.

But now Jim and Jennifer were worth a million dollars. They paid for their children's education and weddings, and financed their first cars and first homes, and looked forward to a comfortable retirement.

This was the fulfillment of The American Dream.

A new century, a new world

When the 21st century dawned the world had changed drastically from the world Jim had grown up in. His parents wouldn't have recognized it, and his distant ancestor from Ireland would have found it unbelievable.

What had been science fiction had become off-the-shelf everyday technology. There was both more equality — and less. Almost everybody had more money — but not nearly enough. Nor was one telephone, one car, or even one television enough for most people. The proliferation of roads, cars, and shopping malls transformed the city, and people's lives. Air travel was common (speed was paramount), computers ubiquitous, and families and neighbors insignificant, nearly obsolete.

Distrust and fear were everywhere: a single case of Tylenol tampering and a razor blade in a trick-or-treat apple had launched a tsunami of caution, even paranoia. Children no longer walked to school, and seldom played outside. When they did, extreme care was required; protective helmets were mandatory for riding bicycles or roller skating. Ball games were played on regulation fields, with real balls; the games were not only scheduled, but the players wore uniforms, and there was adult supervision. Most of the old ways of having fun, of being children, had died.

But then, in Jim O'Brien's boyhood neighborhood, even the elm trees were dead.

In one way it began at 12:30 p.m. on Friday, November 22, 1963, in Dallas, Texas. A large part of the American Dream was shattered. Many thought assassinations were isolated events in small, backward, far-away places or long-ago times; surely an American president was immune to such a primitive act: it couldn't happen here.

They were proven tragically wrong. Anything is possible.

For most Americans, life went on as if nothing had changed. Then, at 8:46 a.m. on Tuesday, September 11, 2001, America saw another event that "couldn't happen here." The confirmed death toll was 2,996, including 19 hijackers. Airlines were grounded: the skies, free of contrails, were eerily quiet. Stock markets were closed for four days, and stocks lost $1.4 trillion in the week after reopening. Physical damage was calculated to be $23 billion, but economists could even put a price tag on the human lives lost: $15 billion.

Again, life went on. But was America in 2001 the same as it was in 1950? Obviously, those who hadn't been born yet in 1950 had no basis for comparison: for them, life was "normal." Many who grew up before 1950, like the O'Briens, weren't so sure. They had already seen events they had been led to believe "couldn't happen here." Again they learned that anything is possible.

Then came the Crash of 2008.

Chapter 2: The Crash of 2008

As the 21st century dawned, Americans were comfortable, and hopeful, following a five-year boom period. There was nothing to indicate how tumultuous the first decade of the new century would become.

The Dow Jones Industrial Average reached 1,000 for the first time in November, 1972, and 2,000 in January of 1987, 14 years later. But in the next 12 years it added, not just another 1,000, but *nine* thousand. And then another 3,000 was tacked on before the crash.

Jim and Jennifer O'Brien had not been involved in the stock market to any extent. Their home and farm were paid for, they had no other debts, and they had emergency funds tucked away in laddered CDs, but their modest income didn't provide for more than that. Their main investment was their business: they put most of their eggs in one basket, and carefully guarded that basket.

When the business was sold, some of the funds went into stocks, not to get rich but for diversification; where else could they stash it so it would be available in their old age? And for a few years, the investment paid off handsomely.

The DJIA went from 1,000 in 1972 to 2,000 in 1987; 3,000 arrived in April, 1991; 4,000 in February, 1995; 5,000 in November of the same year; 6,000 in October of '96, 7,000 in February, 1997, 8,000 that July, 9,000 in May of '98, 10,000 in March of '99, and 11,000 just a little over a month later.

In January of 2001 it stood at 10,645, but on Dec. 31, 2002 it was 8,341 — the 1st 3-year consecutive loss since 1939-41. On October 9, 2007, it hit an

all-time high of 14,164.53; in March of '09, just 17 months later, it had plunged more than 50% to 6,547, where it had been in 1996.

In spite of this remarkable creation of wealth, most people had no savings to invest. Among those who had anything left after the plunge, many (including the O'Briens) swore off stocks forever: retirees and those close to retirement grimly realized that they would never recover their shattered nest eggs.

Much of the $9.3 trillion that simply vanished into thin air represented nickels and dimes squirreled away over the years by ordinary average citizens who had been told by experts that they *must* be in stocks in order to enjoy a comfortable retirement. After the crash, many gave up the idea of retiring at all, comfortable or otherwise.

Smaller or less sophisticated savers favored bank certificates of deposit. These paid around 6.5% in early 2001. By late 2011, many rates were less than .03%. Anyone planning to collect even a meager income from a modest investment in CDs was sadly disappointed. Capitalism was not delivering as promised.

The O'Briens were much better off than most people, but they remembered their heritage. Not having a great deal of faith in the stock markets in the first place, they were stoic when their easy profits were eroded, but when the plunging market started eating into their principle, they became more concerned. Now in their seventies, would they be financially ruined and forced to spend their final years in poverty? They bailed out at the very bottom, with a loss of more than $100,000.

Most retirees who had saved for their old age expected to earn some interest on those savings, perhaps even enough to live on. A million dollars in a CD or other investment earning 5.4% would provide $54,000 a year, roughly the median income of an American household. However, that same $1 million at the 2012 rate of .03% pays $300 a year. *Cat World* estimates that it costs $1,040 a year to keep a cat.

The housing boom

But the biggest story was in housing, a major component of the American Dream. Every generation of O'Briens aspired to own a home; not all of them attained that goal.

In 1963 the median home value was around $18,000; by 2001 it had soared to $147,800 (and the average was $207,000). That was nothing: by 2007 the median price of a new home was $247,900, an increase of $100,000 in just six years. The *average* was $313,600, meaning some were far more expensive than that; in some areas, million-dollar homes became common.

The O'Briens had never spent more than $100,000 on a house: they considered the inflated prices to be ridiculous. And they were right.

The bubble burst. In 2010 the median home price was back down to $221,800, the average to $272,900. But there were few buyers.

Although everyone who owned real estate was affected to one degree or another — some long-time owners only *felt* rich when prices went up, and they merely felt poor when prices retreated— the real problems concerned those who had either purchased homes during the boom or had taken advantage of the increased value to get a second mortgage. These numbers were huge. Government encouragement of home ownership in some cases actually forced lending institutions to ease up on restrictions, with the result that many homes were purchased with very low down payments, or even none at all; by people who weren't even required to prove their ability to repay the loan, which many could not.

According to *Chicago Fed Letter*, from the Federal Reserve Bank of Chicago, the annual real return from stocks between 1960-2005 was 5.4%, and from housing, 5.6%. Most people who were retired, or approaching retirement, would reasonably expect those numbers to remain fairly steady in the future. They did not.

The same letter noted that people aged 51-65 in 2006 had 54% of their wealth in housing, 23% in stocks, and 13% in businesses. All suffered large price declines over the period 2006-2010.

These weren't considered problems at the time because, we were all assured by the experts, housing prices could go only in one direction: up.

A good many took advantage of this by "flipping," the practice of buying a property, waiting for the price to go up (in some cases only a matter of months, or even weeks), then reselling it at a profit. This was capitalism, pure and simple. Later analysis showed that flippers were much more numerous than had been thought, and were a major factor in the housing bubble. A house was no longer a home to live in: it was a piggy bank just waiting to be smashed.

The problems arose when the market ran out of fuel, meaning new buyers. (The ultimate fuel of capitalism is *people*, human lives.) The bottom of the barrel had been scraped, leading to stagnant and even falling prices.

As potential profits evaporated, speculators dropped out, further constricting the market. Falling prices meant many of those unqualified buyers owed more than the property was now worth. As of September 2011, there were 10.7 million of those "underwater" mortgages. An additional 2.4 million borrowers had less than 5 percent equity in their homes, according to CoreLogic. Foreclosures soared. Financial institutions holding sub-prime mortgages were in trouble. People who had planned to sell their homes and move into retirement homes were trapped: their houses were worth far less than expected, or they couldn't be sold at all.

Six million home sales a year was once considered a healthy market. After 2008 the average fell to five million or less.

The housing boom was over. But in accordance with the butterfly effect, the webs that connect everything to everything else, it wasn't confined to real estate.

Every time a house was sold the real estate and banking people made a profit. Every new house that was built employed excavators, workers in concrete, and of course carpenters, plumbers and electricians. Those homes needed windows, siding, roofing and water heaters as well as carpeting, bathroom fixtures and kitchen cabinetry. The owners purchased stoves, refrigerators, freezers, and new furniture.

When the housing boom ended, all of the people involved in producing, selling, transporting and installing all of these had less work.

The unemployment rate in 2001 was 3.97%. At the end of 2008 it was 7.2%, after the year's loss of 2,590,000 jobs, the worst ever except for 1945. But it wasn't over.

By 2010 unemployment approached 10%, although by that time many had given up looking and weren't counted as "unemployed," while many others who had lost jobs and were fortunate enough to find new ones rarely made as much money as they had before. The actual "misery index" was much worse than it appeared from the numbers: some estimates placed unemployment at 20%.

And then there was gold, that "barbarous relic" even its detractors regard as an indicator of investor fear and uncertainty. Very few financial experts recommended investing in gold. In 2001 the yellow metal sold for about $300 an ounce, a range it had hovered around for years. By 2007 it was $600; in 2010 $1,100, and in 2011 one ounce was worth more than $1,800.

The grim outlook on employment

The economy was devastating for those who were about to quit working as well as for those who had already retired and had managed to save a little to supplement the social security checks that many, quite frankly, had never expected to see anyway. It was worse for those who had never managed, or in some cases never bothered, to save. But it was equally disastrous for those just entering their working years.

The unemployment rate for people under the age of 24 was higher than the average throughout this period. It was higher still for those with only a high school education, but arguably more crushing for college graduates, who not only expected but had been "promised" better: after all, part of the tradition of the American Dream was that every new generation would live better than the previous one. Follow the rules, get an education, and you shall be rewarded. That wasn't happening.

To make it worse, roughly a third of these recent graduates had student loans, averaging more than $25,000. It became common for adults in their 20s and 30s to not only put off marriage, but to move back in with their parents, putting economic and emotional strains on both generations.

Older Americans — many who had grown up during the lean post-depression and war years and still retained some sense of frugality — resigned themselves to the knowledge that they would never regain what they had lost. Many put off retiring; many who had already retired went back to work... if they could find work. The others could only hunker down and survive as best they could.

Many Americans who had saved for years to enjoy a decent retirement and weren't comfortable with the ups and downs of the stock market simply stashed their savings in the "safest investment in the world," U.S. Treasury bills. As of 2007 they were paying 4.64%, so an investment of $500,000 generated an annual return of $23,200. By 2012 the interest rate was 0.03%; the same $500,000 of retirement savings returned $150 a year. As some disgruntled retirees noted, this amounted to a 100% tax on savers, a tax not enacted by Congress but by actions of the Federal Reserve... which then used that money to bail out irresponsible banks, spendthrift homeowners, and bloated car companies.

Younger Americans — who had come of age during a period of surging wealth and opportunity (not to mention technological wonders and conveniences they had come to take for granted) — saw what was happening and became disillusioned with the American Dream. They knew they wouldn't live as well as their parents, and they saw that saving was pointless.

Those in the middle who hadn't lost their jobs or their homes? There should be one word that describes feelings of relief at still being employed, but extreme nervousness about future prospects; compassion for those without jobs or homes, and gratitude that they weren't among them; concern for their own standard of living, and the prospects of retirement in particular; and above all, fear; an inverted *schadenfreude* combined with a certain *angst* and a whirlwind of other emotions. That there is no such word confirms that we have never experienced such turmoil, and that the people who invent new words still haven't caught on.

Jim and Jennifer were far from destitute, but also much less secure than they had been, with diminished assets and drastically reduced income despite their careful planning and frugality. Even more disconcerting, several of their children and children's spouses had lost their jobs or had been downsized; and their grandchildren were even worse off. The one who dropped out of high school was now in prison, but even the college graduates were either unemployed or underemployed, and several had moved back in with their parents. Jim sometimes wondered how much progress had actually been made: was the American Dream nothing but a shooting star that lit up the night sky for only a few brief moments before fizzling out?

Most disturbing of all, even though those previous generations had started out with little material wealth, they had something the latest generation did not: hope, and opportunity.

But wait a minute: ups and downs have always occurred! They're part of the capitalist democratic System. Besides, this is America, the land of plenty, the home of the can-do attitude, the land of opportunity! Just wait until we get some new leadership, a few new laws to control those crooks on Wall Street, and a way to make the greedy capitalist thieves share their obscene and ill-gotten wealth with the rest of us, and everything will be okay again. We'll get back to normal.

That's what most Americans think. They're mistaken. The world as they knew it no longer exists. Now they must learn to live with the *New Normal*.

Chapter 3: If cheerleaders won games...

Most Americans know that they live in the greatest nation the world has ever seen: the most educated, the healthiest, the strongest militarily, the most righteous and above all, the richest. They know this because it's been drilled into them since childhood.

They know this — even though most of it is not true.

Facts: Ranking countries by gross domestic products at purchasing power parity per capita involves estimates and can vary, but the United States routinely comes in seventh or lower, behind countries such as Qatar, Brunei, and Norway. The U.S. never tops a list of the world's healthiest countries: according to an analysis by Forbes magazine, it's number 11. Infant mortality: 47th — 6.06 deaths per 1,000 live births, compared to 4.9 for Cuba, 4.16 for South Korea, 3.73 in the Czech Republic and 1.79 in Monaco. Education: Based on the percentage with an associate's degree or higher, the U.S. is 6th (behind Russia, Canada, Israel, Japan and New Zealand); The Paris-based Organisation for Economic Co-operation and Development (OECD) PISA tests involving 470,000 15-year-olds from 65 countries ranking for the U.S.: Reading, 14th; math, 25th; science, 17th.

The United States does rank number one in two categories: military might, with a defense budget of $692,000,000,000 and 1,477,000 personnel on active duty with nearly as many in reserves (108 per 100,000 citizens); and the world's highest per capita prison population (715 per 100,000).

This could go on and on, even in specific industries... or just comparing the U.S. and China. Yes, the U.S. was number 1 in steel production at one time — but not since 1973. The next year it was overtaken by the USSR. Today (2010 figures) it's number 3, with 80 million metric tons compared to China's 627 million metric tons.

Auto production: China, 18.3 million; U.S., 7.8 million; U.S. rank, 3rd.

High-technology exports (aerospace, computers, pharmaceuticals etc.) in 2009: China, $348 billion; U.S., $142 billion.

Coal: China, 3.24 billion short tons; U.S., 985 million tons; cotton (2011): China, 7.3 million metric tons; U.S., 3.4 million metric tons.

China even produces more beer than the U.S. (443.8 million hectoliters vs. 227.8 million hectoliters), but the potentially most embarrassing of all, *communist* China raised $73 billion in Initial Public Offerings in its three stock markets in 2011, while the democratic-capitalist New York Stock Exchange and NASDAQ accounted for $30.7 billion. The U.S. lost this leadership in 2009.

Almost everybody knows that the world is going to hell in a handbasket, we need to create more jobs, housing prices must rise again, capitalism has run amok, the System is broken, and politicians aren't doing enough to fix any of it.

Not all of this is true, either.

America was "different" from other countries from its inception in terms of its size, natural resources and people, but the expression "American exceptionalism" wasn't used until 1929, by Joseph Stalin — not surprisingly, in a pejorative way. (He was admonishing the American Communist Party for acting like America was independent of Marxism because of its natural resources, industry, and classless society.) Today, Americans in general act like they're independent of the laws of nature due to some special dispensation from the gods.

President Barrack Obama landed in hot water in late 2011 when he said that while he believed in American exceptionalism, it was no different from British exceptionalism or Greek exceptionalism or any other country's patriotism. He quickly softened his stance because — well, because Americans *know* they are exceptional. Presidential candidate Ron Paul was even more broadly honest — and even more viciously castigated.

If enthusiastic cheerleaders won games, the U.S. would have a good shot at being #1 in everything.

For a mind-blowing exposé of the extent to which Americans are brainwashed, and how, see *Lies My Teacher Told Me; Everything Your American History Textbook Got Wrong* by James W. Loewen (1995, The New Press). This is an iconoclastic analysis and commentary by a college sociology professor who spent 20 years teaching race relations in Vermont, plus teaching in a mostly-black college in Mississippi, and then two years at the Smithsonian dissecting twelve leading high school textbooks of American history where he found an "embarrassing blend of bland optimism, blind nationalism, and plain misinformation." Americans become imprinted with an idealistic notion of patriotism at an early age, and few ever learn the truth. (Whether due to this book or something else, more Americans today are well aware that some of their most cherished heroes were scoundrels, or at least blemished — knowledge that still gives some patriots apoplexy.) In addition, the emphasis on Eurocentrism and Anglocentrism implies that other societies and cultures contributed little or nothing to civilization, which is far from the truth, an obstacle to understanding the world as it exists, and an unfortunate roadblock to appreciating the considerable achievements of other cultures. Ignoring America's mistreatment and exploitation of other people, particularly Native Americans — a ghastly, largely untold story, well-documented here — is a hindrance to self-knowledge, understanding, and progress. Finally, nefarious government schemes and policies provide ample evidence that America is no more righteous and upstanding than most other countries. Of particular interest is the FBI under J. Edgar Hoover.

Growing up in the 1950s

However, it *was* true, or at least truer than now, arguably reaching its apex in the 1950s. The first members of the Baby Boomer generation (born 1946-1964) were growing up during that period; those were their formative years. To them, the times, and American supremacy, were "normal."

In the late 1930s and early '40s, births averaged around 2.5 million per year. In 1946 they soared to 3.47 million; in 1957 and 1961 there were 4.3 million. Altogether, some 79 million people were born during this period. In 1965 and after, the birth rate plunged, hitting 3.14 million in 1973, the lowest since 1945.

A demographic group of that size obviously affected society — and the economy. And it still did in 2008, when the first Boomers were reaching retirement age.

The Greatest Generation (so-named by tv journalist Tom Brokaw) was born between 1901 and 1924. The Silent Generation was born between 1925-1945; Baby Boomers from 1946-'63; Generation X '64-'79; Gen Y '80s-mid-'90s; and presumably Z. Then what? What could have prompted the positioning of the "Greatest" Generation (after which, logically, none could be greater) with the apex of American exceptionalism?

The 1950s was a period of relative calm and prosperity. Women who had gone to work in business and industry during the war years continued to work outside the home, and their numbers grew by another 18% during the 1950s. With two-income families, the standard of living rose. After the lean years of the Depression and WWII, most people now expected to own a car and a house; they expected their children to attend college. Life was good, most people were sure it would be even better for their children, and the children certainly anticipated that. And for most of their working lives, it was.

About 20% of the population moved each year, from the country as small farms went out of business, to the city where factory jobs were plentiful, and then to the suburbs, where the American Dream awaited. More people were starting families, adding to the need for housing: population soared by 28 million during the decade. Veterans Administration and Federal Housing Administration mortgages made home ownership easier.

College was no longer for the wealthy or the elite... or more people thought of themselves as elite. Either way, the number of college students doubled.

It was the era of the civil rights movement, Joseph McCarthy's stoking of anti-communism hysteria, the U.S./Soviet arms race… and continuing major break-throughs in technology, including the Salk polio vaccine, the near-eradication of TB, and the decoding of the molecular structure of DNA.

It was also the age of television. In 1950, about 150,000 tv sets were sold; in 1951, 10 times as many, 1.5 million. Shopping centers went from eight, after the war, to 3,840 by 1960.

Gross national product went from $200 billion in 1940, to $300 billion in 1950, and more than $500 billion in 1960. In 2011 it exceeded $15,000 billion ($15 trillion).

Not only was the American Dream playing out according to plan: politics also supported the idea of American superiority. Harry S. Truman instituted the Marshall Plan to stimulate economic recovery in war-torn Western Europe to stem the growth of communism there. The Berlin Airlift of 1948 again demonstrated America's wealth and power, and NATO was seen as a diplomatic deterrent to Soviet expansion. When North Korean communists attacked South Korea in June, 1950, the U.S. considered it more than the civil war it appeared to be. The U.S. became involved "to avoid a future war in less advantageous circumstances," referring to China and Russia. Korea was only mildly felt by many Americans; while it was a long and dreary struggle it was nothing like WWI or II; for some time it wasn't even considered a "war:" it was a "police action."

Throughout, government asserted its central role in economic affairs. The Employment Act of 1946 affirmed that it was government policy "to promote maximum employment, production and purchasing power." During this period the U.S. was also behind the creation of the International Monetary Fund (IMF) and the World Bank —"to ensure an open, capitalist international economy." The link between capitalism and democracy couldn't have been made clearer.

In 1953 Dwight D. Eisenhower became president. The hysteria Senator Joseph R. McCarthy (R.-Wis.) created about communist subversion started during the Truman years, but came to full flower in the '50s. Although he and his sensationalized investigations were eventually disgraced, McCarthyism left a lasting effect on the doctrine of American exceptionalism.

On October 4, 1957, most Americans were stunned to learn that the Soviet Union had launched the first Earth satellite, Sputnik. This affected everyone, including Baby Boomers; how could American exceptionalism have been beaten by a technically backwater country like the U.S.S.R.? America's Explorer I reached orbit on January 31, 1958, NASA was created, and education for Baby Boomers was hotwired.

Service workers first outnumbered those who produced goods in the 1950s, and by 1956 white-collar workers outnumbered blue-collar workers. At the same time, the number of farmers plummeted.

Although Eisenhower usually isn't given much credit for doing anything — his tenure was more of the slow-and-steady kind — he is well-remembered in certain circles for some of his parting warnings, which are pertinent here.

"The conjunction of an immense military establishment and a large arms industry is new in the American experience. In the councils of government, we must guard against the acquisition of unwarranted influence, whether sought or unsought, by the military-industrial complex. The potential for the disastrous rise of misplaced power exists and will persist."

Concerned that the military-industrial complex (Eisenhower was the first to use the term) was developing an enormous power to absorb national resources, he issued one last warning. "As we peer into society's future, we — you and I, and our government — must avoid the impulse to live only for today, plundering, for our own ease and convenience, the precious resources of tomorrow."

In 1954 Eisenhower reduced the federal budget to $63.2 billion, the largest amount of the decrease coming from national security. In 1955 he chopped another $5 billion from the defense budget.

The 2010 U.S. budget was $3.55 trillion; defense alone was $663.7 billion.

John F. Kennedy and the New Frontier

The 1950s was a time of great complacency and comfort, befitting the American Dream. It was not to last. In the '60s and '70s great changes took place. The dreams and dashed hopes were encapsulated for many in 1961-1963 in the election, and assassination, of John F. Kennedy. That brief span seemed to signal a sharp break in American life. The idea that America was special and "It couldn't happen here" was badly shaken (as it would be again on 9/11/01). It was a "New Frontier," all right, but not exactly what Kennedy had envisioned.

Lyndon B. Johnson's "Great Society," to be achieved through economics, drastically increased federal spending for Medicare, Food Stamps, and numerous education incentives, as well as the "War on Poverty."

The 1973-74 oil embargo by OPEC caused long lines at gas stations and an energy crisis, as well as inflation and stagnant business activity, which became "stagflation." President Nixon resigned in disgrace. And the war in Vietnam dragged on, affecting the attitudes of many young people. The American trade deficit swelled. American exceptionalism seemed distant. The American Dream was fading.

One constant was the American fascination with war. The Vietnam era was considered over by 1975, but by 1979 there was a war on inflation and a war on drugs, and of course Americans kept singing their unsingable war-like national anthem, mostly at war-like athletic contests.

In 1979 the Federal Reserve tightened the money supply, causing interest rates to rise. This tamed inflation, but slowed business, resulting in an economic recession that lasted until 1982. That year, business bankruptcies rose 50% over the previous year.

It was capitalism's turn to affect democracy: the economic turmoil resulted in the defeat of Jimmy Carter and the election of Ronald Reagan, who became well-known, if not universally loved, for his embrace of supply-side economics. This centered on tax cuts. The primary benefits went to the people who pay taxes, namely, the wealthy, the theory being that this would lead to higher investment, more jobs, and greater wealth all around.

While cutting taxes, social programs were also slashed, with a view to downsizing a bloated and intrusive government. One exception: there were large increases in military spending.

The federal budget deficit went from $74,000 million in 1980 to $221,000 million in 1986. Some economists considered this a recipe for inflation, but the Federal Reserve took charge. Previously almost unheard of, the Fed played a major role under Paul Volcker, then Alan Greenspan, and continuing to Ben Bernanke.

During the '80s the trade deficit swelled, Japan and other Asian economies challenged the United States, there was a weather-related farm crisis and a savings & loan crisis, all changing the face of capitalism. But some of the biggest moves in American capitalism came from "corporate raiders," capitalists who bought companies with depressed stock prices, dismantled them, and sold off the pieces. Controversy arose: did this practice destroy companies and put people out of work, or did selling them off enable investors, who usually profited handsomely, to reinvest those gains in more productive capitalist enterprises? As so often happens, the answer depended on your perspective.

The economy grew, corporate profits rose, and the stock market surged in the 1990s.

But by 2008, America's exceptionalism, such as it had been, was in the past. Even the cheerleaders were losing their enthusiasm. There was a New Normal. But what did that mean?

Chapter 4: Waiting for the recovery

Had the previous chapter skipped from the 1950s to the present without all those little steps in between, the contrast would have been far more jarring. This does not make the actual changes any less dramatic: it simply means that most of the people who lived through them hardly noticed them — like the legendary frog in the kettle of cold water doesn't know it's getting boiled. If that frog were tossed into a pot of boiling water it would notice it immediately and jump out... as would any American who went to sleep in 1959 and woke up in 2009. In any event yes, there was a time when the American Dream loomed large; many felt it was within their grasp, and some had achieved it. Somehow, it slipped away.

Capitalism's "creative destruction"

All of the foregoing might explain why, as of early 2012, most Americans were still waiting — although with increasing impatience — for the "recovery" from the Great Recession. There was general agreement (at least tacitly) that the American Dream had faded. The conclusion was that the System must be broken. The prevailing sentiment was that it would be fixed as soon as Washington and/or Wall Street got their act together and made the repairs.

Ironically, that solution is no solution at all; some economists think it's counter-productive.

The key to understanding this can be found in Austrian economist Joseph Shumpeter's 1942 book, *Capitalism, Socialism, and Democracy*, in which he describes "creative destruction" as being an essential element of capitalism. This simply means that as new technologies and jobs are created, old ones are destroyed. In with the telephone, out with the telegraph;

automobiles come in, carriages and buggy whips go out; computers replace adding machines, slide rules, filing cabinets, paper, and much, much more.

In other words, lost jobs, ruined companies and vanishing industries are essential parts of capitalism, growth, and economic progress. If this is what we're seeing in 2012, then this is only the beginning: we have a long way to go.

Let creative destruction run its course

The oddity — and the great danger inherent in the current concerns about job creation — is that societies that allow creative destruction to run its course become more productive and wealthier, while those societies that attempt to soften the harsher realities of creative destruction by trying to preserve jobs or protect industries stagnate and decline. Shumpeter says the pain and the gain are inextricably linked: new industries are not created without sweeping away the preexisting order.

If this theory is correct, and if we are indeed in such a period now, then it follows that our financial predicament will get much worse before it gets any better, no matter what happens and no matter what anyone does. Environmental considerations, which capitalism considers mere collateral damage, make the prognosis even worse.

No politician is going to condone hunkering down until the storm passes and capitalism gets "back on track." But the compulsion to do something, do anything at all — which is what the mass of voters want — can only make matters worse, according to Schumpeter's theory. Implementing policies to resist economic change only blocks the natural process of creative destruction. It actually prolongs the pain, and delays the gain, a lose-lose situation. (Watch the U.S. Postal Service for a real-life demonstration of this.)

Is the past prologue?

Will the jobs eliminated by creative destruction be replaced by whatever comes next? In the past, that seems to have been the case.

In 1900, 40 of every 100 Americans were engaged in farming. Today it's less than two. And we eat more, and better, and export more too. Blacksmiths went from 238,000 in 1910 to just a handful, today. In 1900 there were 102,000 cobblers; today, there aren't enough to count.

At the same time, in 1900 there were zero airplane pilots and mechanics; in 2002 there were 255,000. Auto mechanics went from zero to 867,000. And as recently as 1990 the total number of webmasters was zilch; today there are more than half a million. So to some extent, new technologies that eliminated old jobs created new ones. But can that continue when jobs disappear at a dizzying clip and workers become redundant? Even more pertinent is this seldom-considered question: if we have become so efficient at providing life's necessities with so few workers, what can the surplus workers do that will benefit humanity?

While we're pondering that, old jobs continue to disappear. Practically every job I myself worked at during a widely varied working life has either disappeared, or has become unrecognizable, from working on a pea viner in the 1950s to the magazine business I retired from in 2000.

My first experience as a capitalist

There probably isn't a person alive today who hasn't been touched by the explosive appearance of the electronic revolution, of which computers are just one component. Most people, especially older ones (like Jim O'Brien and me) have at least one story to tell about how different things were in "the old days." Here's one of mine. (As a multi-tasker, usually holding two or three jobs at a time, I have several.)

When I first started in the printing and publishing industry in 1961, letterpress printing (the kind "invented" by Gutenberg in 1450) was still the norm, and the Linotype machine hadn't changed much since Merganthaler devised the first one in 1884. I had never used an electric typewriter, in journalism school or as a reporter on a metropolitan daily newspaper. (We also used 4 x 5 Speed Graphic cameras — 35mm film didn't provide the quality needed for newspaper photography — and we learned to set type, by hand, from a California job case.) A process called offset lithography had been around for a while, but was just starting to make an inroad in commercial printing: most real printers still scoffed at it. Being young and fresh out of college, I wasn't afraid of a new technology.

My new magazine was set in hot metal (that is, Linotype). Reproduction proofs were made, meaning only one copy was printed using the metal type. I cut these long columns of type into pieces, arranged them on a grid representing magazine pages, and glued them into place using rubber cement. The printer photographed these "flats," assembled the negatives, and from those made metal plates that would be used for the printing. (The plates actually printed on a rubber blanket, which then "offset" the ink onto the paper.) It involved a lot of work... but it would get worse.

Textbooks vs. the real world

Like many recent college graduates, I learned that the real world seldom follows the textbook models. I knew how to write and produce a magazine, but I didn't know how to get people to read it. I needed readers (I didn't want advertising) in order to pay the printer, as well as the postage and everything else, to say nothing of myself. At the time my only source of income was odd jobs — putting up or taking down storm windows, raking leaves, washing dishes at a synagogue — at the then-current rate of 75¢ an hour.

Long story shortened: I put out the next few issues on a used mimeograph, an old office machine using a master produced on an ordinary manual typewriter. After a while (and after getting a real job, with a salary) I was able to buy a small office offset duplicator, that did "real" printing, on an 8-1/2 x 11-inch sheet. I got a credit union loan. The credit union wasn't allowed to make business loans; it was a "furniture" loan. But that was all right, because we kept the press in the bedroom of our rented farmhouse.

The business progressed from there, eventually being located in its own building, with several presses (including one that printed four magazine pages at a time on a 17 x 22-inch sheet). But even when it progressed beyond that, to farming out some of the really big jobs to a much larger printer with huge multi-million-dollar four-color web presses, the magazines (there were six, at one point) were made basically the same way, by pasting up type on flats, with three exceptions.

The least important in retrospect, although it was a wonderful improvement at the time, was replacing the rubber cement with hot wax, which was not only less messy but also allowed blocks of type to be taken up and repositioned as necessary. The other was going from a drafting table, with T-squares and triangles, to light tables. Glass-topped tables, lighted from below, enabled the paste-up artist to position type on a pre-printed grid, much faster and more accurately.

Advances in typesetting

A much more important change involved type. After that first issue when we couldn't afford Linotype we reverted to an ordinary typewriter. That continued even when it was no longer required by the mimeograph. At one point, in order to make it "look" more like printing, we justified the columns. This meant typing the article in the desired format, then retyping it, adding spaces between words as needed to make a flush right margin. Later, an electric typewriter improved the print quality, somewhat.

Soon after, an IBM carbon ribbon typewriter presented a much smoother and cleaner look; and the IBM Selectric, which not only used a carbon ribbon, and not only had interchangeable balls to provide different fonts, but also *proportional spacing* like real type (an *i* takes up less space than an *m*), was surely the last word in typographical technology.

Except that it wasn't. Other forms of "cold type" (as opposed to the Linotype which used a molten mix of lead, tin and antimony) had been gaining acceptance in the 1960s. Much like the Luddite weavers of the early 1800s, traditional printers and typesetters resisted, claiming that the quality of their skilled work couldn't be compared to the shoddy results of the new, cheaper methods. In most cases that opinion was justified. But progress came swiftly.

We bought a machine that set type photographically — a Compugraphic — using a variety of fonts on film strips to print long columns of type on photographic paper, which then had to go through a developing processor in a darkroom, and dried, before being cut into the pieces needed to make a magazine page, just as had been done with the Linotype. With this system corrections had to be set and run through the same process, then painstakingly cut, waxed and pasted over the typos, very picky work usually employing an X-Acto knife. It goes without saying that, as had been the case with Linotype, writers and editors typed everything first, and sometimes more than once, to provide clean copy for the typesetter.

An advantage was that this machine was capable of setting headline-size type. Before, headlines were set by transferring rub-off letters, one at a time, from sheets of acetate onto the flat. Any type blocks over 12 points were kept very short because of the time and labor involved. In the very early impoverished days, we even cut letters from a box of corn flakes and rubber cemented them onto a page, so machine-set headline type was a very welcome improvement.

Desktop computers? Ha!

It was during this period that one of our editors returned from a seminar and told me that some day, every one of our employees would have a desktop computer. I laughed. To me, even the electric typewriter was too new-fangled. I certainly wasn't going to get involved with computers for writing, and the IBM 360 we used for mailing lists, like the Compugraphic, would never fit on a desktop. Neither of these two large and expensive machines could do anything but their assigned tasks. They even had their own air-conditioned rooms!

By the time the Compugraphic went kaput (which didn't take long, and it was not an inexpensive machine), it was obsolete. Adding to our woes, the business was in a slump, and money was even scarcer than usual. What were the options?

Enter the Macintosh

As fate would have it, that was in 1984, when Apple Computer Inc. (now Apple, Inc.) introduced the Macintosh, touting it as a computer that could set type. As usual, real printers scoffed: the type quality was lousy, compared to Linotype. But it was an absolutely astounding advance if only because the writing and typesetting were done on the same machine, and with corrections so easily made, our workload was cut in half, even though we still printed out columns of type, cut them up and pasted them into forms on the light table as before.

Using a page layout program, Adobe PageMaker, was even more amazing. With the labor saved, who cared or even knew that 128k was laughable, the tiny screen even worse, the floppy disks a joke? But the 128k was soon replaced by 512k, the Mac by the MacPlus, the SE, the SE/30, LCV, Quadra... I lost track a long time ago.

Me, the guy who had hoped to one day own a Linotype and a decent used flatbed letterpress that would last another lifetime or two, swore never to get behind in the computer game. Since business was improving, we grabbed every new development as soon as it came out, to maintain our cutting edge. I recall the first hard disk (external, of course) because the 20 MB capacity was amazing, the relief from floppy disk switching was such a blessing... and the price was "only" $3,000. A monitor that showed a full 8-1/2 x 11 page was obviously a boon: I can't imagine, now, laying out a magazine page on that tiny 9-inch 512 x 342 pixel monochrome screen. But soon we had monitors displaying a full 11x17 spread.

There was a crude scanner, then much better scanners, and then color computers and scanners. A color cover photo engraving that at one time had set us back $3-$4,000 and several days could now be done on a desktop for virtually nothing, in minutes.

I retired in 2000. By then, every employee had a desktop computer. Today the editors work from remote locations and the magazines are sent to the printing company in digital form

via satellite. I wouldn't be qualified for even the most routine
job in my old company without a lot of retraining. But of
course, they don't hire old men, any more than they use old
Linotypes. And the end is nowhere in sight.

Because of my penchant for multi-tasking, I simultaneously
put in 15 years in the telephone industry… and you can
imagine how *that* has changed since 1961.

Can we live without jobs?

It's true that almost nobody *makes* anything any more. The
fact that we can not only survive but actually flourish with
two farmers per 100 people instead of 40 and with vastly
reduced numbers of workers in manufacturing industries
suggests that we have reached the saturation point with
manufactured "stuff"; we simply can't make use of more, even
with widespread pleonexia, or greediness, which we'll
examine in detail later. (Economists will say that off-shoring
jobs, which some readers might be thinking of here, is not a
legitimate part of this discussion and "buying American" has
nothing to do with a solution.) This saturation of material
goods has given way to a service economy, a post-industrial
society.

Now the question is becoming how many *services* can we
use, or tolerate? Surely there must be a limit to the number of
ball players and rock stars a nation can put up with, as well as
the number of burger flippers and big box store greeters, or
even prison guards. Will we end up taking in each other's
laundry? Where is the job satisfaction and joy of living in that?

A cusp point for humanity

Clearly, the current creative destruction is no mere blip in
the upward progress of the American Dream, or even of
capitalism. It's a cataclysmic event that is shaking the very
foundations of society, and civilization itself. Humanity has
reached a major cusp point, akin to the dawn of the Industrial
Revolution, but potentially far more potent.

There are no political solutions, but politicians will have to
deal with the fallout. There are no technical solutions, but

technicians will have to struggle to stay ahead of the tsunami. Capitalists will have a field day because this is their milieu (although many will be tearing out their hair, trying to get ahead of the game), but they can provide no cure. Most significantly, there is no turning back, or even stemming the flow, and the speed of change increases exponentially. We all have to learn to deal with that.

It's frightening, but also exciting, to be alive at such a momentous time in history. The question is, what are we going to do with this frightening, exciting opportunity? To understand that we must know more about the System that is collapsing around our ears.

Chapter 5: Understanding the Capitalist Democratic System

The importance of the sliding scale

We Americans are taught, in some cases even brainwashed, to be very proud and protective of the capitalist democracy System we live under, but many have not learned enough for a true understanding. Many economists like to say that "Capitalism is one of those subjects everybody knows something about and most of it's wrong." This often affects our judgment in matters of public policy as well as dealing with businesses.

Dr. Roger B. Butters, president of the Nebraska Council on Economic Education and Assistant Professor of Economics at the University of Nebraska-Lincoln, has pointed out that like so many other things in our educational system, capitalism teaching is designed to be memorized and then recognized on a multiple-choice exam. That kind of knowledge doesn't reflect reality, and it doesn't help us understand the real world. (The ancient Greek philosophers wouldn't even consider that "knowledge;" it's merely "know-how," which is quite different.)

My father often told me, "The man who knows *how* will always have a job... working for the man who knows *why*."

He explains that the heart of capitalism is the private ownership of property, which is one end of a spectrum. At the opposite end is communism, the public ownership of property. No country can be purely capitalistic, and none can be completely devoid of capitalism: they all exist somewhere along the continuum.

Most societies have started out very close to the communist end of the scale, with very little personal property save for clothes, weapons and utensils. Land in particular is owned in common, or more properly is not "owned" by anyone. Remember Chief Seattle's oft-repeated quote: "How can you buy or sell the sky, the warmth of the land? The idea is strange to us. If we do not own the freshness of the air and the sparkle of the water, how can you buy them? Every part of the Earth is sacred to my people."

In sharp contrast to this philosophy, capitalism is very keen on private ownership of land. Since no one has yet figured out how to buy fresh air and sparkling water (except for the bottled kind), capitalism merely uses those (mostly as sewers) at no charge, with no cost to anyone — except to those who feel they have a right to clean air and water. But more on that later.

A food surplus is needed

Not until technology allows a food surplus does a commercial society arise, sliding the economy from the communist side of the scale toward the capitalist side. It never goes all the way. Some people who rail against "socialism" in America seem to forget this. The capitalist community owns much in common: roads, schools, parks and fire trucks are usually owned by the government, that is, all of the people, even among people who claim to be pure capitalists. It's not a question of one or the other: the only question is where you are on that sliding scale.

A number of other economic concepts often appear to be beyond the grasp of many people, even though they've been exposed to them. "There is no such thing as a free lunch" is often forgotten when money comes "from Washington." The only source of Washington's money is *you*. By the same token, "profit" is not a dirty word: businesses that don't make a profit don't stay in business.

Democracy on the continuum

Democracy likewise lies at one end of a continuum, with totalitarianism at the other, but again with all actual societies located at least a bit from the very ends. Some Americans have been careful to identify their system of government not as a democracy but as a democratic republic. But here again a society can move, sometimes quite freely and with little fanfare, along that continuum.

Capitalism has been defined as an economic system in which trade and industry are controlled by private owners, for profit. Although this works best in a democracy, that's not a prerequisite: a prime example today is communist China. While not all capitalist countries are democratic, democracies are invariably capitalistic.

Democracy can be regarded as a form of government in which all adult citizens have an equal say in the decisions that affect their lives. This worked fine in ancient Greece, although women and slaves were not included, and the philosophers of the time (Plato in particular) thought it would become unwieldy with a population of more than 10,000 or so. A democratic republic maintains (and in our case today extends) that equality, but it functions with the masses electing representatives. An elected head of state serves for a limited time, as opposed to a monarchy or dictatorship.

The United States of America flourished under this system of democratic capitalism for 200 years. It worked so well that few dared to mention that both democracy and capitalism had been criticized by highly respected thinkers throughout the ages, from Aristotle to such Americans as John Adams and Alexander Hamilton.

This is not the same as the more recent brouhaha concerning the "exceptionalism" of America. Exceptionalism is simply nationalism, or patriotism; in no way does patriotism address the basic technical pros and cons of either capitalism or democracy.

In *The Federalist* Papers James Madison argued (like Aristotle and Plato) that a democracy weakened as it grew larger, and suffered more than a republic from factions that would inevitably arise in such a system. Joseph Shumpeter argued that ordinary citizens are not fit to rule because they are not well-educated on important topics and have no clear views. Plato made the same point about two thousand years earlier when he suggested special rigorous training of leaders, pointing out that if you wouldn't entrust your body to a doctor who wasn't well-qualified by education and experience, why would you entrust your political life to an untrained politician?

This seems like an even more serious problem today, when there is so much more to know and so much more that affects our lives and laws, and yet overspecialization has made even the most educated — perhaps *especially* the most educated — like the three blind men describing the elephant. In many of today's heated debates we might wish for a naïve but honest little boy who doesn't hesitate to proclaim that the emperor has no clothes.

This System, this mix of capitalism and democracy but both located at some distance from the pure forms on the ends of the continuums, pervades our lives. It controls us from before birth to after death. There is no escape, even for a Thoreau or a Robinson Crusoe. We have no control: the System rules. We are not only its servants, but its slaves.

However, for the most part this servitude is not only gladly tolerated but eagerly embraced. After all, the thinking goes, who wouldn't want to live in the Land of the Free, where food and gas and housing, necessities and luxuries alike, are widely available and affordable to the vast majority of the population? If you don't like it here, the refrain goes, go live in Russia or China. The American System is beyond reproach.

According to an article titled "Brain Drain Reverses Course, Flows Away from America" (Reuters, Dec. 6, 2011) the percentage of Americans aged 25 to 34 actively planning to relocate outside the U.S. has quintupled in the last two years because they no longer see the U.S. as the land of opportunity. And an earlier story

**detailed how a growing number of retirees are making their nest
eggs stretch further by relocating to places such as Panama and
Costa Rica.**

Except when it doesn't seem to be working quite right, and
when life as we came to know it is turned upside down, as
happened in 2008. Since the old rules no longer apply, the
thinking goes, the System must be broken; let's fix it.

But wait: What's *really* happening? What, actually, is not
working, how did it break down, and what can we do to
repair it? To investigate these questions we must briefly
review how the System functions today, and how it came to
this point.

The history of money

Ever since a group of families became a clan and then a tribe,
there has been a commercial aspect to society, some form of
trade or exchange that reallocated resources. If I kill a hairy
mammoth and you don't, we'll share the meat — because my
family couldn't use all of it, because it's in my best interest to
keep you alive to participate in the next battle against our
common enemy, and because maybe next week *you* will kill a
hairy mammoth and I won't, and you'll share the meat with
me.

As the science of food production progressed and the
division of labor expanded beyond simple sexual roles,
surpluses became more common. The first step toward a
commercial society was barter, often involving cattle, probably
more than 10,000 years ago. Then came the concept of money.

If I wanted some of your surplus rye or barley when it
ripened in the fall, I couldn't trade for it with my wool because
I sheared my sheep in the spring. But if we agree that
something — let's say a cowry shell — represents a certain
value, a set amount of wool or grain, I can "buy" your grain at
harvest time, and you can use that cowry shell "money" to
buy my wool next spring.

Money, in various and often ludicrous forms, was used
thousands of years ago. Rai, the doughnut-shaped carved

stones weighing thousands of pounds found on the island of Yap, are well-known curiosities. Today we have something equally strange and even more worthless: much of the world's money consists of nothing more than bits and bytes in a computer. But even paper fiat money, as everyone now knows, isn't worth the paper it's printed on except by common consent and good will.

Money can be defined as "a medium of exchange." Odd fact: Nearly all money originates as *credit*. (But credit cards are not counted as money.) Ponder this: By the end of 2011 American homes were worth nearly $7 trillion less than they were five years earlier, a 25% decline; the stock markets lost more than $9 trillion. Where did all that "money" go? In one sense, it never really existed.

In spite of this long history of money and trade, until relatively recent times few people were touched by either. Most people produced life's necessities on a subsistence level and had little to trade, and little need or incentive to trade.

That slowly changed as technology progressed. When people were able to produce more food than they needed for themselves on a regular basis, some of them became weavers, or brewers or cheese-makers. It became essential to exchange such goods for their basic sustenance. Then came merchants and shopkeepers, those who didn't produce anything at all, but served as links between the artisans and consumers.

The next big step came scarcely 300 years ago, when machines began to replace artisans, beginning with the weaving of cloth. The artisan weavers didn't own the machines: in fact they resisted them, in many cases destroying them, during the time of the Luddites. While it might be argued or at least supposed that the weavers were in the best position to design and build such machines, that never occurred to them: weaving cloth with unskilled labor, and at a rate that would put many craftsmen out of work, would require not only thinking way outside the box but a suspension of belief in their own worth: it was unthinkable.

But capitalism had been born, and it could not be stopped.

The Agricultural and Industrial Revolutions

Agriculture had slowly evolved through the ages: domesticated animals replaced hunting; planting and tending crops replaced gathering; draft animals replaced human labor. Plodding oxen were replaced by much-faster horses, and the old Roman neck harness was replaced by the breast harness which enabled a horse to pull a much heavier load.

Jethro Tull (1674-1741) was one of the first real innovators in the Agricultural Revolution, with his grain drill — a much more efficient and effective way of sowing seeds than the old method of scattering them on the ground by hand — and his version of an improved plow. Lord Townshend developed crop rotation, which eliminated the practice of letting the land lie fallow for long periods. Robert Bakewell (1725-1795) contributed to the revolution with his work on livestock breeding.

The Agricultural Revolution increased English farm output by about three-and a-half-times, freeing up a large workforce for the looming Industrial Revolution.

Cloth becomes an industrial product

The first commodity to be industrialized was cotton. The catalyst was John Kay's flying shuttle, which doubled a weaver's cloth production, making the cloth more abundant and widely available, and cheaper.

In the "butterfly effect" of economics, where *no* thing is *one* thing because everything that happens has consequences, it now took four spinners to keep up with one weaver. James Hargreaves remedied that, and more. In 1764 his "spinning jenny" allowed one person to spin, not one thread at a time, not just two, to keep up with the flying shuttle, but *eight* threads at once, by turning a single wheel. This was later increased to eighty.

More than 20,000 of these machines were in use in Britain by 1778, even though the yarn was usually coarse and weak. This flaw was overcome by Richard Arkwright's "water frame," which produced better yarn faster. The drawback was that it was too large to be operated by hand. As the name implies, it was powered by a water wheel, which limited its use to locations where waterpower was available. In spite of that, and after Samuel Crompton combined the spinning jenny and the water frame into one machine known as "Crompton's mule," within 35 years more than 100,000 power looms were in operation in England and Scotland.

The time was ripe for the steam engine… and we all know the butterfly effect that had on civilization.

By 1812, the cost of cotton yarn had plunged by 90 percent and the number of workers by 80 percent. Much of the raw cotton was imported from the U.S., involving not only slavery but also deflecting land from food production, and contributing to the well-known soil depletion and erosion brought about by constant cotton production. But those webs are another part of the story.

Subsistence farming wasn't easy, but neither was factory labor. Hours were extremely long, even for young children; working conditions were poor and the pay was miserable. Moreover, it was monotonous, unfulfilling, assembly line work. The skill and pride of craftsmanship so valued in the guilds was ground into bitter dust, as the weavers were forced from their looms and onto the assembly lines. Some became Luddites.

The Luddite movement

Luddites were English textile artisans whose resistance to the Industrial Revolution lives on today: anyone opposed to any new technology is still called a "Luddite." The name refers to a mythical Robin Hood-like commoners' hero, Captain (or sometimes General, or even King) Ludd, who in turn was derived from Ned Ludd, a weaver with a temper which was reportedly unleashed on a knitting frame. Years later, whenever a frame was damaged, the joke was that "Ned Ludd did it." Apparently he was very busy around 1811-1812.

The skilled weavers protested that the mechanized looms, which could be operated by cheap, unskilled labor, robbed them not only of their livelihood but their way of life. At that time unemployment in general was high, and economic hardship was fed by events like the long-running war with Napoleon's France. At one point the weavers' movement became so strong and widespread it clashed with the British army.

An agricultural parallel took place in the 1830s during the widespread Swing Riots, where the mechanical victims were threshing machines, although hay ricks, barns, and cattle were also destroyed. According to most accounts, although the riots spread rapidly, they weren't ignited by any single event. Leading the many causes was the progressive impoverishment and displacement of farm workers over a span of 50 years. One sympathetic Lord told parliament that the English laborer was "reduced to a plight more abject than that of any race in Europe." This was in spite of all the supposed blessings of industrialization.

The notion that labor-saving technologies increase unemployment by reducing the demand for labor is considered false by neoclassical economists. This "Luddite fallacy" assumes that employers will make use of technology to reduce the workforce, rather than to increase production. Economist Alex Tabarrok dismissed this by saying "If the Luddite fallacy were true we would all be out of work because productivity has been increasing for two centuries." Hold that thought for now, but keep it in mind: it's important, and we'll revisit it later.

Other thinkers, including Martin Ford and Jeremy Rifkin, suggest that the Luddites were simply 200 years ahead of the times, including their contention that automation made the rich richer and the poor poorer.

Within a very brief span of time industrialism had spread well beyond any possibility to contain or restrict it, and it was not only tolerated, but often welcomed. Mechanization begat more technology, which begat more capitalism, resulting in more mechanization, and the process fed on itself. The System not only fostered but *required* growth, and the growth came faster and faster. Life changed more in one century than it had in the previous 5,000 years.

How fast life changes!

In addition to Thomas Newcomen's atmospheric steam engine (1712) and John Kay's flying shuttle (1733) the 18th century saw the first mercury thermometer, thanks to Gabriel Fahrenheit, in 1724. And in 1776, Scotsman Adam Smith published *An Inquiry into the Nature and Causes of the Wealth of Nations,* often considered the beginning of capitalism. But that was just the beginning.

The 1800s saw the rise of machine tools — tools that made tools, machines that made machines, along with assembly lines and the interchangeable parts those required. (Some people who value craftsmanship and personal job satisfaction say the conveyor belt was invented by the Devil.) Inventions included the light bulb, telephone, typewriter and sewing machine; Volta invented the battery, Trevithick the first steam-powered locomotive, Nicéphore photography, Durand the tin can, John Walker, matches; Joseph Aspdin, Portland cement; and Samuel Fahnestock a soda fountain. Michael Faraday invented the electric dynamo, and Cyrus McCormick built the first commercially successful reaper. The word "scientist" was first used in 1833.

The pace became dizzying in the 20th century. The first year alone ushered in the safety razor, the first radio receiver, and the vacuum cleaner; followed in 1902 by the air conditioner, lie detector, and Teddy Bear; only to be outdone in 1903 by the Wright Brothers' gas-powered airplane and Mary Anderson's windshield wipers. After that, take your pick: the bra *(update: it was recently discovered that the bra is 600 years older than previously thought),* the zipper, pop-up toasters, Pyrex, traffic signal, television (1923), frozen food, Technicolor, aerosol can, penicillin, Scotch tape, jet engine, Polaroid photography, photocopier, helicopter, and radar. The first computer controlled by software appeared in 1941, the first electronic digital computer in 1942, and in 1943, synthetic rubber, the slinky, silly putty and LSD. The mobile phone was invented in

1947, although cell phones weren't sold commercially until 1983 (and they were the size of suitcases).

During the 1950s almost every family in America acquired a television set… and the Diners Club credit card was invented along with super glue and power steering.

By the end of the '60s man had reached the moon. But we also had acrylic paint, Astro-turf, Nutra-sweet, bar code scanners and ATMs.

From agrarian to supercharged

Obviously, this is a very abbreviated list and just as obviously, this is not the end of it. But it's enough to show how very quickly human life changed from a basically agrarian subsistence lifestyle to the supercharged mode of living most of America — and much of the rest of the world — experiences today. We have become so accustomed to all these goods we can hardly imagine living without them, but everyone — even the wealthiest potentates — did, for many thousands of years. We don't need all the "stuff" capitalism provides.

It also demonstrates the multiplier effect, how one thing leads to another in an ever-expanding gush, with constant acceleration. It took thousands of years to combine fire, water, and the wheel to make a steam engine; the first software-controlled computer to the Internet took about 50; and after that, it was "Nellie, hang on to your hat." Today a product becomes "obsolete" within months, or less. In fact there's a new saying: "If it works, it's obsolete."

At the same time, and very much a partner of capitalism, democracy was developing. The thinking of Rousseau and Voltaire fomented not only the French Revolution; they were in large part also responsible for the American Revolution, where a number of sociological, geographic and economic factors allowed democracy to take shape and flourish not only in theory but in practice. A limited form of capitalism is possible in a totalitarian state, but it can only flourish in a democracy; America provided the perfect petri dish to incubate it, and went on from there.

And go on it did, in that such a system demands constant growth in order to survive, and that growth comes faster and faster... until it spins out of control. It consumes the lives it was supposedly "designed" to help (although of course it wasn't *designed* at all, and no one is in charge); it consumes the resources of the nation, and indeed, the planet; and still it continues to grow, until it depletes its fuel: it uses up both the people, and the resources. When anything runs out of fuel, its food, it dies.

Oddly enough, this is an anticipated part of the System. It's the process of creative destruction.

Chapter 6:
Thinking About Capitalism

I have spent a lot of time over the years thinking and writing about self-sufficiency. It wasn't easy, because self-sufficiency is impossible. No one can march off into the wilderness and create a life worth living without a lot of help. Even an independent fellow like Daniel Boone had to acquire a gun that was made by others. The question for a homesteader is not "how can I live a self-sufficient life without outside input?" but rather, "What does capitalism provide that I cannot, will not, or would rather not produce myself, or live without?"

Thinking about this provides some quick reminders about what capitalism is and how it works.

An example I often used is the light bulb. You go into a room, flip a switch, the dark room becomes bright and you scarcely even think about it. Simple.

But could you make a light bulb? Or the electricity to make it work? Or a length of wire?

Leonard E. Read went through the same exercise with a much better and even simpler example: a pencil.

His essay "I, Pencil," published in *The Freeman* in December, 1958, traces the making of a pencil from beginning to end. He describes how the cedar tree is cut down, the wood cut into slats less than ¼-inch thick, tinted and waxed and kiln dried, and grooved to accept eight pieces of lead. The lead — which contains no lead — is complex in itself, and includes graphite from Ceylon, clay from Mississippi, ammonium hydroxide, wetting agents such as sulfonated tallow, all of which is mixed and extruded and baked at 1,850° F. for several hours. To increase strength and smoothness the lead is then treated with a hot mixture containing several ingredients including candelilla wax from Mexico.

The lead is placed in the grooves of the cedar and another slab of cedar is placed over it, like a sandwich. (Now you know how they get the lead in that pencil.) Individual pencils are separated from the slab, and given six coats of lacquer, which as you might expect involves scores of people, including growers of castor beans.

That bit of metal on the end, the ferrule, is brass, which entails the mining of zinc and copper, and all of the processes involved before it reaches the pencil factory. And finally, the "plug," which most of us call the eraser. The main ingredient is not rubber, but "factice," a product made by reacting rape-seed oil from the Dutch East Indies with sulfur chloride. Among the numerous vulcanizing and accelerating agents is pumice, from Italy.

It takes more than a village...
Read doesn't leave it at that: he also includes the scores of people involved in the railroads and ships, the design and manufacture of the machinery, the production of the electricity used and even the men who poured the concrete for the dam of the Pacific Gas & Electric hydroplant that provides the power to the sawmill. He goes so far as to wonder how many cups of coffee are slurped in the making of a pencil... and how many bean pickers and others are involved in *that!*

No single person could make a pencil. It takes millions.

His point is that most of these millions don't even realize they are making a pencil; some perhaps never even saw a pencil. Their motivation is doing whatever they do — digging graphite, piloting a ship, working in a chemical factory or an oil field (paraffin being a by-product of petroleum), tending crops of castor beans or rape — to exchange their tiny bit of knowledge and labor for the goods and services they need or want. For them, the pencil is incidental.

Note how he takes pains to point out that even pencils "Made in the U.S.A." require inputs from around the globe.

That describes *capitalism*. The purpose of capitalism is not to produce "stuff," useful or otherwise; its purpose is to produce profits and more capital. The capitalist — by nature, by definition and in some cases by law — cares little about the end product "pencils" and even less about global warming or the environment; the sole *raison d'etre* of capitalism is profits.

The monster

Capitalism is a dynamic system, constantly recreating itself, like a shape-shifting creature in science fiction. It requires constant growth, like some giant alien blob that oozes over the Earth, consuming everything in its path. No one created it; no one controls it: it's guided by what Adam Smith called the "Invisible Hand." What could be spookier than that!

Capitalism is a monster.

One of its most monstrous characteristics is its insatiable need for growth, which infects the entire economic and political system and has been, for the most part, cheerfully supported by the American Dream.

With economic traditionalism, you work until you get enough, then you quit. (Incidentally, this is the ideal goal of the homesteader.)

Capitalism is just the opposite: there is never "enough." The Greeks called it *pleonexia*, meaning a morbid greediness or selfishness. Extreme cases are now recognized as a psychiatric disorder, but an excessive desire for wealth, the drive to get more than your fair share, and certainly the inability to say "enough!" are all everyday normal components of capitalism. They are an integral part of Mall Mania and after-Thanksgiving Black Friday Midnight Madness. Even in their mildest forms they provide a basis for the aptly-named rat race: a way of life where people are so caught up in a struggle for wealth or power that they have little time or energy for anything else, including *living*.

For individuals, it's a trap with a barb: once hooked, it's almost impossible to escape. This is especially true if consumption involves credit and debt: go into debt and the rat race becomes literal, a treadmill that never stops.

A democratic government is equally entrapped. Growth in GDP — a measure of an entire nation's goods and services — is closely watched in government and economic circles because the theory is that if you're standing still you're going backwards, and going backwards is deadly. (The U.S. has been close to standing still for several years. Anything less than 2% annual growth in GDP is considered poor. Incidentally, China's GDP has been growing at about 10% a year)

"Grow or die"

Until recently, capitalism's need for growth has been a given: almost no one questioned it. "Grow or die" is a law of survival in the marketplace. Then some people realized that the world is running out of resources, including clean air and water, and that the main culprit was unbridled capitalism. Kenneth Boulding said it: "Anyone who believes exponential growth can go on forever in a finite world is either a madman or an economist."

Some economists and other thinkers who agreed began to examine the notion that growth in capitalism is optional, not built in, and pushed the idea of a "steady-state" capitalism, or even something called "de-growth."

Others disagreed: "Since capitalist growth cannot be stopped, or even slowed, and since the market-driven growth is driving us toward collapse, ecological economists should abandon the fantasy of a steady-state capitalism and get on with the project figuring out what a post-capitalist economic democracy could look like…

"Growthmania is a rational and succinct expression of the day-to-day *requirements* of any conceivable kind of capitalism." (Richard Smith, "Beyond Growth or Beyond Capitalism? *real-world economics review,* issue no. 53, 26 June 2010, pp 28-42.)

Putting it another way, constant growth is essential to the System: without growth, capitalism would wither. The amazing thing is that while capitalism satisfies the demands of the marketplace (but in pursuit of profit, not from altruism), it's also capable of *increasing* those demands. Thus it feeds on itself, and on us. Capitalism is a *cannibalistic* monster!

As you might expect, there is a great deal of discussion among economists about capitalism and growth, some of which we'll consider later because it's pertinent to our overall theme. (See Smith, above, p. 33: He claims that if *all* businesses were small, or like regulated utilities, they *could* provide a steady-state economy.) But that's theory and speculation: what's the present reality of constant growth?

The reality is that we live in a consumer society; our wants are endless; and growth seems infinite. However, another part of reality is that satisfying endless wants is a deadly disease; infinite growth cannot come from finite resources; there must be a point at which we cry, "Enough!"

Dissecting how this functions reveals a long list of seemingly innocent components including "what everybody's doing" and keeping up with the Joneses as well as an individual's human weakness for convenience and the existence of capitalism itself, its inherent need for consumers. In many cases two or more are tied together, as with the combination of advertising with the innate human desire for luxury and perceived low cost or the easy availability of credit… all in the service of capitalism, of course.

Satisfying the need for growth

Economic growth occurs in several ways. The first option is market saturation. The theoretical ideal is that every man, woman and child in the country becomes your customer. Then get them to buy more, by offering credit.

After that, an increase in population increases business: more people equals a greater market for goods and services.

Next, this can be stimulated artificially by expanding the market through exports. When there's a coffee shop or burger stand on every street corner at home, start opening them in China or Russia or Bangladesh.

When there are no more markets, expand your offerings. If you're a Walmart, start selling groceries; if McDonald's, offer gourmet coffee.

What then? Well, the System will always come up with new gizmos and gadgets, and improvements to old ones (even if that only means a different size or color) and on rare occasions, something entirely new and useful. Given the competitive nature of the beast, token "new" products outnumber truly new ones by a wide margin, probably by an order of thousands. (Remember, in 2010 the average supermarket carried 38,718 items.)

The speed of growth increases exponentially. By one account, food was first preserved in tin cans in 1772; the can opener wasn't invented until 1855. (In the interim, cans were opened with a chisel and hammer.) If the can had been invented late yesterday the opener would have been here this morning. Now there are manual, electric and cordless can openers; lever-type and rotating wheel, church key and butterfly, space-saver and under-counter; the Star, the Bunker and the bull-head; special models for users with arthritis and the P-38, P-51 and FRED for the military. All of which are becoming obsolete with the introduction of pull-and-tear and pop-top cans, and some formerly-canned products now packaged in pouches.

Along with new products there are new ways to entice shoppers. In the realm of food alone, there are traditional supermarkets; fresh format markets (Whole Foods, Public Greenwise, The Fresh Market); superstores, super warehouses, limited assortment stores (Aldi's, Trader Joe's, Save-A-Lot); as well as non-traditional groceries: wholesale clubs, supercenters (Walmart Supercenters, Super Target, Meijer, Fred Meyer); dollar stores, drug stores, mass merchandisers, and military commissaries. Oh, and the neighborhood small corner grocery store, which probably sells more gas than groceries. *(Source: Food Marketing Institute, which did not include farm stands, farmers' markets, or CSAs.)*

Today the Internet is vying with brick and mortar stores in nearly all categories.

The role of advertising

With all of these businesses competing for your money with all of these products, advertising is essential. The Siren call of advertising is more than legendary: it's part of the culture, almost worn like a second skin. Some experts claim we see so many ads in a day that we ignore them... which makes them even more insidious and likely to affect us on a subconscious level. Figures range from a few hundred "exposures" a day to tens of thousands, depending on who's counting, how, and perhaps why. (Is spending a few seconds scanning the classified ads in a newspaper really "exposure" to all 500 of those sales messages?) A common estimate is 3,000, which as one rational analyst calmly pointed out, would mean that the average person who is awake 1,000 minutes a day would see three ads a minute, all day long. But even some of the lowest guesstimates, minimums of 300-500, constitute an enormous strain on our mentality. That's a lot of noise.

What affects us is not a single ad, but the massive steady stream, on television, billboards, radio, in newspapers and magazines and on the web, on trucks and busses, even on coffee mugs and clothing. Even architecture can be advertising. (What do you think when I say "golden arches"?) There is no escape, and no let-up. The $130 billion (or $200 billion, take your pick, either one is too much to comprehend) spent on advertising annually alters not only our buying habits but our minds.

You might think you don't pay attention to ads, especially the stupid or trivial ones for products you have no interest in... maybe including political ads. You zap tv commercials, flip through magazines, and think you avert your gaze from highway billboards you pass by at 70 per. You think advertising doesn't influence you. If you think that, you're mistaken. You aren't even aware that it's altering your brain.

Advertising aimed at children, primarily on tv, has long been a topic of hot debate. Ads for fast foods and sugary beverages (and those are not only colas, today) aimed at children and adolescents have come in for particular criticism in the war on obesity. But such ads comprise only about a quarter of the total. There isn't as much uproar about the effects of the other three-quarters. There should be. Not only do those ads move tremendous amounts of merchandise of dubious social value to a particularly vulnerable subset of society; they act very much like those miniature supermarket carts with the flags proclaiming "Customer in training." They constitute brain-washing.

Is advertising good, or bad?

In a world where nothing is all black or all white, advertising stands out as a prime example. Noted adman Rosser Reeves said, "Advertising is, actually, a simple phenomenon in terms of economics. It is merely a substitute for a personal sales force — an extension, if you will, of the merchant who cries aloud his wares." William Allen White believed that "Advertising is the genie which is transforming America into a place of comfort, luxury and ease for millions." As Tevye of *Fiddler on the Roof* might say, "You're right."

On the opposite side, Clare Boothe Luce wrote, "Advertising has done more to cause the social unrest of the 20th century than any other single factor." And from Raymond Chandler: "It's pretty obvious that the debasement of the human mind caused by a constant flow of fraudulent advertising is no trivial thing. There is more than one way to conquer a country." And to this Tevye would say, "And you're right too."

When we retort, "What? The two sides can't *both* be right!" Tevye responds, "And you're right too!"

The argument becomes even more contentious when it turns to the question of choice. Carrie P. Snow thought advertising degrades the people it appeals to, because it deprives them of their will to choose. On the opposite side, more than one supporter has claimed that advertising is the very essence of democracy, by giving people choices.

Advertising by itself is neither good nor bad. It's more accurate to say it's good *or* bad, depending on your goals and concerns. In any event, it's the *effects* that concern us. And those effects are dependent on what's being advertised, how, where, when, how much, why, and to whom.

Taken as a whole, advertising is (as Will Rogers said) "the art of convincing people to spend money they don't have for something they don't need." Many ads try to accomplish that with a calculated mix of golden promises and dire threats: promises of everlasting youth and sexiness, ridiculously simple ease, or delirious happiness; or threats of being a social outcast due to bad breath or ring around the collar.

A factory might make shampoo, or lipstick or perfume, but its advertising sells hope. In beginning courses in ad copywriting this is phrased as "Sell the sizzle, not the steak!"

Another form of advertising creates a need and then fills it; presents a problem, then solves it; or as one wag put it, it invents cures for which there is no disease.

Promoting greed, in disguise

Most of all, advertising creates dreams, a desire to turn those dreams into reality, and then offers a way to achieve those dreams.

My dear mother, who not only had a wry wit but was as frugal as anyone else who lived through the Great Depression, often told a story about a door-to-door vacuum cleaner salesman who promised that his machine would cut her work in half.

"Fine, she said. "I'll take two."

She had a broom and a mop, and that's all she needed or wanted. We had a rug and a rug beater (requiring only a clothesline and a young boy), but no carpeting. Her assessment of needs, wants, and advertising promises certainly affected my outlook on all three. Sadly (or alarmingly) too many mothers of more recent generations have not passed on such wisdom, in most cases because they didn't have it themselves. As a result, while most consumers learn how to be cynical of some kinds of advertising, they don't know how to be critical and discerning. They become mindless consumers. And since *everybody* is doing it…

Maslow's hierarchy of needs, which we'll discuss later, includes self-respect, recognition, and acceptance or peer approval. To psychologists, that's only human nature. To an advertiser, all three present a golden opportunity. A desire for acceptance is unavoidable to some degree, in small doses it enhances human life, but it can easily roar out of control. Adolescents are particularly vulnerable, but it's not confined to any age group. Peer pressure mixed with advertising can make a deadly cocktail. Then add easy credit...

We want instant gratification —
and we want it right now

The "buy now pay later" pitch is part of the advertising and marketing bag of tricks. Originally applied to big-ticket items such as farm tractors and cars, it soon trickled down to less expensive goods. With the introduction of credit cards, anything at all could be "purchased" without spending a dime. This trap contains a number of hidden dangers, not the least of which is paying interest on top of the purchase price. But others might be even more insidious.

If you really want something but don't have the cash, one option is to save until you have the money in hand. This has become old-fashioned, even unacceptable, in our age of instant gratification. If you've never done it try it, just once. There's an excellent chance that by the time you accumulate enough to make the purchase you'll change your mind, or even forget about it entirely. The obverse of that coin is buying the thing on credit, lugging it home, tossing it in a drawer or closet, and forgetting about it. Or worse, suffering buyer's remorse: you really didn't want it as badly as you thought you did.

Buying goods we really don't need or want in large part accounts for our overflowing closets and landfills... and the constant growth of capitalism... and the depletion of natural resources. But perceived low costs and easy credit aren't the only culprits. The very ubiquity of both goods and advertising makes avoiding them impossible. Nearly anything you can think of, and some things you never even dreamed of, are close at hand, on store shelves, in vending machines, at the click of a mouse, usually with no cash needed. We can buy almost without thinking, and some people often do.

It's not easy to ignore all of that to become self-sufficient.

The role of ease and luxury

And then there's the all-too-human desire for ease and luxury. Sometimes it's warranted, and extremely worthwhile. All too often it's either a misplaced emotion or a perversion. Once again there must be harmony, a balance between being a sybarite and a puritan.

Taken together, these components of modern merchandising dull our senses, turn off our internal alarms and good sense, and make us reach for our credit cards without even thinking. This is good for the economy, and capitalism. It's bad for the Earth and its environment, including the humans who inhabit it. And what about you, your life?

The components are traps, individually and together, because they entice you to spend your time and money, your *life-force* if you will, in ways and places that keep you from achieving your *real* dreams and goals, the truly important ones that you have set aside because... well, because you don't have the time and/or the money to pursue them!

These traps are insidious because all too often they aren't even recognized as such. One result is that attempted escapes are rare. But even if the attempt is made, escape is difficult, and sometimes nearly impossible. Dig yourself into debt too deeply and you'll never get out: it will bury and crush you. Or simply get on the consumer carousel. Spend every penny as soon as it comes in (and sometimes before) and the merry-go-round will never stop, you'll never get off. In any event, once you're trapped in your material world of escapism, the stuff you once owned now owns you.

Now we face another dilemma. What if we put all this together and decide we don't need all the stuff capitalism provides, and simply quit buying after we have "enough"? We take away the monster's food dish. The monster starves. And we, with it.

This is definitely not looking good.

In October 2011 the Federal Reserve reported that while in the three previous recessions household debt increased after the recovery began — as much as 25% in 1982 and 2001 — after 2009 that number actually decreased 8.6%, or $1.1 trillion. "Millions of Americans have ditched their credit cards, accelerated mortgage payments and cut off credit lines that during the good times were used like a bottomless piggy bank. Many have resorted to a practice once thought old-fashioned — delaying purchases until they have the cash."

This is good, right? Maybe not for modern capitalism. The Wall Street Journal headline on the story was "Penitent Debtors Hobble Recovery in U.S."

But one of the debtors quoted, "talking about her old borrowing habits like a recovering drug addict," said "My life is so much better not having that haunting debt," suggesting that for some at least the old borrowing habits are gone for good, even if "good times" do return. On the third hand, although this "reformed" 36-year-old borrowing addict did pay for her wedding last year with savings, and wiped out the balance on two dozen credit cards, she is still working her way through $50,000 in student loans and the $215,000 left on her mortgage.

During the Great Depression, economist John Maynard Keynes spoke of the paradox of thrift: When everyone turns frugal, everyone suffers. Synchronized thrift slows the economy, according to Keynes, which hobbles income growth and makes people even stingier in a pernicious cycle.

Some economists are concerned about the environment; others are not. Some are alarmed by capitalism's need for constant growth; others are not. Most ordinary people also have ideas on these topics, without having to resort to economic theories. Few would actively choose a polluted and desolate world over a Garden of Eden… but only if achieving the garden didn't interfere too much with their desired lifestyle. Many have grave concerns about the various perceived shortcomings of capitalism — the alarming and increasing gap between haves and have-nots, for example, or the role of banks in foreclosures. But we're trapped: there is no way out, we can't restrain capitalism without losing our cherished way of life.

Is no-growth capitalism possible?

In recent years more and more discussion has been devoted to the possibilities of no-growth capitalism, and "de-growth" and stasis or steady-state capitalism. Some writers have pointed out that we've been in a state of stasis and zero growth since the fall of 2008, and look at the misery that resulted: unemployment, foreclosures, loss of savings, business closures and downsizing, poverty and homelessness, cash-strapped schools and municipalities… If this is what no-growth capitalism looks like, most people proclaim, we'll take the growth, even if it does cause other problems!

From the standpoint of employment alone, capitalism, and economic growth, are considered essential to the American way of life. Even those who desire a clean environment and a sustainable future for their children and grandchildren would hesitate to swap those for unemployment and poverty. And according to common thinking, we can't have it both ways.

Milton Friedman said, "corporations are in business to make money, not save the world." But if in the process of doing business and making money they destroy the world, we have a problem. Capitalism contains the seeds of its own destruction and doesn't care if it destroys the planet in the process; we humans see things a little differently.

A growing number of economic thinkers, particularly those with environmental leanings, have simply given up on capitalism. Richard Smith, in "Beyond Growth or Beyond Capitalism? (*real-world economics review*, issue no. 53, 26 June, 2010) concludes, "Either we save capitalism or we save ourselves. We can't save both."

But are Americans ready for a more copacetic economic system? Most will automatically recoil from the term "socialism."

If this means an impasse, then the future will be very interesting indeed.

Chapter 7: Accounting for homesteaders: A stacked deck

Adam Smith did not invent capitalism. Neither did any of the others who thought and wrote about it in its early days. They described what they saw, coloring it with their own ideas and twists and at times offering opinions and suggestions, but neither alone nor as a group did anyone invent capitalism; there was no central planning; it just grew.

According to one theory it began with the printing press, which in our over-simplified world we say was invented by Johannes Gutenberg in 1450. By then, thousands of books had already been printed in China, some with moveable type, which we also often credit to Gutenberg. The truth is, Gutenberg (a blacksmith and goldsmith) developed a way to mass-produce *metal* type (as opposed to carving it from clay or wood); an oil-based ink required by the new type; and a new press to make use of the other two: he didn't invent printing, but a new printing *system.*

This system obviously revolutionized handwritten bookmaking, and it spread rapidly, resulting in a concurrent spread of knowledge and literacy and schools, as well as papermakers and booksellers and, after all the available ancient Greek and Roman manuscripts had been printed, new writers.

A certain set of conditions and circumstances, in a certain place, at a certain time, acted upon by certain unseen forces — and *poof,* there it is. Like spontaneous combustion. No one created it, no one controls it, and no one can put out the flame.

But that doesn't mean it's inextinguishable. Capitalism can, and must, burn out on its own, (as several early writers on the topic suggested, although seldom for reasons that seem plausible today). It feeds on itself, and thus contains the seeds of its own destruction.

We have glimpsed, briefly, some of the conditions that gave rise to capitalism, and we have seen, even more briefly, some of the indications that it's running out of fuel; now let's look at some of those more closely.

We've paid scant attention to some of the classic arguments against capitalism, reasons why it couldn't, wouldn't or shouldn't last, usually having to do with its most glaring shortcomings such as its tolerance of greed and inequality. Only recently have a few economists considered the insatiable appetite of the monster, the need for constant growth and constantly *accelerating* growth, the consumption of natural resources inherent in that growth, the finiteness of those natural resources. The inevitable conclusion: capitalism is not sustainable.

The Earth belongs to everyone

One aspect of this new emphasis on eco-economics concerns "the Commons," that earth and sky and water Chief Seattle referred to. They "belong" to no one, because they belong to *everyone.*

One factory located on a river discards chemical waste into the river rather than spending money on a disposal system that will not foul the water. That's simply part of the capitalist profit motive: the savings give it an advantage over other factories. Then the other factories must also discard waste into the river in order to remain competitive.

At first no one notices, or at least says much about it, even though the water is used by the townspeople and those who live along its banks for miles downstream as well as those from some distance away who enjoy the river. (Note that in most cases, whether the capitalist enterprise is a mine, a new factory or a shopping mall, two sides are drawn up: jobs vs. nature. If the two are naturally antagonistic or incompatible, and many capitalists believe they are, then the capitalist democratic System has a very serious problem.)

Eventually the water becomes so polluted it's undrinkable, or unusable for any domestic purposes; humans can no longer safely swim in it; they cannot fish in it, the fish have all died;

it's not even pleasant to float on with a canoe or rowboat, nor to live alongside of, nor even to gaze upon. And when the river starts to burn, as the Cuyahoga in Ohio so famously did in 1969, it becomes obvious that something needs to be done.

Actually, the Cuyahoga River burned at least 14 times, the largest fire causing more than $1 million damage to boats and a riverfront office building in 1952. The river didn't attract national attention until *Time* magazine covered the 1969 fire. Economist Paul Krugman called this the start of "environmentalism." (The first Earth Day was in 1970.)

Today, metaphorically burning rivers span the globe: truck and auto emissions foul the air everywhere; coal-burning plants spew pollutants into the air everywhere; open pit mining, deepwater oil spills, deforestation, soil erosion, soil depletion, soil salinization, lowering water tables, the list seems endless. And it continues to grow: the hydraulic fracturing, or "fracking" now being used to squeeze more oil and natural gas out of shale is a case in point. Vast quantities of a special kind of sand are used in the process. That silica sand is found in western Wisconsin. Sand mines have mushroomed in the area, virtually overnight, setting off alarms among the local inhabitants.

Meanwhile there are growing concerns about the fracking itself. Does injecting those millions of gallons of water underground cause earthquakes, as was decided in Britain? Is it morally acceptable to use such awesome amounts of a precious resource for such a purpose? There is now evidence that some of the chemicals used in the process are contributing to water pollution in Wyoming.

Another component is guar bean gum. Its use in vast quantities in the gas and oil fields has had repercussions on growers and the former major users of the bean product, food and beverage manufacturers. And the webs don't end there.

Not so incidentally, what are we to think of the people who have lived in western North Dakota for all of their 70 or 80 years but can no longer afford the rent because the influx of highly-paid Bakken Shale oil field workers has exploded the local economy, ballooning the cost of living even for those not involved in the boom?

All of these, and many more, are problems of capitalism. Adam Smith and even Karl Marx did not and could not have anticipated such problems, and certainly not problems of such magnitude on such a broad scale.

It gets worse: if the teeming masses of China and India, along with the rest of the world, want to share in their version of the American Dream, if we Americans support them because we believe in equality for all or even if only because we believe in capitalism, and if technology continues to find even more ways we can destroy the Commons (or even the entire planet), then where will it end? Maybe "destroying the entire planet" just answered that.

You might not "believe" in global warming: many do not. Nature doesn't care. If it's going to affect the world it will affect believers and non-believers alike. But that's only one part, and perhaps a small part, of the assault on the Commons. What we're really talking about when we discuss man-made global warming is not simply CO_2 in the atmosphere, but the monster of capitalism suffocating the globe in myriad ways. In the big picture, maybe global warming isn't even worth getting excited about. For homestead economist-philosophers, there is much, much more to the story.

Economics of the tomato

Sustainability is one issue with the System. Another is how capitalism has usurped the commons for its own ends, disregarding the non-economic needs and desires of the people. But this type of accounting has another aspect that is just as galling to homesteaders: it also fails to place a value on many of their products and services. Capitalism says "what you're doing doesn't benefit *me* so it doesn't count."

A prime example that was a bone of contention in certain quarters for many years was the role of the full-time housewife. More than a few witty writers examined her many roles (only rarely were there house-husbands then) such as chef, nurse, bookkeeper, purchasing agent, maid, chauffer, etc., and assigned an hourly rate to each. Adding it up often resulted in eye-popping value, which the System totally ignored. According to the rules of the System, anyone who gets a paycheck is a "worker;" anyone who does not get a paycheck, even if performing the same work, is a "non-worker" and doesn't count.

A properly run self-sufficient homestead is a small business, and even when it isn't, it involves useful human labor. Like the housewife, it performs, or renders unnecessary, many tasks capitalism jealously guards as its own. Even if the product or service covers only a few small aspects of life, there is a corresponding effect on capitalism.

When you plant a tomato from seed you saved from last year's tomatoes — it would have to be open-pollinated (non-hybrid) and very likely an "heirloom" variety which capitalism would charge extra for — you are diverting money from the System. In this case the loser is probably a seed company called Seminis, which reportedly accounts for 40% of the U.S. seed market and 75% of the tomatoes in supermarkets. Seminis sells seeds to other seed companies, both large and small, who simply repackage them.

Oh, by the way, Seminis is owned by Monsanto, which also owns Cargill International Seed and DeKalb Genetics, as well as Roundup herbicide (and we'll encounter them again in coming chapters). Maybe a behemoth corporation like that won't even notice that you saved a few seeds from last year's tomatoes… but let's press on anyway, just for the sake of argument.

Incidentally, some seeds and plants are patented, and there are stiff penalties for their unauthorized production. Many people find capitalism's move to corner the market on living things such as plants and animals… shall we say, unsettling?

We're talking about the tangled web of capitalism. You not only deprived Seminis of a seed sale: you also short-circuited the company or companies that function between them and the gardener, the companies that send you their catalogs every year, or have large display racks filled with packets of seeds set up in supermarkets and hardware stores everywhere. Obviously, you are infringing not only on the seed-growing trade, but you're also endangering the paper-making and printing businesses engaged in producing seed packets and catalogs, as well as the truck drivers and dispatchers and diesel mechanics involved in moving those products, and of course the retailers who sell the seeds or, if you ordered them by mail or online, the person who delivers them to your door. (Are you feeling any guilt yet? And are you wondering how such a system can be *efficient?*)

As you plant your seeds, tend the sprouting seedlings, transplant them into the garden and then continue to look after them, you're displacing many other workers and in some cases, machines. (We won't get into what's involved in the machines, nor even the effects of using your own homemade compost instead of commercial fertilizer: just use your imagination.) Many of these tasks are not highly regarded or compensated: some migrant farm workers are little more than slaves. Which might be why most Americans prefer to avoid such labor, even on their own behalf.

Homestead labor: work, or play?

But I would hasten to point out the qualitative differences between migrant labor and homestead labor. The migrant works for a boss, (who also has a boss, named "Capitalism,") working a set schedule of long hours of repetitive labor at an exhausting pace, since the compensation is dependent on the amount picked, currently about $2 a basket. The huge field stretches out to the horizon like the endless conveyor belt of a factory assembly line, which in a way it is. The tomatoes are green (to be ripened later with ethylene gas), and the worker has no interest in or relationship with them except to fill his basket.

In contrast, the homesteader probably strolls through the tomato patch every morning as a matter of pride and pleasure, much as the gentlefolk of yore passed through their formal gardens to relax and perhaps to commune with nature. Watching for and attending to problems with a few dozen tomato plants is more akin to picking a bouquet than to the dehumanizing factory work modern agribusiness makes it. Just as importantly, you, as a home gardener, have a very personal interest in each plant; we might say you have some skin in the game. The tomato becomes a very important and personal part of nature.

And then you find the first, firm, sun-ripened fruit, lifting it from the plant you began nurturing as a seed, feeling its smooth perfection, its fresh warmth from the sun, and inhaling the distinctive perfume of tomato leaves. For many, this annual ritual involves taking the first bite of the first tomato right there in the garden, without washing off the chemicals (there are none), even without salt (which is probably bad for you anyway).

Later, picking a bushel or two at the peak of perfection and before the unrelenting heat of the day is not an onerous chore, but a ritual of joy and wonder, even an act of love.

The karma of the tomato

Canning tomatoes is not an activity many people would choose in place of, say, lounging in the hammock under a shade tree with a glass of iced tea or a cold beer. But if you live in a northern clime and want to enjoy and benefit from tomatoes during the long winter, in soups and stews, as juice and as salsa, with pasta or chili or baked beans, then *somebody* has to preserve them. The independent self-sufficient person does not shrink from the task, but faces it with determination by bearing in mind the future rewards. It's like making firewood in summer: sweating with a chainsaw and splitting maul amidst mosquitoes, ticks and deer flies, while envisioning bitter winds and swirling snow… and a cozy blazing fire of well-cured oak. And as with butchering your own meat, *karma* is involved.

The rewards come after the first frost, when the once-luxuriant plants lie prostrate and blackened, sprawling over themselves and each other like soldiers heaped in a horrendous battlefield massacre. As frost paints over the windowpane in the kitchen where the seeds first sprouted and snow covers the garden, the homesteader gazes over the rows of gleaming glass jars in the root cellar and relives the balmy days of summer.

The entire process circumvents the role of capitalism in the tomato sector of the homesteader's life. Limited to a single person or family, it affects capitalism about as much as a toad crossing an Interstate highway affects the loaded semi bearing down on it. So far as capitalism is concerned, the rewards to the individual are so insignificant they're not even worth scoffing at (although some cheerleaders of capitalism do occasionally draw attention to self-sufficiency by ridiculing the notion of peasants with "40 acres and a mule" feeding the teeming modern world… but more on that later.)

How do we measure efficiency, and profit?

And admittedly, from an economic standpoint, the entire exercise of growing, preserving, and then using a tomato in made-from-scratch cooking seems futile: it's not "efficient," and it's not "profitable." Why do all that work when you can buy a can of tomatoes or a jar of catsup for a couple of bucks?

But that's according to the accounting methods used by traditional capitalism. Those methods only count things that can be measured in dollars and cents and tallied in a profit-and-loss statement. The homesteader uses a different system of bookkeeping based, we might say, on spiritual values as much as or even more than material considerations.

The home-grown tomato doesn't exploit human labor, anywhere along the long line from seed production to the final product in a sealed glass jar and the dinner table. That labor has been provided by the homesteader, not under duress, not in soul-sucking production line boring monotony, but in joyful cooperation, even celebration, with nature. The homesteader can sing while working, not the dirges of the galley slave oarsmen or those of the cotton fields, but the uplifting hymns of freemen rejoicing in their liberty, songs of happiness and satisfaction. The homestead tomato has not abased humanity in the pursuit of profit.

Under ideal conditions, nature provided the tomatoes with needed water; if not, the homesteader watered the tomato plants from a rain barrel, not by drawing down an underground aquifer, a piece of the Commons that has no price. The plant was nourished with organic nutrients that were not only replaceable, not only sustainable, not only did not involve the pollution and devastation of industrially produced chemical fertilizers, but which also did not harm the biosphere: the flora and fauna existing in a healthy fertile soil, the interactive web of insects and birds. The homestead tomato has not abused the Earth in search of profits.

The true cost of goods

Capitalism does not account for the costs incurred by the Commons. This makes many prices artificially low, including the tomato. What you pay for even a hard, gas-ripened and tasteless tomato doesn't include the social costs of near-slave labor, the environmental cost of water and fertilizer needed to grow tomatoes where they shouldn't be grown at all, the unallocated costs of the damage transportation and chemicals wreak on the biosphere.

When — not if, but *when* — these costs are taken into consideration, the price of a tomato in a supermarket will soar, perhaps even to its true cost, maybe even to the cost of a homegrown tomato (which will still retain all the personal and "spiritual" benefits).

Spread this across all of capitalism and all of homesteading and the economic gulf between the two all but vanishes. The truth is, to a homestead accountant, capitalism isn't really so efficient and economical after all. And if capitalist agribusiness is not sustainable, meaning it can't go on forever, either it must change or homesteading will be the *only* option.

The homesteader (who for all we know also spends interminable hours at a conveyor-belt type of job, on an assembly line or at a computer, because few homesteaders can escape the clutches of the System under current conditions) plants each tiny seed with reverence, hope, anticipation, awe, we might say with religious fervor, while at the same time following scientific principles: the seed must be set just so in the environment of a certain kind of soil with just the proper amount of moisture and in a certain temperature range with mandated lumens of light at various stages of growth. The homestead tomato represents a spiritual experience combined with scientific knowledge mixed with human emotions ranging from the wonder in seeing a sprouting seed and the pleasure of the first fresh fruits to the fulfillment of the harvest, the security of the root cellar, and the immense satisfaction in eating a meal made with tomatoes and saying, "I grew them myself."

In other words, homesteading blends many aspects of capitalism into what the thinking person must consider a much saner way of living. The trick is in deciding what to use, and what to discard.

Chapter 8: Shopping bags, carts, and capitalism

Bringing home material goods — whether necessities or luxuries, from compulsive habit or for conspicuous consumption — is one aspect of consumerism. Another is disposing of those goods. Except for consumables like crackers and candles that are actually used up, material possessions are eventually trashed. Ultimately, anything that has been manufactured, by hand or machine, will outlive its usefulness. In some cases it's a nearly straight line from factory to store shelf to your shopping cart to the landfill: one wonders if some day they might even eliminate the middlemen. Those are purchases to avoid, but the System is making that more and more difficult. Sometimes, it's virtually impossible.

The plastic sack

Exhibit A is the ubiquitous plastic sack. Like so much of what we're talking about, this all-too-familiar icon of the throwaway branch of the compulsive consumer society is a fairly recent introduction, which is both interesting and important. Invented by engineer Sten Gustaf Thulin, it was patented by the Swedish company Celloplast in 1965. In typical capitalist fashion other companies saw the potential and wanted in on the action. Petrochemical conglomerate Mobil got the U.S. Celloplast patent overturned in 1977. Kroger was the first grocery chain to use the new bag, but not until 1982. Since then, nobody knows how many millions have been made, used once, and discarded: 22.5 million a month were used in Washington, D.C. alone, before a 5-cent tax was levied in June, 2009. That resulted in a decrease to three million in the first month… 19.5 million bags formerly deemed "essential" simply not being used, in a single month, in just one city. One wonders what else that might be applied to.

They reportedly can take up to 1,000 years to decompose, which could be a blessing in disguise: the process involves breaking into tiny pieces and leaching toxic chemicals into soil, lakes and rivers, and eventually oceans. But this means they continue to pile up.

The Great Pacific Garbage Patch is one of five ocean gyres, or vortexes, where trash accumulates as the result of enormous rotating ocean currents. In the past, rubbish accumulated in gyres biodegraded, but today, plastic constitutes 90 percent of all trash polluting the Earth's seas, and it's not biodegradable. The impact on sea life is considerable.

The bags are taxed or restricted in about a quarter of the world's countries. By 2011 they were banned entirely in Italy and several other countries, and in several areas of the United States, starting with San Francisco in 2007.

The familiar "paper or plastic?" is sometimes answered with "neither," as customers present reusable cloth bags.

This is the kind of situation that keeps capitalism on its toes. Follow the money:

Somebody came up with a cheaper alternative to the traditional paper grocery sack (which incidentally replaced the sturdy wicker shopping basket); more and more stores used the bags to remain competitive. Eventually opposition arose on environmental grounds which, of themselves, have no cost basis in a capitalist economic system but which presented other opportunities: entrepreneurs began selling reusable cloth or canvas bags.

And how did this all start? Return for a moment to the paper bag. According to one story, William H. Deubner, owner of a small grocery store in St. Paul, Minnesota, noticed that his customers' purchases were limited by what they could conveniently carry. His solution was to invent the paper sack, in 1912, featuring a cord looping beneath the bag to not only provide support, but two handles. In true capitalist fashion he patented his bag, abandoned the grocery business for the bag manufacturing business, and by 1915 was selling more than a million bags a year for 5¢ each. (Note that million a year, nationally. Less than a hundred years later more than 22 million plastic bags were used just in Washington, D.C.)

Evolution of the shopping cart

As usual, one bag wasn't enough: there is never "enough" for capitalism. Customers could buy much more with a shopping cart. Oklahoma City grocer Sylvan Nathan Goldman got the idea while looking at a folding wooden chair in his office. All it took was a basket on the seat and wheels on the legs. After a bit of tinkering to make it more elegant, he patented the "folding basket carrier" in 1938.

But capitalism marches on: child's seat added to the cart: 1947. Plastic added to close off the leg holes for the childless shopper: 1952. Color-coordinated plastic cart handles with personalized store names: 1954. And on and on, past the built-in UPC scanner and calculator to the IBM "Stop and Shop Shopping Buddy" smart cart, which allows a shopper to email a grocery list to the store's database from home, and then keeps a running total of purchases as well as the loyalty program benefits, offers information on products or nutritional values, and evaluates the customer's shopping history to suggest whether certain perishable items in the refrigerator at home could be outdated and should be replaced. To cap it off, at the end of a strenuous shopping trip the cart can wirelessly place deli orders to be picked up on the way to the checkout counter. Oh, it also has a GPS and a store map. One reason for all this is to "create a compelling consumer experience."

Add the "compelling experience" to advertising and peer pressure as a force we must learn to ignore. And what once was referred to as the "grocery cart" is now found in nearly every kind of emporium, from hardware to liquor to fabric and clothing stores.

The Packaging Plague

You need something to put into those bags and carts of course. Chances are, no matter what it is, it's packaged. Packaging takes the fast lane from natural resource to trash to the extreme.

Packaging does serve several purposes, at least for capitalists. It protects the product during shipping. When it's on display, it is usually part of the advertising by being distinctive or eye-catching. In some cases it can provide added value (new and improved ketchup bottles and flip-top toothpaste tube caps). It can also be expensive: packaging reportedly represents 40% of the selling price of some cosmetics.

Homesteaders in particular can't help but notice that many food items can be purchased in bulk at half the price of a name-branded packaged product, or even less. Taking it to the extreme, a farmer currently gets about 10¢ a pound for oats; a box of oatmeal often costs 40 times as much. Even if you let capitalism do the processing, boxed oatmeal costs 2-3 times as much as bulk oatmeal.

This very brief diversion from big important ideas like capitalism to a silly little thing like shopping bags demonstrates how even the smallest details can have a great impact, and how everything is tied together in ways we don't usually consider. Even when we aren't paying attention, capitalism has us in its grip.

Chapter 9: Understanding needs, wants, luxuries, and the concept of "Enough"

Satisfying human needs, wants, and luxuries is at the base of both capitalism and democracy, and to such a degree that some people might even presume that's their purpose. It is not. Their sole purpose is survival, self-perpetuation: if they ever actually satisfied humans they'd have no reason to exist. That's why, if they even come close, they must create more needs, wants and luxuries, like the carrot dangling from a stick in front of the donkey. In that sense, human needs serve the System as much as the System serves humans. Or more.

What's good for the capitalist democracy System isn't necessarily what's best for the people living under that System. This disconnect comes with some problems.

Humans have basic physical needs. Without adequate food, water, clothing and shelter, we'd die. "Food" might mean some bread or porridge, "clothing" could consist of an animal skin or a blanket, and a rough lean-to of brush or sheet metal or even cardboard could be considered "shelter." While those would meet our basic needs, the human mind isn't wired to accept that: we always want more, and whatever we perceive as better.

But why? And how has this affected capitalism, our lives, our world? Is the constant quest for more an ideal, or should we be looking at something else? How might this change, for better or worse, in the New Normal? How much is enough?

If we happened to live in a society where these bare minimums were the norm, we probably wouldn't even dream of anything else; at least not until one of our neighbors discovered that a shelter with four walls and a roof was more comfortable than the lean-to. That neighbor might have been smarter, more creative, or more ambitious than us, or he might have made his discovery accidentally, but once the rest of us saw the improvement, we all copied it.

At some point, even four walls and a roof aren't enough. So little by little we add doors, windows, rooms, furniture, central heat, a bathroom with running water...

The dividing line between needs and luxuries

At what point does the shelter meet our actual physical needs? When does it surpass that and become a luxury? And how far can we take this before the needed shelter is an albatross around our neck, requiring far more of our time and effort to pay for and maintain than it's actually worth in terms of our life-effort spent on it, actually *decreasing* our satisfaction, and even our quality of life? Will we toss in the towel at the professional chef's kitchen, the 25-seat home theater, or will we go for the thousand-bottle wine cellar and the indoor lap pool?

Although food and shelter are essential, their definitions are flexible. As with the basic shelter, a simple loaf of bread could keep us alive. But if bread is a basic necessity, a little butter might make it taste better: let's call that a "necessary nicety." But if we're adventurous or bored or somehow accidentally add some lettuce... a slice of tomato... a few strips of bacon... how "necessary" are those? And what about white or whole wheat, and maybe some mayo?

The line between needs and wants can become blurred, and the further divisions between wants, necessary niceties, affordable luxuries and luxuries that are restricted to the very wealthy (or the fantasies of average people) are even fuzzier. Even a grilled cheese sandwich can be problematical. Plain white factory-made bread could be replaced by the Roquefort and almond sourdough bread from Harrod's of London that sells for $24.50 a loaf. A substitute for Velveeta processed cheese might be *pule,* a Siberian product made from donkey milk and selling for around $616 a pound.

Statistics have shown that an average family in Houston spends twice as much on food as the average in Detroit. They don't eat twice as much: they just *spend* twice as much. And as more than one chef has glumly noted, by the next morning it all ends up the same anyway.

We are a nation of consumers; Earth is becoming a world of consumers; capitalism is entirely dependent not only on consumption but on continual growth of consumption. Infinite growth is impossible on a finite planet. At some point, anyone facing the New Normal will be forced to think about this dilemma and ask, "How much is enough?" As with everything else, it's multi-faceted, there are trade-offs, and there are innumerable fascinating webs.

Needs are more easily met, today

In 1901 nearly 80% of the average American's income (less for the rich, more for the poor) was spent on basic needs: 40% on food, 20% on housing, 20% on apparel. By 2003 those basic needs used only 50% of income, with 13% on food (and almost half of that for dining out), just 4% on clothes, and a whopping 33% on housing (and housing costs increased for the next five years). In addition, transportation went from near zero to 22%.

What this tells us is that we are covering our essential needs much more quickly and easily in terms of life-force spent or hours worked, so that fully half of our income is available for wants and luxuries. If dining out is seen as a want, necessary nicety or luxury, and the increase in housing expense is due to more spacious and luxurious shelter, then we're spending even less than 50% of our income on bare necessities. Note also that the cost of food dropped by 27 points, clothing by 16, and transportation became a "necessity." It would be reasonable to wonder why and how these changes occurred, and what the other half of our income is spent on. The answers deal not only with economics, but psychology.

The Maslow Pyramid

In 1943 American psychologist Abraham Maslow published a "hierarchy of needs" pyramid that has been reprinted in nearly every basic psychology textbook since then. The pyramid is built on a foundation of basic human needs, such as food and water, sleep and sex. The next layer includes safety and security, which is topped by love and belonging, and then esteem. At the peak is what Maslow called "self-actualization." Until the lower levels are satisfied, the upper levels remain elusive or out of reach but to be complete human beings, we need all of them.

Looking at it another way, the basic essentials for survival are physical. The rest is psychological, or "all in our heads." But as we have just seen, even the necessities have a psychological tinge. Returning to the above examples, progressing from a lean-to to an enclosed hut might or might not be a faint forerunner of the conspicuous consumption found in so many present-day pseudo-castles, but there are parallels. Certainly a BLT tastes better than a crust of dry bread, but at what point does taste matter less than the psychological satisfaction, or even excitement, of eating something other people don't even know about or can't afford?

Capitalism is well aware of the connection, and not only at the deep core level: marketers have been using psychology since the days of Sigmund Freud; their sophistication today would amaze many consumers who seldom bother to consider how they're being played. One root is conspicuous consumption, with variations: a sense of competition, or a feeling of not being left out of the crowd. The second is the rise of recreational shopping, which in some cases becomes an actual psychological disorder, *pleonexia*. And even when not actively involved in promoting consumption, capitalism makes it oh, so easy!

Conspicuous consumption

At first blush conspicuous consumption might appear to be egotistical, perhaps a desperate grab for esteem and the respect of others, which Maslow considered needs, but like everything else, there is that slippery sliding scale.

Thorstein Veblen, who first used the term in his 1899 book *Theory of the Leisure Class,* would no doubt be astounded at some of the examples of his theory today. He cited the use of silver eating utensils when those made of cheaper materials served the same purpose. Today there is everything from "name brand" clothes for kids to $354,000 Lamborghini automobiles to multi-million-dollar second homes. Like the food, eventually these will all end up the same, joining their less expensive counterparts on the trash heap.

The psychology of luxuries

But it gets more complicated. What if you happen to *enjoy* good cheese, or a fine wine? They simply add a little extra pleasure to your life. What's ostentatious about that? They could be on the borderline between necessary niceties and affordable luxuries. Just recognizing that they are not basic necessities and that you could live just as well without them probably adds to their cachet. So does enjoying them only occasionally, instead of on a regular basis. In fact, when luxuries become routine we become accustomed to them, we accept them and become jaded: they are no longer "special." In fact, their withdrawal can make having to survive on mere necessary niceties seem, to some people, like the most abject poverty. This is a psychological, not an economic problem.

The distinction isn't always easy to define, although H. L. Mencken did a fine job with one aspect of it in his essay, "Professor Veblen," from *Prejudices, First Series, 1919.* Mocking the notion that conspicuous consumption is "the use of money or other resources by people to display a higher social status than others," Mencken asked "Do I prefer kissing a pretty girl to kissing a charwoman because even a janitor may kiss a charwoman — or because the pretty girl looks better, smells better and kisses better?" The same reasoning might apply to cheese.

This can take a sinister turn. It has been suggested that "beautiful people" make life miserable for us normal people because we compare them to our own ordinary spouses and ourselves. Not that we don't try to emulate them: Americans spend $10 billion a year on cosmetic surgery, not to mention diet plans, exercise regimes, lotions and potions and other wild notions, all in an effort to be "beautiful." But many of us would be happier if we weren't constantly confronted with those impossibly perfect specimens of the young human animal, mostly in air-brushed advertising, of course.

No one can escape

Robert H. Frank touches on the same phenomena in *Luxury Fever: Why Money Fails to Satisfy in an Era of Excess* (1999). He optimistically thinks there are still some ordinary regular people who regard the consumer society, and conspicuous consumption in particular, as not only silly but downright stupid, but posits that even those people can't escape. Opulent McMansions attract attention and make news, but most people don't give serious consideration to a dwelling listed for $10 or $20 million. But then, how come the average American home today is twice as large — and far more expensive — than its counterpart in the 1950s? Sure, a $354,000 12-cylinder Lamborghini Diablo would look good sitting in the driveway, and it would certainly impress the neighbors, but most of us have a better grip on reality. The problem is, that reality now includes the fact that the *average* car costs $22,000, up more than 75% in a decade.

He goes on to say that no matter what your income and no matter how immune you think you are to conspicuous consumption, you can't escape. Consumer excess affects not only your home and car, but the kinds of gifts you're expected to give at weddings and birthdays, what you spend on an anniversary dinner or a bottle of wine to mark a special occasion, the kind of sneakers your kids are willing to be seen in and the suit you wear to a job interview.

One of the bothersome webs we get entangled in here is that in recent years the wealthy have been doing very well indeed; the average American has been treading water; and the "wealth" (such as it is) of the bottom 5th has declined 10%. In a "trickle-down" economy, ostentatious wealth seeps down too, unfortunately, even when the money doesn't.

Recreational shopping

To the various levels of conspicuous consumption we must add recreational shopping, which likewise can be divided into smaller sections along our ever-present sliding scales. This one, on the surface, is "just for fun," with several offshoots. But in another context, it becomes a new element in the American Dream, and according to at least one analysis, even a patriotic duty. And in the extreme, it's a certifiable disease.

Surveys show that 70% of Americans shop for the fun of it, even when there is no need to. Even when they don't make a purchase, it's entertainment. (There are, perhaps in odd contrast, people who detest shopping in any form, but they're a minority.) These people are of tremendous importance to the national economy, and to retailers in particular: in recent years they have accounted for 70% of the entire U.S. economy.

Everyone, whether they enjoy it or not, must shop for necessities (or delegate someone else to do the dirty work): food, clothing, cleaning supplies and toiletries, etc. Most of these also get involved in entertainment and recreational products: fishing tackle, books, CDs, etc. But the recreational shopper is special. In fact, five "personality types" have been identified:

• The *Uber shopper* is highly motivated, shops the most, spends the most, and gets the most enjoyment out of the shopping experience. According to the research firm Unity Marketing:

• The *Therapeutic shopper* considers shopping an escape from everyday life, and enjoys browsing almost as much as buying. (*Shopping* and *buying* are not the same.)

• The *Discerning shopper* likes to research purchases and comparison shops.

• *Bargain hunter* rarely pays the full price because she knows where the discounts are and is always on the prowl for the best deals.

• *Reluctant shoppers* (more men than women) shop less often than the others and often have to be coaxed into a store, but once there, they find it a source of entertainment.

You didn't know marketers dissect shoppers like that? Ha! That's nothing. Another research group unveiled four new types of holiday shoppers even before the end of the 2011 season (which began before the leftover turkey had a chance to cool). They spent about $470 billion in the fourth year of a "weak" U. S. economy.

The bargain hunters have cranked it up a notch, according to America's Research Group. Not content with ordinary bargains, the *bargain timers* believe the best deals come at the beginning and the end of the season.

The *midnight buyers* didn't wait for Black Friday morning: 24% of the Friday shoppers were ready for action by midnight on Thanksgiving Day, up from 9.5% the year before. The biggest reason was that more stores, and bigger stores, were open then, in an effort to outdo each other.

The returners, as you might judge from the name, are not among the most favored of customers. They load their carts in a shopping frenzy, but later suffer buyer's remorse. Retailers handed back 9.9 cents for every dollar they took in… up from 9.8 cents a year earlier, and about 7 cents in "normal" times.

The "me" shopper blended in with the Christmas crowds, but their purchases were for #1. Spending on non-gift items rose 16 percent, to $130.43 per person. Many stores encouraged this with advertising, and even a "treat yourself Tuesday" … after getting all worn out on Black Friday, and Cyber Monday. Recreation can be hard work.

Compulsive buying disorder

There is also a great deal of information on truly compulsive shoppers, those who are certifiably sick with addictive out-of-control shopping, or *oniomania* (Greek: *onios*, for sale; *mania*, insanity), now commonly called compulsive buying disorder (CBD). By some estimates, as many as 1 in 12 Americans suffer from this condition, 80-90 percent of them women. The symptoms include:

• Spending unconscionable sums of money you don't have on stuff you don't need;

• Having closets and drawers and shelves filled with stuff that has never been used, with the tags still attached, and probably still in the original packaging;

• Carrying several credit cards, all maxed out;

• Having a prior addiction, such as alcohol, gambling, or eating disorders.

That last item is revealing: some psychologists consider *shopaholic* an accurate term because it really is an addiction. Others consider it an impulse control disorder, or an obsessive-compulsive disorder. What it is *not* is a joke about women shoppers.

Apparently much of the problem is related to low self-esteem and insecurity, which often begins in childhood. It's a substitution of material goods for personal relationships. And since afterward the shopper often feels guilt, regret or depression — and the shopping is a form of self-medication for such conditions — the addict resorts to another purchase in what becomes a vicious circle.

In 2006 a woman in Pennsylvania was sentenced to 27 months in jail for embezzling $1.5 million from the credit union where she worked, to buy hundreds of pairs of shoes, thousands of books, 58 coats — and 16 chainsaws plus a $25,000 John Deere tractor. Clearly, this condition involves much more than financial disorganization or irresponsibility.

Not surprisingly, social conditions play an important role. First described in the early 1900s, only recently has it received much attention, or become widespread. Capitalism — ubiquitous advertising, inviting stores, bright signs, endless variety, blowout sales and easy credit — ostensibly encourages such behavior. Quitting entirely, taking the sliding scale to the extreme, is virtually impossible: in our society shopping in one form or another is as natural as getting dressed in the morning.

And cutting back on shopping while surrounded by a capitalist democracy society must be even more difficult than staying off the booze when you're surrounded by drinking buddies at a hunting camp or ballgame. Shopping is not just a part of our culture: it shapes, defines, supports and embodies it: "I shop, therefore I am."

The zombie craze

As a good example of just how crazy our capitalist System really is, consider zombies. A small and weird cult (the cult classic movie *Night of the Living Dead* was made in 1968) became a major force, in the culture, and economically.

While pinning down the economic impact of something like this is nearly impossible, just adding up the take from movies (est. $2.5 billion), video games (another $2.5 billion), comics and tv ($50 million), Halloween costumes ($500 million in the past four years), comes to $5.55 billion, without even getting to the books, conventions and other events, digital stuff and of course, merchandise, reportedly involving some 411,000 products (CafePress.com).

According to one theory (as put forward by bestselling zombie genre author Max Brooks), zombies are a reflection of "our very real anxieties of these crazy scary times. A zombie story gives people a fictional lens to see the real problems of the world. You can deal with societal breakdown, famine, disease, chaos in the streets, but as long as the catalyst for all of them is zombies, you can still sleep."

This, as much as anything, describes the times we live in. A more rational approach to the New Normal isn't likely, but one can hope.

A New American Dream?

In *American Dreams in Mississippi*, Ted Ownby acknowledges our consumer culture by incorporating it into four new versions of the American Dream:

• The *Dream of Abundance*, that overflowing cornucopia of manufactured goods available to all Americans, making them proud to be the richest society on Earth;

• The *Dream of a Democracy of Goods*, where everyone has access to the same products regardless of class in any form or measure;

• The *Dream of Freedom of Choice*, allowing people to fashion their own lifestyle with a wide variety of products; and

• The *Dream of Novelty*, referring to the excitement of ever-changing fashions, new models, and unexpected new products.

Several writers have taken this further, observing that Americans, in sharp contrast to most other nations, take shopping to be almost a patriotic duty and indeed, President George W. Bush said as much when, after the attack of 9/11, he urged Americans not to let terrorists keep them from living the American lifestyle: go to Disney World, he said.

Economist John Maynard Keynes introduced the quaint notion of deficit spending, suggesting that governments go into debt to invest in public works and hire the unemployed to keep the conveyor belt of capitalism moving. After the Great Depression, and again after WWII, officials in Washington extended this to individuals, demonstrating democracy's ability to control capitalism simply by jawboning. During the war, Americans were urged to be frugal and to save, especially with U.S. Savings Bonds and Postal Savings (which was discontinued in 1966, although other countries still maintain similar systems). But afterwards the message changed: spend, spend, spend, to revive the economy!

This reverberated again in 2001 when President Bush urged American to whip out their credit cards to reverse the drop in spending that resulted from 9/11, making spending a patriotic duty. That attitude continued into 2008, but by then many Americans were no longer in the mood for that kind of patriotism.

Many politicians, most consumers, and credit card companies love deficit spending. Or they did. The U.S. personal savings rate went from 1.5% in June, 2004, to 0% one year later. (The rate in Japan was over 11%.) Still later it turned negative for the first time since the Great Depression. By 2010 it had clawed its way up to 5%, not entirely because consumers finally "got religion." One significant factor was that credit card companies tightened up during the financial crisis. Rapidly shifting from mass mailings (young children, and in some cases even family dogs who happened to be on rented mailing lists were reportedly pre-approved for credit cards), they rejected a large number of new applicants, and even canceled the accounts of existing cardholders, sometimes due to a single late payment. There were higher-than-ever credit qualifications. Americans began to shun credit card debt, abandoning the use of plastic as a lifestyle choice.

But did they learn the meaning of "enough?"

The magic money: credit cards

According to some historians, "credit cards" go way back, as far as 1890; but since these were transactions between a merchant and a customer, it's hard to see where they differed from simply running up a tab, which was common among local grocers (as well as taverns) in the U.S. until well into the 20th century. Cards issued by oil companies appeared in the 1920s. The first *bank* card is traced to 1946. The Diner's Club card, good only at certain restaurants, was introduced in 1950. Not until 1958 did we see American Express and BankAmericard (now Visa).

Just 50 years later (2008) a Federal Reserve Bank of Boston survey counted 176.8 million credit card holders, each with an average of 3.5 cards. (More consumers have debit cards than credit cards.) However, a 2010 poll revealed that 29% of Americans did not have a credit card, an increase of more than 10% from a year earlier.

A few other stats: The average debt per household: $15,799; average APR on a new card offer: 14.89%; total U.S. revolving debt (credit cards accounting for 98% of that): $2.43 trillion (as of May, 2011, Federal Reserve report). And in light of our interest in changes over time and generational differences, note that the average age at which a U.S. consumer under 35 first acquired a credit card is 20.8 years; the average consumer over 65 didn't get a card until age 40.6.

The average consumer has a total of 13 credit obligations, nine of which are credit cards (including department store cards and gas cards); the others are installment loans (car, mortgage, student, etc.). The average unpaid card balance in December, 2009, was $3,389; the median was $90.

In 2007 97% of consumers had used a credit card within the past year. In 2008, that number dropped precipitously to 72%. And in the month before the Sept. 2008 survey, just 51% of the 18-24 age group used a credit card. This is a startling demonstration of how rapidly things can change (including almost any element of a New Normal).

According to Fitch Ratings, credit card defaults hit 11.37% in early 2010, and 26% of all adults (58 million) admit to not paying all of their bills on time; when finances are tight, 59% opt to pay their credit card bills last. This resulted in (as of March, 2009) a national card debt of $950 billion… resulting in a brain-searing *13.9% of total consumer income going to service this debt!* This is like exchanging a $100 bill for ones, and then throwing 14 of them in the trash can.

And perhaps not insignificantly, in 2009 total bankruptcy filings reached 1.4 million. However, in 2007, even before the Great Recession officially began, 14.7% of U.S. families had debt exceeding 40% of their income. The downturn would only make it worse.

So, have we had "enough" yet?

The question of "enough" is primarily philosophical: it doesn't exist in the economic lexicon… unless you go back to Adam Smith's warning that capitalism's focus on growth could lead to "the endless pursuit of unnecessary things." This suggests that there's a dividing line between necessary and unnecessary things; we can take that line to be the point of "enough;" but this gives us no clue whatsoever what that point might be.

Neither do the philosophers, really.

Lao Tzu: He who knows that enough is enough will always have enough."

Mahatma Gandhi: "Earth provides enough to satisfy every man's need, but not every man's greed."

Epicurus : "Nothing is enough for the man to whom enough is too little."

Still clear as mud. But the problem is obvious: here we have yet another sliding scale; one that not only involves the continuum of not enough, just enough, and too much; but also what's available and on what terms; as well as who, what and where we are, in space and time. The challenge is finding the point where all of this is balanced; the sweet spot, or the Goldilocks position: not too hot, not too cold, just right.

It doesn't help one bit that the sweet spot could potentially be different for every individual on the planet. Therefore laws, regulations, financial formulae or advice of any kind dealing with economics or anything else, nothing can set the limits that could describe "enough."

And yet, such limits necessarily exist. They're necessary because of the finite nature of the planet; because even if infinite growth were possible, capitalism would become so bloated it could no longer function; and most of all, because the whole of human history has amply demonstrated that exceeding the limits of enough, even when unseen or unknown, is detrimental to the human condition and to happiness.

Are Americans happy? Not according to numerous surveys and studies such as the World Happiness Survey conducted by London School of Economics. In that particular research, the U.S. ranked a miserable 46th.

America's 46th place is well behind Britain's 32, and light-years behind Ghana, Latvia, Croatia and Estonia. The happiest people in the world live in... are you ready? ... Bangladesh.

Bangladesh is one of the poorest countries on the planet. Median wage is 58¢ an hour; per capita income is $1,700 a year. Even the most impoverished Americans wouldn't dream of visiting, much less living there. How could those people be considered "happy"?

One clue lies in the "hierarchy of needs" pyramid devised by psychologist Abraham Maslow, described earlier. The World Values Survey, which has been conducted in almost 100 countries

since 1981 and is used by governments and such institutions as the World Bank and the United Nations, notes that happiness is rising in most countries, due, they claim, to "the extent to which people perceive that they have free choice," which in turn is linked to such factors as economic development and democratization.

But that isn't happening in the United States. Why not? One important element in the happiness quotient is a feeling of empowerment, a sense that one is in charge of one's own destiny. Another is a sense of equality, a feeling that the playing field is level. In the U.S., both have been severely impaired in recent years.

Limits also exist because of the economic principle that there is no free lunch: everything has a price, and everything is a trade-off. If you want to spend your day off on the golf course or shopping, then you can't spend it in the garden or fishing. Without such limitations, maybe some people would be even *more* given to excess.

Finding the balance of "enough" is not a priority for most Americans (or anyone else). Achieving such a balance is even more difficult in a society rife with advertising, peer pressure, and the overall desire for ease and convenience and efficiency. But one part of the equation alluded to above, and inherent in the invisible hand of capitalism, is the dependence of the sweet spot on "what's available and on what terms," or at what cost.

If, for any reason whatsoever, any of the delicate mechanisms that keep the capitalist democracy society chugging along would happen to develop a convulsion or even a tic, everything would be thrown off kilter. Individuals would have no need to find a balance, any more than they do now... except that the "just right" Goldilocks point would be far lower on the scale than at present. "Enough" would be much less than it is now.

Some people would consider that a disaster. But those who had already discovered and embraced that point would notice little difference: while some people panic, or certainly worry and complain during a power outage, the Amish don't even know it's occurring. And the amazing thing is that if *everybody* would be satisfied with just enough instead of maximum consumption, certain tics and convulsions might be avoided.

But it's not necessary to become Amish, or a Luddite. Recall that "the millionaire next door," described in a 1996 book of that name by Thomas Stanley and William Danko, is a family that lives well below its means, meaning frugally. Conspicuous consumption isn't even on the table: "It's much easier to *appear* wealthy than to *be* wealthy."

This, and other components of the "secrets" of this group are highly likely to be a part of the New Normal, because they make sense... and because there aren't many other options.

Chapter 10: Working for a living, or a life?

The homestead philosophy posits that the primary reward of work should be well-being rather than money.

"Do what you love and the money will follow" is a popular saying.

In a capitalist society there is no such thing as "enough," or even "too much;" the System, and its minions, always want "more."

All three of these ideas have an impact on whether you're working to make a living, or to make a life.

One of life's givens is that everybody has to work for a living. Granted, some work harder than others, and in different ways: while some are earning their daily bread deep underground in a coal mine, others are frantically working the floor of the New York Stock Exchange; one is a professional nurse or teacher while another is a professional in Reno, or elsewhere.

Some are highly compensated: in 2011, John Hammergren of McKesson (a distributor of pharmaceuticals and health care I.T.) took home $131 million. Many others can find only part-time jobs at minimum wage and manage to survive on less than $10,000 a year, and millions who are desperately seeking any employment whatsoever are living on handouts.

Some workers are highly skilled or talented: not many are qualified to be rocket scientists, brain surgeons, or great artists. Then there are jobs that require little or no thought, or even physical effort. Some are so boring they challenge the worker's humanity. Henry Ford said about his assembly line, "The only thing I don't like about this is that I have to hire a whole man, when all I need are his hands." If you are a whole man but an employer wants only your hands, you don't have much of a life.

With these facts, it's not surprising that one of the first things we wonder about someone we meet for the first time is, "what do you do?" To put it bluntly, our classless society classes people by occupation. Your occupation identifies you. It might tell how much education you have, what kind of house you live in, and of course, how much money you probably make. You are what you do.

Add to this the fact that most Americans spend more time on work than anything else. They see more of their co-workers than they see of their own families. Most think more about their work than anything else.

And then there's that paycheck. Where would you be without it?

We are not only defined by our jobs: we *are* our jobs. Or our jobs are us.

Work is an essential part of life. Even the very rich often insist that their heirs get a job. Even when it's not required to make a living, it's needed to make a life. And if it takes up so much of our life, it should obviously be something pleasant and desirable. So why do so many who work under capitalism utterly loathe their jobs, and why do they continue to "slave" in the "salt mines?"

One more question: What's the difference between grubbing in the woods for roots and berries and grubbing in the marketplace for a paycheck? The answer: not much.

The subsistence farming myth

The quaint notion that subsistence farmers spent all of their time working just to get enough to eat is a myth: even birds don't do that. Today it's well known that even primitive peoples in past ages spent much of their time on creative activities: making pots and baskets and clothing, or even purely artistic non-utilitarian goods (although perhaps of religious significance) such as statues, totem poles and jewelry. They were dancers, and musicians, and storytellers. They had religions, and politics. They probably had more leisure than most of today's hard-working Americans. If you work in an office or factory and look forward to the few days of the year you can spend hunting or fishing, you might not want to be reminded that for many, hunting and fishing was their *work*.

Many thinkers, from ancient Greece to the present, have speculated that somewhere between 3-5 hours a day is all that's required to sustain a human life. Some historians claim that was the average workday of a merchant in colonial America (while the men, women and children working in factories in England commonly put in 60-70 hours a week). The "ideal life" of Scott and Helen Nearing and many others like them consisted of a few hours of essential "bread labor" required for physical survival; several hours of mental activity or intellectual endeavors, i.e. studying or writing; and then some time for personal re-creation (literally), whether playing a musical instrument, woodworking, or watching a movie.

So why does the hapless American get up, get dressed, maybe grab a bite to eat, commute to a job, work all day, drive back home, perhaps stopping to shop on the way, then do whatever needs to be done depending on the presence of a spouse, children, pets or other obligations, then fall into bed and repeat it all again the next day? Why is "leisure" spent plopped in front of a tv? After a while, many people start to think there should be more to life — and they're right. But they find it impossible to change. They are enslaved by capitalism's tender trap.

The Tender Trap

There have recently been about 13 million unemployed Americans who would love to have a job, any job (plus many who would be more discriminating). So the roughly 130 million who do have a job, and a paycheck, must at least pretend to be grateful. Even if the gratitude is heartfelt, the job is still a trap.

Do you remember your first paycheck, from your first real job? Whether you were fresh out of high school or out of college, holding that amount of money in your hand was an awesome feeling, compared with the non-monetary rewards of sitting in a classroom or lecture hall. In most cases this elation was somewhat dampened by the usual new worker's introduction to FICA and its effect on the bottom line, but that's something else. You had *money*. And in comparison with whatever pittance you managed to survive on as a student, you were *rich*.

So of course you could have a car, and an apartment, and maybe a few toys. If you were one of those who already had lots of "stuff," you just got more.

Cars require gas, maintenance, repairs, insurance, licensing. Apartments or houses require rent, and perhaps utilities or other costs in addition: cable tv, or internet service, laundry. If you're on your own for the first time you either scrounge household items from your parents, or you buy them: a kitchen table, a chair, a microwave, a plate and cup and silverware... and of course, food.

So all that money disappears. You are literally forced to go back to work the next day to get more.

And that quickly disappears too, especially if you try to keep up with your peers, or if you're a sucker for advertising, or if you have no control over your buying urges. Or maybe you're just unlucky: you're in a traffic accident, you need a wisdom tooth pulled, or your second-hand refrigerator conks out. Suddenly, you're in debt.

All the opportunities for purchasing material goods we have mentioned, and will mention in pages yet to come, are clamoring for your attention. In many cases they might entail a credit card, which is where the big trouble often starts. Splurge just a little, get just a little behind, start the interest clock running, and you're trapped but good. Do you remember hearing, probably in high school, about indentured servants who were never able to gain their freedom? Now you are one!

The only way out is to continue working. But the way the System works, you'll never come out ahead — *unless you get off the treadmill.*

Members of Generation Y appear to be particularly interested in this, perhaps because of their early experiences. They're less tolerant than older workers of a stuffy 9-5 gig in a corporate cubicle... let alone an assembly line... and they're more concerned with flexibility, mobility, and what has become known as "work/life balance." Many even say they would rather work fewer hours for less pay in order to have more time for things that are more important to them.

Some companies are accommodating this relatively new outlook, with flex-time, paternity leave as well as more maternity leave, time off for personal and family needs, and even job-sharing. Telecommuting has become common in many fields. If this spreads, as many believe it will, it will put a new face on capitalism, and on life.

Unemployment takes a terrible toll on those it affects, but unemployment is not an aberration: it's an essential element of capitalism. Political leaders like to keep it below a certain level to keep the System going and to keep people happy, but an unemployment rate of zero would indicate serious problems within the System.

Escaping from the Rat Race

But even this isn't enough for some workers. Owning a small business has been a part of the American Dream for many generations.

A hundred years ago it was relatively simple: a young man learned a trade, hung out a sign, and he was in business. Often there was little choice: it was that, going to work for somebody else who had started a small business (perhaps with the dream or hope of someday taking it over), or farming. There were few giant corporations, they weren't nearly as gigantic as they are today, and since they were invariably located in or near large cities, vast areas of the country had little or no direct contact with them.

When I started out in the telephone industry with one of my many sideline businesses, the field was dominated by "Ma Bell," with General Telephone a distant second: In 1951 AT&T became the first American corporation to have one million stockholders. But even then there were still more than 1,500 small, "independent" local phone companies, many of them mom and pop operations. By the time I shuttered the business, 15 years later, there were fewer than 500. Today, there are barely 150.

By the 1950s the corporate world was the place for smart and ambitious young people to be. That's where the action was, the promotions and opportunities, and the money. It was capitalism at its best. It was the American Dream.

But the situation that gave us the term "man in the grey flannel suit" (from a book, 1955, and movie, 1956) also spawned the term "rat race," to denote life on a treadmill, running furiously but getting nowhere. Many wanted out. Only a few made it.

A lawyer who hated his job fulfilled a dream by buying and running a hardware store. A business executive took over a bed & breakfast. A truck driver increased the satisfaction he got out of life by becoming a nurse. (And then he wrote a book about it.) But these were the exceptions.

For most people, these were daring moves, especially if a family or other responsibilities were involved. Starting a business requires time and money; if the reason for starting one is because you don't have enough time or money... well, that's a conundrum. It's like being unable to get a job because of lack of experience, but the reason for the lack of experience is that you can't get a job. It's a vicious circle, and a catch-22 trap.

The risk factor

And then there's the risk. "Everybody knows" that most new businesses fail. That might not be true: none of the several businesses I started and ran "failed" in the sense of going bankrupt; they closed for other reasons: one was sold, some simply weren't profitable enough to bother with and I didn't have the time or inclination to develop them because I had my fingers in too many other pies. In the statistics, all of these are treated the same.

Yes, of course, some new businesses don't last very long. But since when is the possibility of failure an excuse to do nothing? Since capitalism began providing virtual cradle-to-grave security — to those who play by its rules. And that's a trap of the worst kind, because the poor victim doesn't even recognize it as such.

Opportunities abound

Recent developments have made starting a business somewhat easier, especially those connected in some way with the Internet. While some entrepreneurs think big — they fantasize about being the next Google or Facebook — and pursue huge sums of start-up money from venture capitalists, the vast majority have reverted to 100 years ago: they simply hang out a sign. Today that usually means having a presence in the "social media" — Facebook, Google+, LinkedIn, etc. — but it can also be taken literally, perhaps with a few classified ads in the local paper and a business card or small notice pinned to local bulletin boards. (This is in rural areas; surely there are similar opportunities in cities.)

Dun & Bradstreet claims to have 23 million U.S. small businesses in its database.

What kinds of businesses? There are people who will fix vacuum cleaners, old clocks, or lawn mowers. Our area has a wine maker, a cheese maker, a baker and a sausage maker. One fellow rents white doves for weddings. (They're actually homing pigeons: they're released, and back in the cote before the champagne is gone.) Some people have a saying, "If you can think of it, you can sell it on the web." But you can also find a need in your own neighborhood, and fill it. Or build a better mousetrap and have the world beat a path to your door.

Of course this is capitalism! But it's *controlled*. I never wanted any of my businesses to get big; being the richest guy in the cemetery was never my goal. I just wanted to make enough money to live on, doing things I enjoyed, and being my own boss… so I'd have both the time and wherewithal to follow other pursuits that made a *life*. I didn't achieve that until my late 20's, but that still gave me more than 40 years of living, and when I retired, some people said, "How will we know the difference?" That's what I call living!

But now, those Baby Boomers reaching retirement age are discouraged, and almost a third of them tell pollsters they doubt that they'll be able to retire at all, ever. That's sad, and worse: it means the capitalist traps have chewed them up and spit them out, and their lives have been misspent. After a certain point of no return, there is little hope for recovery. Their only solution is to do more with less…

Do more with less

But wait! That's also the solution at the *beginning*, the way to become your own boss, whether that means starting your own business or simply taking charge of your destiny and wresting your life from the capitalist traps to live life *your* way.

It's also how homesteaders have been living at least since the Great Depression and the war years. That time distinction is important, because the key to all we're talking about is *taking charge* of your life. The hardships and deprivations and shortages of the Depression and war years were imposed from outside, which is considered poverty. Homesteaders, seeing consciously or not how capitalism impacted their lives, took matters into their own hands. They grabbed capitalism by the throat, shook it and said, "Enough!" That's simplifying your life. The difference is mainly one of attitude, but attitude makes all the difference in the world.

This was all made clear in a wildly popular book, *Your Money or Your Life,* by Vicki Robin and Joe Dominquez, published in 1992. Both homesteading and simple living had been around for years, especially after the halcyon 1950s, but this book simplified, clarified, and most importantly codified the process, boiling it down into nine simple steps. Human nature seems to understand things better when they're reduced to "steps," even though the real world seldom works that way. In this book, that doesn't matter: the important point is understanding that the stuff you buy, the money you buy it with, the work you do to obtain that money, and the hours of your life, are all one and the same and therefore interchangeable. The nine steps help you see how to manipulate them, swap and barter and rearrange them, not to get out of work, but to free yourself to do a different kind of work.

Take control of your life

The gist of this book — and homesteading, and simple living — is that in order to live life your way and not according to the dictates of the System or society, you must take control. To escape the clutches of capitalism, you must be aware of what you're spending... not only in terms of dollars and cents, but in the "life-force" expended to acquire that money.

Some of the book is outdated: nobody is going to live very high on the hog with the interest generated by a bank savings account with the interest rates being offered today, thanks to the recession-fighting policies of the Federal Reserve. But the basic ideas are timeless: get out of debt and build up savings; adjust your economic priorities and live well with less; recognize and deal with conflicts between values and lifestyles; attain a "wholeness" of livelihood and lifestyle; and save the planet while saving money.

Homesteaders were doing this, perhaps intuitively, long before 1992 when this book was published, which suggests that it's just common sense, information everybody is aware of. The fact that actually realizing it had such an explosive effect on so many people is an indication of the tight grip capitalism has not only on our wallets and bank accounts, but on our minds: it has become *unnatural* to think of work as anything but a job and employment for the sole purpose of acquiring money, which has no value until it's exchanged for goods... which might or might not enhance our lives.

Seen from this viewpoint, getting out of the rat race isn't really about escaping from a job; it's escaping *to* a new kind of more meaningful, personally fulfilling kind of work. This leads us to the mantra, "Do what you love, the money will follow."

This too was a book, by Marsha Sinetar, from 1989. While not always literally true, here again the idea is "liberation," which is basically breaking the links that chain you to capitalism and taking charge of your own life. And when that happens, even if the money doesn't follow in the amounts some might expect or desire, it really doesn't matter very much: money can't buy happiness. And sometimes, when you finally learn how to think about it, enough really is enough.

Chapter 11: Transportation: Are we there yet?

"Go west, young man!" And east, and north, and south...

Americans love mobility, specifically the personal auto. Getting the keys to the car, or even a whole car, is a major rite of passage. Gaining the right to drive is a much more potent sign of adulthood than the right to vote, drink alcohol, join the military or get married: it's the beginning of *living.* At the end of the ride, giving up the right to drive is taken as a sure sign that it's all over.

This is changing. Some states are making it harder for teens to get drivers' licenses, and a growing number of 20-somethings have little interest in owning a car. Instead, they stay home, use social networks, and/or move to big cities where mass transit makes more sense, ecologically and financially as well as in terms of hassles. If this continues, the New Normal could see some dramatic transportation-related changes... with all the repercussions alluded to in this chapter. Some people are saying they have had enough, and it's about time!

Between these two landmark events, throughout life, the capitalism of the automobile encases us like a snuggie. Capitalism invented the auto, it has lived by the auto, and it would probably die without the auto, because it's unlikely that anything could entirely replace it in the economy; at the very least, it would be a vastly different economy. The two are so closely aligned that even a bit of a fever in one can cause grave illness in the other: auto sales are one of the most closely-watched economic barometers in the country.

And yet, a few chapters back we saw that transportation costs went from near zero percent of a family's 1901 budget to 22% a hundred years later — an astounding increase, with an equally astounding impact on our lives and the environment.

We know the various success stories associated with the auto industry — Henry Ford's assembly line, the Eisenhower Interstate Highway System, and the countless technical improvements that have been made and are still being made in vehicles themselves. But so far as capitalism is concerned, this hardly scratches the surface. Dig under that surface just a bit and you might be astounded to see what an overpowering role the automobile plays in our society.

But historically, there is much more to transportation, and the development of the American democratic capitalist System, than the auto.

A brief history of transportation

Commerce and transportation go hand-in-hand. Even in the most primitive commercial society trade goods must be carried from where they are gathered or produced — fish and salt from the sea, pipestone from northeastern Minnesota, spices and silks from the East — to where they will be used. In the process routes used by animals became footpaths, then wagon trails, and then roads and four-lane highways.

By 500 BCE the Roman *viae* were known for their scope — they stretched for more than 50,000 miles — as well as their advanced engineering. Their *agger* foundations consisted of several layers designed to provide drainage, making the roads more durable, and usable in all weather, by merchants as well as by armies. The Roman network of roads was longer than today's Interstate System (which stretches only 46,567 miles), but even more amazing, some of those roads are still in use today, 2,500 years later. (Makes you wonder what Romans thought about Roman Exceptionalism… as well as how our modern roads can have potholes within a few years of their construction.)

But never fear, America: size isn't everything. The Interstate System might not be as long as the Roman system, but it is easily the greatest public works project ever, at a cost of $128.9 billion.

The Eisenhower Interstate Highway System is somewhat misnamed, since Ike had little to do with it: the idea started with FDR in 1938; President Eisenhower signed the Federal-Aid Highway Act of 1956, which authorized funding, but the project had progressed significantly before he became involved. The name was made official by President George H. W. Bush in 1990.

And in the interests of further feeding the whole man by offering a bit of history, in this case smashing myths, it's not true that national defense played a role in the creation of the Interstate. Eisenhower did not pattern the U.S. Interstate System after the German *autobahn*, and defense didn't enter into it until the Cold War. Also, according to the U.S. Department of Transportation, the popular notion that there's a law or regulation dictating that one of every five miles be straight and wide enough to land an airplane simply isn't true.

Roads of water

According to popular myth the first "roads" in America were deer trails, which were followed by humans on foot, and later by carts and wagons. When eventually the roads were paved, they followed the original deer paths, which explains why many highways are so crooked.

In the early days, however, rivers were more important than trails and paths. Settlements, villages, and eventually cities were located on important waterways such as the Ohio and Mississippi.

But rivers were inadequate for a rapidly growing nation. Water transportation was greatly extended during the Canal Age (1790-1855). New York City might not have become the world center of capitalism had it not been for the opening of the Erie Canal in 1826. This waterway bridged the Appalachians, opening the Great Lakes to commerce that was funneled through New York, contributing to its explosive growth.

By the 1800s, decimation of the forests of the Eastern seaboard constituted an energy crisis. There was plenty of coal in Pennsylvania, scarcely 100 miles away. But transporting it was so difficult and expensive, it was cheaper to import coal from England, all the way across the Atlantic. Two hundred years later, capitalism still faces similar quandaries.

In the Midwest, the 100-mile-long Illinois & Michigan Canal opened in 1848 with a shipment of sugar from New Orleans to LaSalle on the Mississippi and Illinois Rivers, through the canal to Chicago, and from there to Buffalo, New York, via the Great Lakes. Chicago became the transportation hub of the Midwest. And, just like the story of the deer trail and modern highways, Chicago later became a railroad hub, a highway hub, and an airline hub — all because of a canal 30 feet wide, six feet deep and less than 100 miles long, which moved goods and people at 3-5 miles per hour.

Capitalism, democracy, and a canal

This, of course, is the canal that made the Fox-Wisconsin waterway we discussed earlier obsolete almost before it was finished but it had other effects as well. Let's detour a moment to reflect on some other aspects of the capitalist democracy System as related to this canal.

Until 1900, Chicago's sewage was dumped into Lake Michigan, which was also the source of the city's drinking water. With the growth of both population and medical technology, the potential for typhoid fever, cholera and dysentery became a concern. The Chicago Drainage Canal (later called the Chicago Sanitary and Ship Canal) famously reversed the flow of the Chicago River, carrying the sewage into the Des Plaines and Illinois Rivers, to the Mississippi and the Gulf of Mexico, and to the oceans, which as everyone knows are vast and bottomless and thus oblivious to any puny acts of mankind — even though at the time it was the largest earth-moving operation ever undertaken in North America.

Missouri applied for an injunction against the opening, to no avail. But when Chicago drew more water from Lake

Michigan than the U.S. Army Corp of Engineers had authorized (to flush the sewage faster), it raised alarms for shipping on the Great Lakes and the St. Lawrence Seaway. States downstream from the canal naturally wanted the increased flow to dilute and move the sewage; those in the other direction (toward the Atlantic Ocean) wanted a lesser flow through the canal so there would be more water for shipping on the St. Lawrence. In 1930 management of the canal was turned over to the U.S. Army Corps of Engineers, which reduced the flow from Lake Michigan, but not enough to affect navigation. This forced Chicago to improve its treatment of raw sewage.

The St. Lawrence Seaway, which opened in 1959, allowed ocean-going ships to penetrate the continent all the way to Lake Superior. However, that waterway had always been an important route for explorers and fur traders, and a series of canals opened it to larger vessels as early as 1871. Incidentally, the opening of the St. Lawrence Seaway rendered the Erie Canal obsolete, leading to a severe economic decline along that route: waterways were still important in the 1960s, and remain so today. In addition, the ocean-going vessels that reached the Great Lakes brought with them non-native ecology-threatening environmental scourges including sea lamprey, alewife, zebra mussel, round goby, Eurasian ruffe, and at least 20 others, as well as such plants as Eurasian milfoil and purple loosestrife. And that's why we pay attention to webs that connect everything to everything else.

Even so, fecal matter discharged into the canal is only lightly treated: there is no disinfection stage at any of the three main sewage treatment plants. Signs along the canals warn that the water is not suitable for "any human contact."

The fecal coliform colonies don't seem to affect Asian carp, those 50-pound leaping fish originally introduced in America to reduce algae growth in farmed catfish ponds in Arkansas. This is part of capitalism too: they escaped into the Mississippi and, should they reach the Great Lakes, they'd devastate the biology of that massive freshwater chain, including the $7 billion a year recreational and commercial fishing industries.

When Michigan filed a lawsuit seeking immediate closure of the canal to avert this, Illinois counter-sued, arguing that closure would upset the movement of millions of tons of iron ore, coal, and grain totaling more than $1.5 billion a year. Of course that would mean the loss of hundreds, maybe thousands, of jobs. Jobs are always a big concern in a consumer society: without jobs, who's going to buy all that stuff capitalism provides? Or pay taxes.

In January, 2010 the U.S. Supreme Court rejected Michigan's request, and in August, 2011, the U.S. Court of Appeals also rejected the preliminary injunction.

Capitalism 1; Nature 0. Again. And the webs continue to fan out.

Then, the automobile…

So rivers and canals, and obviously ocean transport, are still of immense importance to commerce. But they pale next to the automobile.

The modern web of roads demonstrates how growth begets more growth as well as providing an example of the interconnection of many things that at first glance don't seem to be related.

By the mid-1950s large numbers of people were moving to the suburbs. Existing roads became overcrowded and were modernized and expanded, while new highways were constructed. This made it even easier to commute to the suburbs, and it became a spiral.

The Interstate System took this even further. Wider, smoother, straighter, faster yet safer roads extended the suburbs well beyond where they would have been without such easy access.

More roads beget more traffic — most families now need two cars, at least — which begets still more roads. We're still widening, repairing, and improving them, as well as continuing to build new ones, along with parking lots.

There are 1 billion cars, trucks and busses on the world's roads. If every country had the same number of vehicles per capita as the

U.S., there would be 5.5 billion. Both capitalism and democracy would like to see equality achieved by raising the number to 5.5 billion, rather than by lowering U.S. car ownership. But when you factor in all the resources involved in and surrounding the automobile, could the planet survive such an assault?

The U.S. has 248 million autos, or 809 per 1,000 people. (Only Monaco has more). China has 46 per 1,000, about what the U.S. had in 1917.

Both roads and suburbs destroy farmland and wilderness, imperiling the biosphere, changing drainage patterns and increasing runoff, altering water tables and increasing pollution. Space used by the average garage and driveway could grow enough food to feed the owner's family (see Chapter 20). We might also mention that the green lawns and golf courses of suburbia consume more fertilizer than major farm crops... but the webs of complexity go on forever and we don't have that much time. Neither, unfortunately, does the planet.

By one estimate, cars kill one million birds, animals, reptiles and amphibians — daily. In Florida only about 300 key deer survive, a number that decreases by about one a week, due to cars. An estimated 60 million birds a year are auto fatalities.

The homogenization of America

But we'll make time for this diversion: the impact of the automobile on the homogenization of America. From early on, one of the most common criticisms of capitalism was that it destroyed local pride and identity, including communities and cultures. Those critics (some going back to ancient Greece, even before "capitalism" as we know it) couldn't possibly have foreseen the heights this would reach because of a hamburger... and the introduction of McDonald's.

We really can't blame Richard and Maurice (the McDonald brothers) for this, especially on top of saddling them with the onus of popularizing the fast food industry (see Chapter 18). But their example spawned the franchise industry, and the cookie-cutter businesses (echoing the cookie-cutter houses of

suburbia) that make nearly any stretch of highway or strip
mall in America identical to any other. A traveler looking for a
Mom and Pop diner offering a bowl of good homemade soup
along any major routes might just as well look for cheap gas:
it's usually a waste of time.

In the nature of webs again, this wasn't the work of the
McDonald brothers or Ray Kroc, but a result of the mechanics
of capitalism. Whether it really makes any difference or not is
a matter of opinion (and probably much further debate), but if
we pine for the perhaps romantic world of small family-run
local businesses and diverse culture across the national
landscape, or simply decry the encroachment of big box stores
and the proliferation of ticky-tacky businesses of every
specialty, then we should be aware of how it all came about.
Blame the auto.

Or maybe the whole highway system, because trucks played
a role too. Some food historians consider the 1950s the nadir of
American cuisine not only because of fast food, but the mass
distribution of *processed* food, thanks to fast and convenient
transportation. Food processors such as Oscar Mayer grew like
mold on an old loaf of preservative-free bread.

**Researchers now suspect that tailpipe exhaust fumes, especially
the tiny carbon particles already implicated in heart disease, cancer
and respiratory ailments, might also injure brain cells. There is
evidence that traffic fumes affect mental capacity, intelligence, and
emotional stability. (That could explain a lot.)**

**Although cars and trucks today generate only 1/10th of the
pollution of 1970, more people are on the road, and stuck in traffic
more often. In the 10 worst U.S. traffic corridors, drivers spend 140
hours a year idling in traffic.**

The webs reach well beyond the environment and culture.

Today, thanks to all of the above, nearly 70 percent of our
petroleum consumption is devoted to moving people and
goods from one place to another. Here's my reaction to this as
voiced in *The Complete Idiot's Guide to Self-Sufficient Living*:

"The automobile led to rampant population dispersal and desecration of the countryside; it enabled fast food, franchises, and the homogenization of America, and ultimately, the world; it is responsible for using prodigious amounts of resources that include not only the materials, workers and money used to build cars but also land and material for roads, parking lots and garages. That's in addition to emissions and the effects on the social fabric of the nation, including the automobile's major role in the industrial economy. We have squandered, wasted, burnt up, misused, dissipated, thrown away, poured down the drain and lost awesome and unconscionable amounts of resources, just to get from one place to another. In the process, we have created an unsustainable economic system, a consumer society that consumes our lives."

The automobile's grip on the economy is easily seen on even a brief ride through any town in America, or even from your armchair: just scan the Yellow Pages, under "Automobiles." You'll find air conditioning, body shops, customizing, dealers (new and used), detailing, electric service, leasing, oil and lube services, mufflers, parts, radiators, repairs, restoration, seat covers, tops, tires, towing, windshield repair, and of course insurance and car washes — and gas stations and junkyards. This doesn't include road construction, maintenance and repair. And most police forces and ERs wouldn't be nearly as busy if there were fewer automobiles on the roads. What would capitalism be without the auto!

More money is spent on automotive advertising than any other category: $13,026,000,000 in 2010.

Learning how to live in the New Normal requires taking a long, serious look at how we use transportation. Is it possible to reduce, or even eliminate, the 1,500-mile trip most food takes between the farm and the supermarket? (It's amazing to think that most garlic sold in the U.S. is grown in China. Anyone with a few square feet of dirt can grow a year's supply with minimal effort.) If you can't or won't grow your own food, you can at least support local farmers and gardeners.

If you can't eliminate commuting by working at home, use mass transit, ride a bike, or walk. If that's not in the cards, make a greater effort to carpool. At the very least, plan trips, to reduce mileage. Along with using a vehicle that sips instead of guzzles, obviously.

Electric cars don't meet the driving requirements of most Americans. In an odd twist, what's negative for the cars is positive for school busses. For many drivers, cars don't go far enough on a single charge; most school busses have fairly short routes, and those routes are the same every day, reducing the risk of running out of battery power before making it back to the garage... where they sit all day, providing plenty of time to recharge their batteries. And those frequent stops that are horrible on fuel efficiency for gas or diesel engines actually extend the range of electric vehicles, since applying the brakes charges the batteries. The biggest problem is that they cost about 60% more than a conventional diesel bus.

However, this could take us on another grand adventure of "what might have been" history, including the fascinating story of how GM bought up, and eliminated, the vibrant electric streetcar industry so it could sell more cars and busses.

Car sharing, and even bicycle sharing, in several forms, are becoming common in many progressive cities. Perhaps even more indicative of what to expect in the New Normal, the real estate industry has introduced "walkability scores" which evaluate the proximity of a home to frequently visited locations: shopping, entertainment, even the workplace. What is most interesting and encouraging to a futurist homesteader, walk scores are being promoted not only for saving gas and auto expense, but also the environment, and even better, they are touted for promoting more vibrant, socially connected communities, which is just the opposite of the automobile. How much this will shape the New Normal remains to be seen, but it's a hopeful sign.

Chapter 12: A house is to live in

The dream of home ownership is often rooted in childhood: in doll houses, tree houses and "forts" and club houses of every description. Whether made of blankets or cardboard, tree branches or real lumber, these spaces most often come with a sense of privacy — and a certain sense of possession. If a man's home is his castle, a kid's hideout is at least a mansion.

But this doesn't even begin to explain the complex emotional, financial, legal and historical factors behind the major component of the American Dream, a home of one's own.

Private ownership of land was spotty in colonial America. Not only were different parts of the colonies settled by people with widely varied backgrounds and expectations regarding ownership; recall that the rightful owners, the natives, had no concept of private property whatsoever, no dreams of home ownership. "What is this you call property?" Massasoit is said to have asked the Plymouth colonists in the 1620s. "It cannot be the Earth, for the land is our mother, nourishing all her children, beasts, birds, fish and all men. The woods, the streams, everything on it belong to everybody and is for the use of all. How can one man say it belongs to him?"

The King of England had other ideas.

In 1681, King Charles II ceded a large chunk of his American real estate to William Penn to satisfy a debt owed to Penn's father, a knighted British admiral — a long, complicated and fascinating story in itself, considering that Penn had previously been imprisoned for disputes with the authorities — making him the world's largest non-royal private landowner, with more than 45,000 square miles. Within six months he had parceled out 300,000 acres of that, mostly to Quakers, but eventually including other persecuted minorities: Amish, Mennonites, Catholics, Jews, Lutherans and Huguenots from France, Holland, Germany and other countries. All were governed by his famous "Framework of Government," which many historians consider one of the foundations of the United States of America a century later. (William Penn doesn't get nearly as much credit for the founding of America as he deserves.)

It's not hard to imagine a downtrodden and landless European immigrant gazing upon the American frontier for the first time and not seeing a single post, mound or marker indicating the metes and bounds that delineated private property in the old country: the land of opportunity, indeed! For such people, actually owning land, and a home, in their native countries would have been unthinkable. Although many of these outcasts were indentured servants and little more than slaves, here, it was at least possible; there was land enough for everyone.

The American Dream developed from such seeds, and continued through the Homestead Act of 1862, the promotion and sale of lands granted by the government to the railroads, to such latter-day attractions as mortgage interest deductions on income tax and government-sponsored programs including Fannie Mae and Freddie Mac. The government actively encouraged home ownership and the dream; it made better citizens, and it was an important part of the capitalist democratic System.

Evolution of the American home

The first of these homes were exceeding simple, although they must have appeared sumptuous when compared with the even more primitive dwellings of the native population; people who merely dwell on the land without owning it aren't given to elaborate constructions. It's common for a society to build shelters made of readily available materials. The stone houses many of the immigrants were accustomed to could have been built in some locations, but would have required a great deal of time and labor. The Scandinavian style of building with logs was ideal for the heavily forested new colonies.

As time passed, farms became established, stockaded settlements became villages and towns, wealth increased... and sawmills, brickyards and by the early 1800s, factories that made window glass, became common. Even then however, especially on the frontier (about as far west as Iowa), an average home might be about 16 by 24 feet (the size of many a master bedroom, today), of log construction, with a dirt floor and a fireplace (no stove). And don't even think about a bathroom or running water, or electricity.

Housing in the cities

The cities were another story, but not because the homes were any more luxurious. By 1860, 20 percent of the U.S. population already lived in cities, attracted by labor-hungry factories. By 1890 that figure reached 40 percent of a much larger population, mostly new immigrants.

Most people in cities like New York lived in overcrowded tenements, in ghettos or slums, without heat or plumbing. Disease was rampant, and wooden buildings were often firetraps. (The Great Chicago Fire of 1871 killed hundreds, and left 100,000 homeless.) The demand for lumber during that period resulted in the denuding of the virgin pine forests of the Upper Great Lakes Region.

The housing situation was somewhat better away from the slum and factory areas, with neat frame houses, a patch of lawn, and even a tree or two. Beyond the means of most people, these homes were inhabited by the middle class — the doctors, lawyers, and others with special skills.

And then there were the millionaires — 200 along Chicago's lakefront alone, and many in huge houses on New York's 5th Avenue, as well as the South's storied plantations — who lived very much like European royalty. (George Washington Vanderbilt's Biltmore in Asheville, North Carolina, takes the cake in this department. Built between 1889 and 1895 with 250 rooms, it's still the largest home in America.) But into the 1900s even the "royalty" were roughing it compared to most people today, including those living in "poverty." Everything is relative.

By 1950 that 384 sq. ft. average log cabin had ballooned into a 983 sq. ft. average house, with separate bedrooms for parents and children, a bathroom with a tub, central heat, rolled glass windows (instead of the wavy crown glass used before the early 1800s), and electricity, providing power not only for lights and radios but for motors that ran everything from refrigerators and water pumps to laundry machines and kitchen appliances… and television.

By 2005, a mere 55 years later, that average home had more than doubled again, to 2,434 square feet.

In early American homes not only did all the children share a room: they often shared a bed. (Actually, the bed was often shared with overnight guests as well.) By 2005, kids had their own rooms, and as often as not their own bathrooms and tvs, as well as computers… and cell phones. The newer larger homes had walk-in closets as large as some entire domiciles used to be. Most were air-conditioned. And we haven't even touched on new construction materials (including insulation), sybaritic bathrooms, professional chef's kitchens, or other furnishings and amenities: swimming pools were considered necessities even in some water-starved regions.

Given these improvements and additions, it's not surprising that the average cost of a home went from $8,450 in 1950 to $264,000 in 2005. We can strip out the effects of inflation by looking at the cost of housing compared to income in both periods. In 1950 the average house cost about 2-1/2 times the average household income; in 2005, that figure was nearly 5-3/4. So the average home still cost more than twice as much in terms of the life-force expended.

Upward mobility

What accounted for these astonishing changes? It's logical that larger, more elaborate houses would cost more than simpler, smaller ones, but is it logical to expect average people to live in, and work and pay for, much more housing than they actually require in order to live a meaningful existence?

Even if conspicuous consumption plays a large role, how much is enough? There were several forces at work, related to both capitalism and democracy.

Mansions and castles have existed since the beginning of architecture, of course, but commoners could scarcely even dream of those. Even into the 20th century, ordinary people didn't exactly covet the mansions of the very wealthy on Chicago's lakefront or New York's 5th Avenue: getting out of a tenement to a small cottage with a rose bush and a white picket fence and a few square feet of lawn was dream enough for most.

In *Architecture Through the Ages,* Cabot Hamlin points out that most ancient Greeks who lived in cities lived in what amounted to crowded tenements, and even the better places were quite simple. However, they spent their days engaged in discussions of philosophy, art, literature and politics, and attending plays and lectures, in beautiful, restful, public spaces, with monumental architecture and fabulous gardens, sculpture and fountains. This enriched their lives far more than spending money, materials, and effort on what was in reality only a place to sleep and hang their chitons. (Greeks didn't wear togas).

These aspirations increased with the rise of suburbia in the mid-1900s, when both the houses and the lawns became larger. At the same time, rising prosperity, as well as new materials and technologies, raised housing to ever-higher levels of comfort, convenience and luxury, for both the upper and lower classes.

An American home was considered far more than a place to sleep, even in bedroom suburbs, no matter how little time was spent in it. A house was a sign of achievement, even when it didn't involve conspicuous consumption. It was considered an investment: renting was like flushing money down the toilet. And it was part of America itself, part of the intangible promise of America. Homeowners were more stable, took better care of their property, took more interest in the community and became better citizens. A 1920s government study concluded that a single-family home with a yard and a room for each child was the optimal condition for raising children... and that would help stop the spread of communism. Later, Franklin D. Roosevelt said, "A nation of homeowners is unconquerable." Government definitely had a self-interest in the dream.

The Great Depression and World War II interfered with that dream: by then housing starts had gone from one million a year to 100,000... and it was the beginning of the baby boom. Something had to be done. Thus arose the suburbs.

The leading innovator and proponent of this type of housing was William Levitt, whose famous "Levittown" set the pace. The rise and proliferation of suburbs is another complex story, too long to discuss here, but important for the multifarious webs connecting it to all aspects of American life and society, including capitalism and democracy. The needs of the people met with the capitalism of a pioneer developer and melded with the guaranteed loans provided by a democratic government, through the National Housing Act of 1949, setting the stage for decades to come.

Government help

In his State of the Union address, President Harry S. Truman cited the need for the Act by observing that, "five million people are still living in slums and firetraps. Three million families share their homes with others." The Act provided for slum clearance and new public housing (that turned out to be not as successful as had been hoped, such as Chicago's Cabrini-Green, since demolished); increasing authorization for the Federal Housing Administration (FHA) mortgage insurance (Title II); and permitting the FHA to provide financing for rural homeowners.

The seedier capitalist side of home ownership was evident even in William Penn's time: glowing descriptions of the New World, designed to lure hesitant prospects, didn't prepare them for the harsh realities they faced if they made the move. Many brochures and other ads from the railroads, selling land to newcomers on the

East Coast as well as enticing new immigrants from Europe, were even more questionable: photographs of humongous cabbages and turnips grown in the rich and fertile virgin soils of the New World gave little indication of the hardships to be encountered on the new frontier.

The stakes were upped in 1995 when President Bill Clinton announced a National Homeownership Strategy to create 8 million new homeowners in five years, through an "unprecedented collaboration of private and public housing industry organizations." It would help middle-income and even lower-income families that had been excluded from the American Dream because they simply didn't have enough money, especially in light of the constantly escalating cost of housing. The goal was to increase home ownership from about 65 percent, to 67.5 percent. That goal was reached as an average, despite racial differences.

President George W. Bush not only continued the program but expanded it, speaking of an "ownership society." Between 2002 and 2006 the government spent $412 million on its American Dream Downpayment Inititative to help first-time homebuyers; $176 million on "housing counseling;" and more than $440 billion committed to Fannie Mae, Freddie Mac, and other government-backed mortgage players. (By 2012, home ownership had reverted back to a 15-year low.)

Meanwhile, Ameriquest (its slogan was "Proud Sponsor of the American Dream") became the first subprime lender ("no-document" loans) to have its loans financed by Fannie Mae. Seven years later, in 2006, it paid $325 million to settle charges of predatory lending. It went out of business in 2008.

In another glimpse of capitalism, in 2003 the head of mortgage lender Countrywide Financial said, "We wanted to make the American Dream of home ownership something tangible — something to which people could do much more than just aspire." Angelo Mozilo went on to explain that his company wanted to be more than a corporation that made mortgage loans; it wanted to be a force making positive differences in people's lives. "Our goal was, and still is, to demonstrate that there is a unique role in the private sector for public service."

Countrywide made nearly $100 billion in subprime loans between 2005 and 2007, and in 2010, paid the Securities and Exchange Commission $67.5 million to settle charges of insider trading, misleading investors, and disclosure violation.

The Federal government took over ("rescued") Fannie and Freddie in September 2008 due to "a capital deficiency." In the next three years, that cost taxpayers nearly $151 billion.

Why capitalism loved the housing bubble

Any discussion of the Great Recession invariably results in a futile attempt to assign blame (as if one culprit could be singled out), which most often points to the Housing Bubble. To be sure, although it's just one piece of the puzzle, that bubble did play a large role in the crash, and continues to affect the lives of most Americans.

In a nutshell, the bubble combined the innate greed of capitalism with the democratic goal of keeping people happy (or at least hopeful) and the American Dream, in which ownership of a home was paramount. The government encouraged home ownership with financial incentives and relaxed lending requirements, and capitalist bankers were only too happy to step up to the plate to meet the challenge. The greed of the masses, which included low or even no down payments and a cocky assurance that home prices could only go higher, forever, made buying a house look like taking candy from a baby. In reality, the buyers were the babes...and instead of candy-stealing it was a slaughter of the innocents.

Capitalism loved it: This was the kind of activity that branch of the System was designed for: finding a need (even if it meant helping to create it), and filling it... at a profit, of course. Government loved it: The people were happy, and happy people don't start revolutions. The people loved it: they enjoyed ever-larger and more expensive homes, and most were getting wealthy, effortlessly, simply by becoming a homeowner and watching that property appreciate in value.

The housing boom gushed money everywhere. Widespread buying created business for Realtors and bankers. As buyers began to feel more "prosperous" they bought ever-more expensive dwellings, sometimes "flipping" or reselling a recently purchased property only months or even weeks after the purchase: prices rose that fast in some markets. Naturally, when it was sold again, the real estate and banking people profited again.

Others who profited were home builders and makers and purveyors of everything that goes into a house: wood and concrete and drywall, copper pipes and wiring and electrical fixtures, kitchen appliances and plumbing supplies and fixtures, carpeting and furniture, as well as landscaping products and services.

It became common to refinance a home only to use the "found" money to buy a boat or take an expensive vacation, so then even those sectors that had nothing to do with housing profited from the housing boom. Stock markets soared because people "felt" rich.

When the markets reached unsustainable heights — when some people woke up and realized that houses simply weren't worth that much in terms of the amount of life-force now required, when there were no more buyers — it all unraveled, and quickly. As prices plummeted, builders and real estate agents were idled; carpenters, plumbers and electricians were out of work; and people who made, sold, delivered or installed household appliances and furniture were laid off. Not only was everyone suddenly poorer: many were worse off than before.

What we should have learned when it popped

For many people the collapse of the real estate market was no surprise: something about it didn't smell right from the beginning. Making money isn't supposed to be that easy; when it is, something's wrong. For the tradition-bound, the very idea of young people just starting out, with no accumulated assets, getting loans for homes costing hundreds of thousands of dollars bordered on insanity.

Then too, in the old tradition a home was a hallowed place, a fortress of security in several senses of the term, a lifetime investment. Now, for many, it had become a mere brief stopover, with little or no emotional attachment and certainly no sense of family or history, or in many cases even pride — beyond the vanity of conspicuous consumption. Homes were treated like piggy banks just begging to be robbed.

Although no one can fairly judge or comment on the thoughts or goals of another, keeping up with the Joneses, peer pressure, and blatant conspicuous consumption shared the guilt with greed in the housing bubble. There is no other explanation for the McMansions, a.k.a Hummer Houses and Starter Castles, that sprouted on vacant land — or worse, in fertile corn or alfalfa fields that will never again grow food. (One result of the crash was housing developers' panic selling of thousands of acres of land acquired during the boom — back to the agriculturists they had purchased it from — with losses of millions of dollars.)

Many McMansions replaced older homes in established neighborhoods, often creating a backlash. Marin County, California; DeKalb County, Georgia; and Austin, Texas are a few of the jurisdictions that placed strict limits on megahouses. When Marin County's "big and tall ordinance" was enacted in 1997, 4,000 square feet was considered a large house. Now, according to the Marin County Community Development Agency, 6,000- to 8,000-square-foot home proposals are common, and they have gone as high as 14,000 square feet. Aspen, Colorado, was considering a 15,000-square-foot cap… after a Saudi prince built a 55,000-square-foot place.

McMansions aren't the only problem. Keeping up with the Joneses and conspicuous consumption are much worse when the resulting activity is unaffordable, which much of the housing boom was for many, because of the inflated prices and easy credit. The cost was not only financial. The psychological toll and stress had wide-ranging effects, including, according to one study, on the sex lives of anxious and overextended homeowners.

Peer pressure has a price. Conspicuous consumption is for losers. There is no such thing as a free lunch, and anything that sounds too good to be true probably is. These are all lessons to be learned, or relearned. But the most important of all is the admonition to not spend money you don't have. Wisely used, credit can be useful. But used with wild abandon and in huge amounts, that useful lever becomes a dangerous weapon. Relying on future price appreciation makes it even worse.

Finally, few people realize that they pay more than twice the "selling price" of a house through compound interest.

Home ownership peaked at 69.2 percent in 2004 (76 percent for whites, 49 percent for African-Americans, and 48 percent for Hispanic-Americans). After the boom came the bust; by 2011 home ownership had fallen to 66.5 percent, and it was still going down. (Remember that "owned" often means mortgaged, and almost a quarter of all mortgages were underwater.) The benefits of ownership vs. renting came under serious scrutiny. For many, home ownership was no longer a part of the American Dream. But it was not relinquished quietly.

Barrack Obama referred to the American Dream in his first presidential speech in 2008, when dark clouds already loomed over his nascent administration. A year later, when the first wave of foreclosures became apparent, he still clung to the metaphor when announcing a $75 billion plan to deal with the housing crisis.

The National Association of Realtors reported that in 2011, 76 percent of homebuyers believed owning a home was as good as or better than an investment in stock, which isn't saying much. Similarly, a National Association of Home Builders survey indicated that 9 of 10 Americans still said home ownership was an important part of the American Dream; 73 percent believed the government should promote home ownership through tax incentives, which has been the case for almost a century.

In contrast to this cheerleading by vested interests, foreclosures continue in 2012; nearly 24 percent of Americans have underwater mortgages; their homes are not building wealth, but destroying it. The value of American homes decreased more than $1.1 trillion in 2010, another $680 billion in 2011, and the trend continues. The home ownership rate is less today than it was 15 years ago, in spite of the efforts of the capitalist-democracy, and it's likely to decrease further: according to yet another poll, some 80 million Echo boomers (b. 1980-1995) have no interest in home ownership, and the 10-15 percent who are, hope to buy land outside a city. Moreover, almost all want "modest" places (to buy or rent) that are close to activities and will save energy. Quite a switch from the McMansions.

This in itself signals a sea change in housing of the future, in the New Normal. Is it possible that a major and important segment of the population will shout *"Enough!"* and put their money where their mouth is?

Your ecological footprint
MacMansions are expensive not only for the owners (which is how we commonly and mistakenly refer to mortgagees). They are unsustainable, and not only from a financial standpoint. They are a drain on the planet and therefore affect every living being, including those living in the humblest of shelters.

The larger the structure, the more wood, cement, copper, iron, glass and other materials are needed, all materials taken from the Earth, most often far from the building site, and undergoing manufacturing and transportation, both of which have further effects on the planet. The more elaborate the structure, the more complex, refined and expensive the materials.

Doubling the size of a house theoretically doubles the amount of materials used; however, today's homes house smaller families: the space per person has *more* than doubled. A larger building usually uses more land; and more energy to heat and cool. Taxes are higher. Larger lawns involve more fertilizer, herbicides, water, and fossil fuel for mowers that spew far more pollution than cars and trucks.

More luxurious components push the costs up even further. Mega-mansions can easily run 5-10 times the size of the average home, with dazzling amenities: pools and spas, home theaters and wine cellars, imported materials and of course, furnishings to fill all that space. The garage alone could shelter an entire village of aborigines.

Living in one room at a time

How much is enough? No one can wear more than one pair of pants or one pair of shoes at a time. If you need one loaf of bread to live on, two loaves would be too much. And no matter how large your house, you can only live in one room at a time.

Regardless of how many rooms you actually have access to, the principle applies: any space not being used at the moment has a cost with no current return on investment; a cost in terms of the money you spent on it and are even now spending on it in terms of heat, taxes, upkeep, etc.; a cost in terms of the Earth's resources that have gone into it. Know what you can afford, and what price you are willing to pay, for all of this. Then draw the line.

Many economists have pointed out that without air conditioning, much of the population growth in the South and West never would have occurred. Follow the webs on that one! Water, electricity, food distribution... Texas, with its massive drought, is home to the fastest-growing cities in the U.S.

What we're talking about is being aware, even dimly, that housing has many costs that even a good real estate agent will not, and *can* not, explain to you. It's part of the art of living, the part our technology-proficient capitalistic democratic society overlooks in favor of material things that can be measured, counted, added to a net worth statement, with a price tag... and a profit potential. It's another one of the many things "everybody knows" but almost nobody pays any attention to... except deep within their psyches, at their most private moments.

There are a few encouraging signs that leaders of the New Normal will be those who say "Enough!" Car and even bike rental or sharing is becoming very popular in several progressive cities, and "walkability" is a now commonly referred to in urban real estate: the ease, convenience and safety of reaching shops, entertainment centers, workplaces, places of worship and whatever else is important to any given individual, on foot. Mass transit is getting a second chance. In the suburbs and countryside, vast ecologically destructive lawns are giving way to natural landscaping (prairie or desert, depending on location), vegetables and edible landscaping, and rain gardens. Roof gardens are proliferating. No one can say where these developments might lead in the future, but one thing is clear: The American Dream is already vastly changed, and continues to evolve. A New Normal is emerging.

Chapter 13: Health and nutrition

Capitalism requires continuous growth to survive, but infinite growth on a finite planet is impossible. That bottleneck makes thinking about the future of capitalism intriguing. Nowhere is it more interesting than when it becomes involved with health.

The various aspects of human health are curiously correlated with some of the major themes of this book: most current health concerns appeared only recently in the span of human history; all are connected by many far-reaching webs, including capitalism and democracy; they have changed drastically in the past few decades, often growing in geometric progression; new reports on America's health problems, nutrition, medical discoveries and technologies, and of course, health care, are issued almost daily. In spite of all this, eventually, everyone dies.

No one can predict the future, but not very many would wager against the bet that health considerations will play a large role in the New Normal.

Considering how much attention is devoted to health and health care (two entirely different topics), not only in medical circles but in economics and perhaps most of all today, politics, it's surprising that until about 1920, such topics were seldom even considered. So once again we can look to the relatively recent past to better understand the whirlwind changes that have taken place in the span of a single human lifetime (a very healthy human, to be sure, although 100th birthdays are no longer rare) and therefore, hopefully, gain a better perspective on any possible future.

The blunt fact is, from the appearance of the first human until roughly 1920, there wasn't much "health care" to be had. Nutrition barely showed up on the radar, and the germ theory of disease was new and suspect. By the 1920s some vitamins had been discovered (starting with vitamin A, around 1913), although they weren't very well understood and almost no one knew what to do with or about them.

Bacteriology, antisepsis and immunology were known, but not many people, even the educated, put much stock in them. *(Web alert: See Magnus Swenson's experience with this regarding the Madison, Wisconsin, water supply in 1880, in Chapter 19.)* Surgery, when performed at all, was generally performed in the home, even into the 1920s, usually with little concern for sanitation, much less for sterilization. Even such "simple" technologies as blood pressure measurement and X-rays were new, largely untested, and far from universally accepted or endorsed. Younger people in particular might be astounded to learn that insulin was isolated only in 1922, sulfa wasn't developed until 1935, and not until 1946 did we have large-scale production of synthetic penicillin (although come to think of it, those were all a long, long time ago, by current standards of young people.)

The polio story
One disease worth a closer examination is paralytic poliomyelitis. Anyone who wasn't there at the time can't imagine the terror felt around 1952, especially by parents — second only to the terror caused by the atomic bomb — when there were nearly 58,000 cases of "infantile paralysis," leaving 3,145 dead and 21,269 paralyzed, most of them children. First recorded in 1835, polio became an annual summertime plague, with epidemics in 1914 and 1919. The March of Dimes was founded in 1938 to find a vaccine, but little progress was made in stemming the disease. By 1952, nearly everyone knew at least one person in an "iron lung." Among the most famous victims: President Franklin D. Roosevelt, violinist Itzhak Perlman, and writer Arthur C. Clarke. Families of victims

were quarantined; some parents were barred from attending their child's funeral.

The Salk vaccine was perfected in 1955. By 1962 polio was practically extinct.

Again, note the time frame. In the 1950s, something just snapped.

Few people of any age today will remember the controversy between Drs. Jonas Salk (whose vaccine used killed virus) and Albert Sabin, who used a live virus. In the beginning, the American Medical Association (and others) backed the Sabin vaccine.

When asked (by Edward R. Murrow) in a 1955 interview who owned the patent to the vaccine, Dr. Salk's reply was more reminiscent of Chief Seattle than any of today's giant pharmaceutical corporations: "There is no patent. Could you patent the sun?" He became an international hero.

Conspicuous consumption of a different kind: **Salk's prospective father-in-law, a prominent dentist, considered the son of Russian-Jewish immigrant parents beneath his daughter's social status; accordingly, he insisted that the marriage not take place until Salk took a middle name, and was able to use the title M.D. on the wedding invitations. Donna Lindsay married Jonas Edward Salk, M.D., the day after his graduation.**

After they divorced in 1968, he dropped the middle name, married the former mistress of Pablo Picasso, artist Francoise Gilot, and became interested in what he called "teleological evolution," another web altogether.

The origins of health insurance

Even a brief dip into history makes it easier to understand why (1,) so little was spent on medical care; and (2,) so few people had health insurance; and (3,) insurance companies had almost no interest in health insurance.

However, those companies did provide *sickness* insurance. The main cost of illness was not medical bills, but loss of pay. Lost pay was four times more than medical costs, according to a 1919 study in Illinois. Sickness insurance provided income replacement in case of illness or disability.

Despite the lack of public demand for health insurance, some groups (such as the American Association for Labor Legislation) lobbied for compulsory health insurance, which was already adopted in many European countries. They received little support from the people they presumed to protect, meaning from the democratic system. They received *negative* support from physicians, pharmacists, and commercial insurance companies, meaning capitalism. (One argument the insurance industry voiced in 1919: the health insurance "opportunities for fraud upset all statistical calculations... health and sickness are vague terms open to endless construction. Death is clearly defined, but to say what shall constitute such loss of health as will justify insurance compensation is no easy task.")

Medical costs increase

Economic webs played a huge role in the rising cost of medical care beginning around 1920. As population shifted from rural to urban areas, hospitals became more accessible... and more essential, because city residences were often much smaller than rural homes with less room to care for ailing family members (although doctors still made house calls). Advances in medical technology increased the importance of hospitals. And medical doctors underwent *vast* changes in education and methods employed, as well as in their use of technology. The drop from a very large number of poorly qualified doctors to a much smaller number of better qualified ones was reflected in the number of medical schools: from 131 in 1910, to 81 in 1922. This was related to physician licensure, education and accreditation of medical schools, which restricted the number of qualified practitioners, with concomitant increased costs.

At the same time, hospitals were being held to higher standards with accreditation by the newly-formed American College of Surgeons (ACS). In 1918, only 13 percent of the 692 large hospitals examined were approved; by 1932, 93 percent of 1,600 hospitals met the ACS requirements.

All of this led to a new image of medicine as being "precise, scientific and effective" (Rosenberg, 1987), which increased not only the hope and expectations of being healed, not only the demand for hospital care — but also the cost.

One result was a plan developed by Dallas teachers and Baylor University Hospital. Baylor provided 21 days of hospitalization for $6 flat. This was considered "prepayment" rather than insurance but, benefiting both patient and hospital during the Depression years of the 1930s, the idea spread.

It did, however, foster competition among hospitals, and where there were several in an area, they began to cooperate. Eventually this evolved into Blue Cross.

Health care gets more complicated

Here the webs become more like a bucket of worms. In a nutshell, Blue Cross plans benefited from enabling legislation freeing them from organizing under the more restrictive laws for insurance companies, or the reserve requirements of stock companies. Health care then involved not only medical science, economics and capitalism, but government intervention.

Blue Shield — insurance for physician services — developed separately, later, and more slowly, partly as a way for physicians to protect themselves from competition with Blue Cross but also to fend off compulsory insurance, whose advocates had been encouraged by the enactment of social security legislation, both considerations rooted in capitalism. Blue Shield also gained enabling legislation. The original fee in 1939: $1.70 a month.

The capitalist democratic System became even more involved in the 1940s. Commercial insurance companies (the ones who earlier said there were too many opportunities for fraud and too many problems relating to adverse selection) saw the profit opportunity they were missing, and entered the field… making lemonade out of a lemon, viz., the restrictions on their for-profit status.

Being nonprofits, Blue Cross and Blue Shield were required to charge everyone the same premium, no matter what their health status. Commercial companies avoided this "adverse selection" by selling insurance to employed workers; i.e., relatively young, healthy people.

They were able to charge sicker people higher premiums, and healthier people lower premiums, thus undercutting the Blues... and since there are more healthy people than sick people, their business boomed. By 1951 commercial health insurance plans passed the Blue Cross Blue Shield plans, with roughly 41 million each. By 1958, nearly 75 percent of Americans had health insurance.

And more than 50 years later, universal — as in "compulsory" — health insurance is still a contentious issue.

The leading health problems

But why, despite all our medical advances and scientific knowledge and supposedly better education, do so many Americans continue to get sick? A look at the leading health problems offers some clues.

Heart disease is the biggest problem for both men and women, killing more people than all forms of cancer combined, according to the American Heart Association. The leading causes are smoking, and diets high in fat and sodium.

Cancer is number two, with lung cancer the most prevalent. Women have a high incidence of breast and colorectal cancers, according to the Mayo Clinic. Risks are increased by smoking, unhealthy diet, and not using sunscreen.

Stroke is number three for women, number four for men. Again, smoking, excess weight, lack of exercise and an unhealthy diet are major culprits.

Number four on the list is *respiratory diseases,* collectively referred to as COPD, or chronic obstructive pulmonary disease. The biggest risk factor? Smoking.

Injuries are next, with the leading cause of fatalities involving auto accidents, many of which could be prevented. Poisoning and falls are next in importance.

Type 2 diabetes can cause kidney damage, heart disease, blindness, and death. The preventive prescription: lose excess weight, exercise, and eat a healthy diet.

Next is *Alzheimer's disease,* although it's the fifth leading cause of death among women, and tenth for men. The cause is still unknown, although there seems to be a link with heart disease and head injuries.

The top ten is rounded out with *influenza and pneumonia, kidney disease, and septicemia,* the only three (except for injuries) with no apparent connection to smoking, exercise or diet.

The role of smoking

In 1901, Americans smoked 3.5 billion cigarettes and six billion cigars: four of five men smoked at least one cigar a day; cigarettes were for poorer folks. (They still are: as of 2010, the median household income for smokers is $33,748, compared to $53,864 for non-smokers.) There were said to be 300,000 brands of cigars on the market, but Buck Duke sold nine out of ten cigarettes. (That's a lot of cigar brands, but with six billion made, that would average 20,000 per brand, and if most were hand-made, it's reasonable.) In 1904, Duke formed the American Tobacco Co. by merging Consolidated and American & Continental; the next year he added Lucky Strike; in 1907, Pall Mall.

There was, however, an anti-cigarette movement as early as 1900. There was strong anti-cigarette activity in 43 of the 45 states, and Washington, Iowa, Tennessee and North Dakota outlawed their sale. A popular notion spread by the activists held that cigarette tobacco was often mixed with opium or some other drug, and that wrappers had been saturated in a solution of arsenic... a charge repeated by a U. S. Supreme Court justice when upholding Tennessee's sales ban.

On the other hand, in 1905, tobacco was removed from the official U.S. listing of drugs, removing it from FDA supervision... the price that had to be paid to get tobacco state legislators to support the Food and Drug Act of 1906. (Democracy is a confusing form of government.)

In 1906, the Kentucky "Night Riders," a group of angry tobacco farmers, wore hoods and rode horses on raids terrorizing other farmers who sold tobacco to the price-gouging American Tobacco Co. Barns were burned, fields destroyed, and people were lynched.

In 1907 Teddy Roosevelt's Justice Department filed anti-trust charges against Duke's $240 million a year American Tobacco Co. monopoly. The case went all the way to the U.S. Supreme Court, which deemed the company in violation of the Sherman Antitrust Act in 1911.

Women did not smoke. In 1904 a New York judge sentenced a woman to 30 days in jail for smoking in front of her children; another was arrested for smoking in an automobile on 5th Avenue.

The webs become even more tangled: in 1912, R. J. Reynolds outfoxed Wall St. raiders by introducing an employee stock/profit-sharing plan, which eventually made many employees wealthy. That same year, book matches were perfected, making smoking more portable. *And,* Dr. Isaac Adler was the first to strongly suggest that lung cancer is related to smoking. By 1914 the lung cancer death rate was 0.6 per 100,000. That was also the peak year of the cigar business, with 24,000 factories in the U.S.

Tons of tobacco.... For the war effort

When the U.S. entered WWI in 1917, General John J. Pershing considered tobacco to be essential: "You ask me what we need to win this war. I answer tobacco as much as bullets... We must have thousands of tons without delay." In 1918, the War Department bought the entire output of Bull Durham tobacco. Virtually an entire generation returned from the war addicted to cigarettes.

By 1925 women were included, with a ladies' brand: Marlboro, "As mild as May." One ad asked, "Has smoking any more to do with a woman's morals than has the color of her hair?" Another: "Women quickly develop discerning taste. That is why Marlboros now ride in so many limousines, attend so many bridge parties, and repose in so many handbags." (Marlboro's switch from feminine to masculine — "The Marlboro Man" appeared in 1962 — remains one of the classic examples of the power of advertising.) By 1928 Lucky Strike suggested, "Reach for a Lucky instead of a sweet."

Women's college Bryn Mawr scuttled its smoking ban. In 1927, Kansas became the last state to drop its law forbidding cigarette sales.

By 1950, more than 50% of all American men smoked, as well as 33% of the women. Daily cigarette consumption was 10 per capita. And *JAMA* (Journal of the American Medical Association) published the first major study that definitely linked smoking to lung cancer.

In 1952, Lorillard introduced Kent, and the Micronite filter, claiming that, "No other cigarette approaches such a degree of health protection." The secret filtering ingredient: asbestos. By the middle of the decade there were a number of lawsuits against tobacco companies, usually citing their advertising claims.

Asbestos litigation is another matter entirely, the most drawn-out and expensive mass tort in U.S. history, involving more than 8,000 defendants, 700,000 claimants, God-only-knows how many lawyers, and as much as $275 billion.

By 1960, the distribution of free cigarettes at annual medical and public health meetings was discontinued, but free mini-packets were still handed out — on airplanes.

In 1999, about 18 percent of Americans still smoked 415 billion cigarettes. About 10 million people smoked 203 billion cigars. Tobacco expenditures were $47.1 billion. Settlement payments, federal, state and local taxes on cigarettes for fiscal year 2009 came to more than $44.3 billion. Between 1998 and 2009 the average cost of a pack of cigarettes went from $2.09 to $5.86. (When I was in the Marine Corps in 1956 we paid 10¢ a pack. When it got up to 20¢, I quit.) Since 2001, 48 states have increased tobacco taxes. And smoking is implicated in the four leading causes of death in the United States.

The American Lung Association estimates that active smoking is responsible for 90 percent of lung cancer cases. (Radon gets the blame for nine percent, and occupational exposure to carcinogens accounts for most of the rest.)

The American Cancer Society reported (in 2012) that 14 percent of cancer patients were still lighting up five months after being diagnosed with cancer.

Many non-smokers find that hard to fathom. The researchers explained that many of these people are heavy smokers, they're nicotine addicted, and they're surrounded by other smokers, which makes quitting more difficult. Some insist on denying that smoking had anything to do with their disease; others figure, "I'm dying anyway, why stop now?" even though quitting has the potential to increase the efficacy of chemo and radiation and might even double the chances for survival.

Will power isn't enough; and often, patches, chewing gum, hypnosis, Chantix (varenicline), cessation groups, lozenges, acupuncture and prayer aren't enough either.

More webs: **In a capitalist democracy, *jobs* are always a prime concern. In 1994 tobacco interests pointed out that the leaf was grown on 124,270 farms, employing more than half a million farm families plus seasonal labor, using 672,880 acres, producing the seventh-largest cash crop, with a value of almost $2.7 billion. (Compare that with the $47 billion total expenditure listed above. Another 43,000± people were employed in tobacco manufacturing.)**

In addition, it takes about 250 man-hours per acre to produce tobacco, compared to about three man-hours to grow and harvest an acre of wheat. Using the same criteria to compare homesteads and backyard vegetable growing to industrial agribusiness would make small-scale food production look pretty darn good!

You want more webs? We got 'em! **About 31 percent of the receipts from tobacco sales went to some form of excise or sales tax: close to $15 billion in 1994. A 1990 Price Waterhouse analysis estimated that the tobacco industry generated $51.5 billion of the Gross National Product and that 681,353 workers were involved in producing and delivering tobacco products and associated goods and services.**

Incidentally, technically speaking, there is no tobacco subsidy: there were government price support and production controls (not subsidies) until 2005 and the "tobacco buyout," a topic which would get us into foreign tobacco production, falling demand,

health-based court settlements, and more web strands than we'd care to get involved with here.

Given its economic importance, impact on tax revenues, effects on health — and perhaps most of all, its addictive powers — tobacco is likely to continue to affect the webs permeating American life for a long time to come. As of 2012, the U.S. Surgeon General's office reported that almost one in five teenagers smokes cigarettes. Most will become addicted.

The role of nutrition

The health values of certain foods were recognized, in some cases, in ancient times. Hippocrates described scurvy in 400 BC, but not until 1737 did British naval physician James Lind prescribe fresh citrus fruits for sailors suffering from the disease, and another 200 years passed before vitamin C was identified and associated with the fruit. "Vitamines" (*vital amines*) were first described by Polish chemist Casimir Funk in 1911... and again we must remember that some people born then are still alive today: this knowledge is that recent.

So nutrition labeling is obviously and necessarily a new phenomenon; for most people, reading and (sometimes heeding) nutritional labeling is even newer. Most of the agitation surrounding nutrition centers on the overuse of elements such as salt, sugar and fat and a lack of the vitamins found in fresh fruits and vegetables; much of it concerns children; and a favorite target is fast food. Capitalism finds itself smack dab in the middle of all of these.

While nutritionists bemoan double cheeseburgers with bacon and greasy salty fries, some people consider that a delicious meal and nutrition be damned. The restaurateur who doesn't want to lose a sale or a happy customer — but doesn't want to be accused of being cavalier about people's health in pursuit of profits — is caught between a rock and a hard place. Walking that tightrope is a common problem for capitalism. The natural goal is to placate the nutritionists while maintaining profits, not making a profit while improving people's health.

In some cases capitalism doesn't seem to have much to do with it, at least on the surface. Democracy takes control. In 2012 the Colorado state legislature was considering requiring schools to eliminate oleomargarine, vegetable oils and other trans fats from school menus. It doesn't mean a great deal, because the federal government is expected to mandate such a move nationwide.

Then there are such well-known head-scratchers as legislators declaring that catsup is a vegetable.

At the same time, there are plenty of opportunities for entrepreneurs. As of this writing, gluten-free foods have become something of a dietary fad, not necessarily connected with celiac disease, gluten intolerance or wheat allergies. There are gluten-free breads, cakes, pizza, cookies, granola... and Frito-Lay touts the fact that they offer 171 different gluten-free *snacks*.

But the interest in healthful eating offers many other capitalist opportunities. Vending machines now offer juices, smoothies, yogurts, fruits and vegetables. Small farmers who lost money competing with Tyson and Smithfield have found niche markets with free-range chickens and heritage breed turkeys and hogs. And of course there are health food supplements and vitamins… and the anti-aging industry.

Be young, forever

Maybe there's a connection between the ideas of American exceptionalism and personal invulnerability. Both are egocentric, and seem to ignore reality.

Young people are glorified, most notably and blatantly in advertising. Nobody wants to grow old, nobody wants to feel or be considered old, and most people don't even want to be seen with or associated with "senior citizens," which is just one of the euphemisms for the elderly that supposedly softens the idea of being *old*. Old age causes wrinkles, liver spots, hair loss, diminished hearing and eyesight, osteoarthritis and osteoperosis, "turkey neck and grandma arms," and of course, dementia and erectile dysfunction. Who'd want any of that?

Ironically, the only way to avoid growing old is to die young. Finding that even more unacceptable, many Americans fight aging tooth and nail.

Again we see the middle of the 20th century as a turning point: the ranks of the elderly (or at least people over 65) surged, worldwide. Few of these people were willing to age gracefully, or even to act their age. Part of the rationale: how can 65 or even 75 be considered "old," when there are more than 70,000 people over 100 years old, in the U.S. alone? Of those, an estimated 60-70 are over 110! With these stats, "act your age" is no longer a cautionary warning: it's an invitation to boogie. (Several well-known bloggers reportedly started at the age of 107.)

Baby Boomers in particular, it has been said, are very reluctant to accept aging gracefully: some seem quite convinced that with the right kind of living and adequate medical care, they'll live forever. The anti-aging industry, once confined to skin creams and hair dyes, now encompasses everything from food supplements and cosmetic surgery to exercise regimens (and gyms and special equipment) and specially tailored tours, along with specially tailored wardrobes. Wrinkles, sagging skin and crow's feet are not to be tolerated.

An aged appearance is one thing; ageism is something else. While some cultures have more respect for their elders than others, the growing dominance and influence of aging Boomers is having an effect on the New Normal. That too will be interesting to watch.

Life is a bitch... and then you die

Even the best efforts of capitalism can't fend off the inevitable forever, but it hangs on to the very end. Capitalism controls your entire life, and capitalism will bury you — literally.

Of course, few people just "die" any more. They "pass on," in one way or another, depending on their religious and philosophical views. This could be related to not getting old. Nevertheless, they invariably leave a cadaver to be dealt with.

The average U.S. funeral costs $7,500, but averages don't mean much: while the average casket goes for $2,300, they range from $600 to $10,000. The basic service fee for the funeral director averages $1,400 — for being on call 24 hours a day, getting a release on the body and acquiring death certificates and burial permits and all the other paperwork required in a capitalist democracy society, coordinating events with the cemetery, writing and placing obituaries, providing the space for calling hours and perhaps conducting a ceremony, providing a register book, and of course, a hearse, which is most likely leased. Embalming is extra, usually about $600.

None of that includes the cemetery plot, grave digging, or a stone.

Some people are consumed by conspicuous consumption right up to the very end, with elaborate caskets and ceremonies, and monuments.

And then for the hopelessly optimistic, there is cryogenics: freezing a body in anticipation that some day a cure will be found for whatever killed it. Whole body cryropreservation currently runs about $150,000. If you're on a budget, neuropreservation — just your head — averages about $90,000.

Ya gotta admire those capitalists: they never miss an opportunity.

Chapter 14: Education: No child (or adult) left behind

"An educational system isn't worth a great deal if it teaches young people how to make a living but doesn't teach them how to make a life." — *Author Unknown*

Attitudes toward the role of education, and the importance of education itself, have changed drastically throughout history, and especially in the past few decades. At one point the purpose of education was to develop "the whole man," in terms of the arts and sciences. In some cultures, including the beginnings of mandatory public education in the United States, education was aimed at making good citizens. (That remains one of its major mandates, according to *Lies My Teacher Told Me; Everything Your American History Book Got Wrong,* by James W. Loewen, The New Press, 1995.) In more recent times education has been taken over by capitalism to a large degree, in the sense that the System dictates what should be taught.

"For profit" educational companies are also making some headway, and many economists would like to see more progress in the interests of competition: the cost of higher education has been far outpacing inflation. But starting a college or university from scratch is a tremendous undertaking, with reasons related to the prestige factors of schools and tenure of professors, as well as simple start-up costs.

While the need for education is seldom disputed, teaching methods are seldom agreed upon. In today's atmosphere of bloated costs of education, coupled with anemic employment opportunities, the topic of formal education ranks high on many lists of post-industrial worries.

Many refer to the dismal three-decade record of Scholastic Aptitude Test (SAT) scores — which become even more dismal when compared to those of students in Japan and elsewhere — as proof of the dumbing-down of America. Add to that disputes about government involvement and standardized testing (as in "No Child Left Behind") and you have a quagmire that's as confusing and conflicting as anything else arising from the travails of the capitalistic democracy System. But in reality, concerns were widespread even before Rudolf Flesch's *Why Johnny Can't Read* was published in 1955.

According to the *University Catalogue, 1851-1852* from the University of Pennsylvania, freshman were required to be at least 14 years old... and had to pass entrance exams in Latin, Greek, ancient and modern geography, English grammar, arithmetic and elementary algebra. In other words, 150 years ago most graduate students of today wouldn't have qualified as freshmen. Pondering which group is more educated would make a fantastic subject for discussion — if we had any peripatetic philosophers like Socrates today, or even a few more polymaths (non-specialists, people with wide-ranging knowledge). Either our educational system doesn't turn out such people, or the capitalist democratic System silences them, meaning many potentially important ideas go unchallenged and undebated.

Education is both essential and unavoidable. The first children ever born learned from their parents, and that continues today, in varying degrees and with variable success. Basic education today involves not only shoe-tying and potty training, but speech, deportment, looking both ways before crossing the street, and the other skills essential for human existence, as well as the minimal skills required for even the most menial tasks.

Until recently (in terms of human history) the vast majority learned all of life's necessary lessons by working with their elders, whether that meant knapping a flint spear point in a cave, weaving cloth in a medieval cottage, or harnessing work horses on an American farm. We might think of that as career training, and a precursor to capitalist involvement in education for its own purposes.

Formal education, most of which we would now refer to as "liberal" education, was reserved for the very few: the students who listened to Socrates or Confucius in ancient times, or members of the affluent elite attending universities as recently as the 1800s.

Universal public education

Not until masses of emigrants poured in from Europe in the late 1800s did universal public education arise as a means of "Americanizing foreigners." Thus did democracy join up with capitalism in education.

Capitalism's involvement is obvious, and in most cases it's neither a secret nor is it burdened with any guilt. In October, 2011, Dow Chemical donated $250 million to several universities' chemical engineering programs in an effort to draw students to the field. Their impetus: the lure of employment opportunities in other engineering specialties has been draining off chemical engineering candidates.

Major companies routinely endow selected universities. But even high schools are not immune, when local employers complain that their graduates are not equipped (meaning trained) to handle even basic job requirements. (Today, unfortunately, this can refer even to reading and basic math, which brings up problems and concerns beyond the scope of this book.)

This involvement reached fever pitch after the Soviet launch of Sputnik in 1957. Alarmed by falling behind in the space race, in 1958 Congress allocated $1 billion for the National Defense Education Act, the first of more than a dozen programs intended not so much to have better-educated citizens, but to compete with the Soviet Union. The Elementary and Secondary Education Act, signed in 1964, lives on as No Child Left Behind, which is being scrutinized again — or for some, still. The 1960's era focus on gifted students was soon dropped in favor of equality, which many felt meant a further dumbing-down of education and an impossibility in any event: not everyone is equally educable, they said.

In other words, education is not some cut-and-dried process of dumping information into (mostly young) minds: It can be highly selective, and variable. It can have various purposes, which can be at odds. None of this was evident to most people during the heyday of the American Dream, but now, in the post-Dream period, it seems like education is a shambles. Dealing with it is a challenge.

Communications, and writing in particular, have always been the mark of an educated person and are still considered important for almost any job that involves dealing with people. But the state of writing in America has reached such an abysmal stage that even some editors apparently don't know the difference between *its* and *it's*, or the quite different meanings of *weather, wether,* and *whether*, and perhaps even *wither* and *whither*. Having spent more than half a century as an editor and author, I'm appalled to encounter even Ph.D.'s who can't spell.

And then there's all that nonsense about short sentences and simple words: even professional writers are supposed to write for 12-year-olds. Apparently, anyone who wants to read an adult sentence or encounter a challenging word is expected to read only 19th and early 20th century writers, in which case what's the point of even learning to read or write above an 8th grade level? Of even greater concern, when I was young, learning to write well was considered an important means of learning to *think*.

The Internet and texting have exacerbated the debacle.

The New Normal is people who are overly educated in one or two esoteric areas, but who write, and think, like children.

What's the purpose?

Many aspects of formal education are controversial, especially among the experts, which as we have seen, is the normal pattern. (Experts in any field often dismiss us plebes for our ignorance, even while disagreeing among themselves. This emphasizes the importance of doing your own thinking.)

One controversial aspect is the *purpose* of schooling. For some the answer is simple: The purpose of education is to cover all the government standards, improve performance on government tests, and to produce a competitive workforce. Others maintain that "the purpose of education is to appropriately prepare our children for the future." Still another view: "To make the world a better place."

The purpose of education as *you* see it determines your attitude toward it, and therefore how you approach it.

A discussion of the purpose of education often covers three types: 1, a "classical" education, where a student learns how to think; 2, training for a career or profession; and 3, preparation for responsible citizenship, or, according to one interpretation, a means of perpetuating the established social and economic System.

A fourth aspect — learning for learning's sake, or to become a more complete or higher form of human being, or just for the thrill of discovery, or as one educator put it, the "bliss" of learning — might or might not be a combination of the first three. But once you're "out of school" this becomes the most important purpose and benefit of education… and arguably, the most neglected. For the masses, early formal education is so awful it turns them off from learning for the rest of their lives. They never do come to appreciate the pure pleasure involved.

The *purposes* of education cannot be separated from *types* of education. This might refer to formal and informal, or to home schooling (an option with obvious appeal to many homesteaders), or by looking into "skimming" and "submergence" as different levels of learning. We might even consider brainwashing, which certainly enters into this. But let's look at the two most commonly debated, under various titles. Call them learning how to think, and learning how to do something useful, or if you prefer, professional training versus a liberal education, or simply training and education.

One way to tell the difference between education and training, according to storied Washington D.C. fire chief Dennis Rubin: Would you rather have your daughter take sex education, or sex training? And recall Pete Seeger's explanation of the difference

between education and experience: Education, he said, is what you
get when you read the fine print; experience is what you get when
you don't.

Learning to "make a living"

Much of today's education is aimed at "making a living,"
just as in the time of the guilds, but the technology is much
different. Instead of learning to tan leather or fashion useful
goods from metal, modern students must learn the skills
needed to become biomedical engineers or bankruptcy
lawyers. In our post-industrial society, services are more
important than goods. The System is adapting to that.

Perhaps it has adapted too well. During the period when
every child was encouraged to get a college education, college
prep courses crowded out shop courses. Capitalists who hire
the shop-type people are becoming concerned, and there are
signs that is changing yet again.

The problem is, what skills will be needed, or even usable, in
the foreseeable future? The whirling spiral of the speeded-up
System is so tornadic, how can we even deal with it?

Today this is exemplified by the apocryphal stories of people
with masters' degrees flipping burgers for a living. The
unemployment rate for all 18-24-year-olds in 2010 was 17%.
What makes it worse is that the recent graduate with a student
loan — about two-thirds of the total — owes an average of
$25,250. One 2011 Occupy Wall Street protestor in Boston had
a master's degree, $60,000 in loan debt, and no job. Even those
who do land a job in their chosen field can expect to be paying
on the loan for the next eleven years.

A college education, as part of the American Dream, is
becoming as debatable as home ownership. Again, this is not
new: Generation–Xers who have been complaining about this
for years were labeled as whiners: now, more people
understand what they were talking about.

During the 1950s and '60s, the number of workers with high
school and college degrees increased greatly — part of that
American Dream, again. The number of jobs requiring higher
education did not. Using Census reports from 1950 and 1970,

researchers Thurow and Lucas studied the numbers of workers, by educational level, in occupations ranked by income. By 1970 those with college educations had become increasingly occupied at the lower levels; those with only elementary or high school educations were even less likely than before to be in the upper levels. There was much more concentration at the bottom of the pile.

That was in 1970. It's far worse now. And today, in addition to the diploma, you need to pass a personality test, drug test, and criminal background check, and prove that you are not an illegal alien or a terrorist, even if the job is just pushing a broom.

It's important to note that what we're talking about is *know-how,* not *knowledge* in the strictest sense. Many a college graduate is woefully uneducated, in the classic sense.

"I think everyone should go to college and get a degree and then spend six months as a bartender and six months as a cabdriver. Then they would really be educated." — *Al McGuire, College Basketball Coach*

Given these facts (and many more like them, just as depressing or worse), what should the role of education be? In an out-of-control system that's changing with blinding speed, what course of action makes the most sense? Whether you are a young adult contemplating the future after high school, already a college student, or the parent of a child just entering the K-12 system, these questions are as difficult to answer as they are unavoidable.

One fact is inescapable: Everybody has to make a living. It's a key tenet of capitalism. (Remember, capitalism and socialism are at opposite ends of the same sliding scale, and despite the concerns of many, we are still deeply entrenched on the capitalist end.) Moreover, (although some people seem unclear on this today) it's a moral obligation. How you earn that living is dependent on many factors, education being only one; and education itself is in turn dependent on many factors.

For example, not everyone has the necessary aptitudes or interests to become a biomedical engineer or a bankruptcy lawyer. Those who don't won't even entertain the notion of training for those jobs. Similarly, not everyone is qualified to be a plumber, welder or diesel mechanic. To be sure, the world, the System, needs all of these, but having said that, the System also requires migrant field hands and slaughterhouse workers and a host of others requiring no education at all. So one of the first tasks of a young adult contemplating the future today is deciding where in that hierarchy he or she would be most comfortable. When the general target is defined, the choices can be narrowed down.

In our so-called "classless" society a college professor is likely to be ranked higher than an automobile mechanic. But it has been pointed out that in certain situations that professor might be inclined to look upon the mechanic who can start his car stalled on the freeway in much the same way as the aborigine regarded the explorer with a thunderstick: the equivalent of a *god!*

There is little argument that on average, college grads earn more than high school grads, who earn more than high school dropouts (with a few exceptions, which we'll look at). As usual, averages are meaningless.

According to a 2010 report issued by the College Board, the median earnings of full-time workers with college degrees were $55,700, $21,900 more than those of workers with only high school diplomas. This study claimed that after working for 11 years, the higher pay of college grads made up for the four student years of lost income, as well as paying off the student loan.

This, of course, is historical. Today, nearly half of young adults with college degrees are not working in their chosen profession. (However, changes in mid-career were becoming common even before the recession, suggesting that putting all your eggs in one basket with a too-specialized degree might not be wise under any circumstances in a rapidly changing world.) Only 47 percent earned more than $30,000 last year, but they have historically high debt: nearly 10 percent leave college with more than $40,000 in debt, typically meaning monthly payments of $460.

A significant minority of college graduates don't earn as much as those with less education, for a variety of reasons. Some degrees are worth less than others in the marketplace, while some non-college skills and trades are in high demand, and pay very well. (Have you hired a plumber, lately?)

Many of us wonder why a ball player or a musician or a business executive can be paid millions, or even hundreds of millions of dollars a year, while teachers and others in supposedly much nobler professions are tossed only crumbs. Surely a dedicated teacher or a caring nurse is worth more than a wild-haired half-naked multi-pierced potty-mouthed rock star who is also doped up most of the time.

The fallacy lies in the assumption that compensation is determined by the value society places on a certain activity. It is not. Compensation is determined by the marketplace, by the law of supply and demand. The public is eager to throw money at a few of the top rock stars and ball players just to see them perform. There are many more dedicated teachers and skilled nurses than there are rock stars, and fewer people standing in line overnight to see them in action. Large supply, smaller demand: That's what makes the difference.

The obvious solution is to stop throwing money at the rock stars, ball players, and overpaid executives and bankers. That we don't is simply another indication of how our capitalist economic System works, and why we should give it some serious thought. The System is working just fine; *people* need to change.

But even then, unless you are on the very brink of entering the workforce, specialization, or overspecialization, is risky. When the first automobiles were produced few people could foresee the demise of the buggy whip industry, and no one could have imagined the day when repairing carburetors would join lamp-lighting in the jobs dustbin of history. But today, not only is what might seem like a stolid and secure occupation not at all a sure thing: even if it survives, it will undoubtedly undergo such tremendous change that it will require consistent re-education and updating.

In 2010 software architect, physician assistant, management consultant, physical therapist and actuary were listed as being among the "best" jobs based on pay, hiring outlook, work environment, stress and physical demands. (Not surprisingly, some workers in these fields *hate* their jobs and bitterly contested the findings in online comments.)

Even when arbitrary and subjective, or even controversial, such lists can be somewhat helpful, or at least interesting. But they're based on *today*: what about tomorrow? And even more dizzying, what hot jobs of tomorrow don't even *exist* today? Shooting at a moving target is one thing, but aiming at one that no one has even thought of yet is impossible.

The value of a liberal education

The changing role of education in earning a living means that without a very specific career goal — dentistry comes to mind as one that might not be automated or outsourced any time soon— specific training could be risky: a broad, general education that provides a background applicable to a wide range of fields would seem to be safer. Be prepared for any opportunity that presents itself, and be prepared to change or adapt on short notice. That's a sensible approach in this climate. It's not the only one.

The college graduate is still most likely to get the best jobs: when there are so many of them, why hire a high school graduate, even if the position doesn't require a degree?

In this line of thinking, a graduate with a knowledge of any of the sciences, including social sciences, and who can communicate effectively, is a more serious contender than one who specialized in Lithuanian Renaissance literature.

This description of a modern liberal education comes from the president of Sarah Lawrence College, Michelle Meyers, who claims that liberal arts colleges provide "an education in which students learn how to learn, an education that emphasizes the forming rather than the filling of minds, an education that renders our graduates adaptive to any marketplace, curious about whatever world is around them, and resourceful enough to change with the times."

It's well known that the richest man in America, Bill Gates, with $59 billion, is a college dropout. What's interesting is how many others became fabulously wealthy, also without college degrees. What's even more revealing is that these are all internet-related. A sampling: Larry Ellison (Oracle $27 billion); Larry Page (Google $18.5B); Michael Dell (Dell); Paul Allen (Microsoft); Steve Jobs (Apple); Jerry Yang (Yahoo); Mark Zuckerberg (Facebook, well known for his $700 million at age 23); Matt Mullenweg (WordPress); Jawed Karim (YouTube); and Shawn Fanning, (Napster).

Hacking out a personal path through this thicket, for yourself or your young child, isn't easy. The only constant is that a good education is better than a poor one.

Critics of modern K-12 education are quick to point out the amount of time wasted in the normal, average school day. Sex education and driver's ed are favorite targets, but others such as self-esteem, personal safety, family life, consumer training, etc. — skills that used to be learned in the home — occupy more than half the day in many high schools. One study claimed that American students spend 1,460 hours on math, science and history during four years of high school, while their peers in Japan spend 3,170 on basic subjects, in France 3,280, and in Germany, 3,528. Even if the comparisons are meaningless, anyone interested in being in control of life, in conserving that life-force consisting of the time we have to actually accomplish our goals, will find this atrocious waste of time inherently abhorrent.

Home schooling

For parents of young children, reclaiming the right to educate one's own offspring is a logical first step. Here's another sliding scale where nothing is either all black or all white: no parent, no matter how inept or uncaring or even cruel, can avoid teaching a child *something,* if only by bad example. At the other end, no parent could devise a home schooling plan that would teach a child everything the child needs to know, or everything the child learns: we all learn from others and the world around us, as well as from books and teachers.

At-home learning, in the family classroom, went out of style about the time women became working-outside-the-home mothers. This doesn't refer to formal, scholastic learning; it means families spent less time together, not only working in the garden and at the dinner table, but even on such tasks as washing dishes. A noisy dishwasher precludes any opportunity for conversation, either weighty or whimsical.

For awhile in the 1950s "family time" might have consisted of an evening gathered in front of the new-fangled and therefore mesmerizing tv, but soon even that was supplanted by separate programs for kids and adults (at the behest of advertisers who wanted certain age groups), then recorded movies just for children, and then youngsters having their very own televisions in their very own rooms.

Add to all this the whirlwind of after-school activities — Girl Scouts, soccer, band practice and on and on — and when would a parent even find an opening?

Many people have changed this by taking other facets of their lives into their own hands. If bringing up a child — educating a person — is as much of a goal as making more money for whatever reason, then parenting becomes a priority and something else has to give. No one drops everything and just *does* this: it's part of the overall plan and pattern of living free, taking control, and consciously ignoring anything that gets in the way of the goal.

The options along a sliding scale are infinite, and because life itself is a system of intertwined systems there are many points where some degree of compromise is essential. That's no reason to not choose any option at all.

It used to be claimed that people who grew up on farms made the best workers: they had more experience with chores and responsibilities than city kids. I wonder how much of this was due to the work on the farm, and how much to the influence of the family, working together. Many homesteaders claim to know the answer.

The world wide web

For many, home schooling isn't an option; for others, a private or charter school might be impossible. But supplemental learning materials, through libraries or on the web, are nearly universally available.

The web could fill a chapter of its own. Not only can a home-schooler take a full load of online courses: many regular public schools encourage, and some *demand* that all students take some courses on the web. Considering budget restraints and other problems, learning via the Internet is a foregone conclusion. This requires a whole new set of skills many of today's students aren't familiar with: a form of independence, self-control, and self-reliance that is just the opposite of what much of society seems to demand, and what most people have become accustomed to. From the standpoint of homesteading and self-sufficiency, it couldn't happen too soon!

Parents must make the time — not *take*, but *make* the time — to oversee and participate at least to some degree, depending upon the age and experience of the student and the difficulty of the material. But there are two other important points:

One is teaching, by example, what you have learned about using time and life-force. Just as a worker who spends half the day chatting and doodling and shuffling papers will accomplish only 50% of the output of a co-worker with better work habits and a better work ethic, so will the student who dawdles and procrastinates.

The other is the importance of doing what you love — not in the sense of just having fun, but delving into it with a certain lust that makes it interesting, even exciting, and therefore most welcome. In the working world it's what makes a person say "I've never worked a day in my life, I love my job that much." For a student it's a gnawing curiosity about how the world works, and the thrill of discovery, the bliss. Great teachers have a knack for instilling these traits, because when they're present, learning isn't an onerous chore: there's no need to assign homework; the eager student will seek it out, independently. When you come right down to it, great teachers are great not because they impart so much information but because they instill a love of learning. Too bad not all parents are a part of this.

The Internet will indubitably play a major role in the New Normal... but will that role be beneficial to individuals and society, or will it be a curse? Benefits will not come automatically: they will only accrue to those who are aware of the options, who can sift and winnow the valuable from the useless or downright dangerous. It requires thinking... and a kind of pre-education to prime the pump and get things started on the right track.

This applies equally to young children, college students, and adults who are still eager to learn — as they very well should be. Learning is not only for getting a job: it's what makes us human. Done right, it's also satisfying, and even fun — which also makes us human. Capitalism can't take that away — unless we let it.

"I didn't go to college at all, any college, and I'm not saying you wasted your time or money, but look at me, I'm a huge celebrity." — *Ellen DeGeneres, Tulane Commencement Speech, 2009*

Chapter 15: In pursuit of creative leisure

Leisure deserves a great deal more thought than most people give it — and there's much more to think about than most people realize. It's important mentally, physically, and economically, even now when most people think they have so little of it: what would it be like to have loads of leisure?

Surprise: a vast army of Americans are retired, most of them faced with more free-time than they know what to do with. As Baby Boomers join them, their ranks will swell... and Baby Boomers have different values (and ideas about leisure) than older generations. In addition, some 20 million people who are un- or underemployed have more leisure than most of them want. How much of this is *creative* leisure?

Then too, some thinkers claim that technological advances will increase leisure for *everyone* in the decades ahead. Taking all of this into account makes leisure a major concern for society and a major component of the New Normal.

While most people recognize the mental and physical health benefits of "time off," not everyone is aware of the tremendous impact our leisure-time activities have on capitalism (and not just during the Super Bowl, either).

Impacting all of this is the seldom-recognized idea that, like capitalism and democracy, leisure lies on a continuum: there is a sliding scale between pure work, and pure leisure. There is also a difference between leisure, recreation, and play.

But that's getting ahead of the story, which is obviously a big one. Let's start with some basic concepts.

In the beginning

It's a common myth that primitive people spent all of their time grubbing for a living. Poppycock. Any homesteader with animals, or any observer of wild animals, is well aware that even the birds and beasts frequently enjoy various forms of leisure: the chickens in their dust bath and the hog in the wallow might be engaged in their particular form of personal grooming, but no one who observes them closely can deny that they're enjoying themselves. Otters, and the young of almost all species, are notorious for their playfulness, but they're not alone. (Pets and other domestic animals with enforced leisure might shed some light on our own future, should we reach a similar stage of being "kept," that is, surviving with little or no effort of our own, which seems to be happening.)

Even in prehistoric times, humans engaged in the arts. There is archaeological evidence that they enjoyed music, personal decorations, and of course, cave paintings and petroglyphs. In more advanced but still primitive societies this expanded greatly, including story telling and religion, huge totem poles and tiny trinkets, elaborate costumes and beautiful pots and baskets. They danced, held contests and played games.

Some scholars have held that merchants in colonial America worked about three hours a day... the amount of time others have determined is sufficient to provide for essential human needs. Capitalism, including conspicuous consumption and over-consumption, has inflated that to current levels.

It is true however, that for most of human history leisure was pretty low-key. Social intercourse, at first around the fire, later at the tavern (wine has been traced to the Stone Age, and beer isn't much younger), and now on the cell phone, has always been a part of human existence. We know games existed since before recorded history, but we can only guess at the popularity of such leisure-time activities as "meditation" (aka "napping"). Whether sex is a leisure-time activity or a necessary part of grubbing for a living will be left to other thinkers.

The continuum of leisure

This demonstrates the sliding scale between work and leisure: is sex work, or play? For some people it's a profession, it's essential to perpetuate the species, but it can also be quite recreational. Yes, clay pots and reed baskets are "essentials" and tools, but what impulse drives the maker to strive for grace and beauty of form, or elaborate decorations, far beyond any practical considerations? Are the goat kids butting heads just playing, or are they preparing for adulthood? The hen fluffing her feathers in a dust bath is controlling parasites, but the look of "aaahhh" on her face is no less blissful than that of a woman being pampered in an exclusive spa.

John Neulinger, in *The Psychology of Leisure* (1974) describes six stages from one end of the continuum to the other: pure leisure, leisure-work, leisure-job, pure work, work-job, and pure job. Homesteaders can simplify this, insofar as it can be simplified at all: there is stuff that absolutely must be done, now; stuff that must be done, but it can wait; stuff that really ought to be taken care of as soon as you get some extra time, and finally, things you'd really enjoy doing even though they aren't essential.

One hurdle in identifying stages of work/leisure is that someone's job can be some else's leisure, and worse, the same task can be considered relaxing fun on one day and an onerous chore the next.

A classic example of the former asks two young boys about two pictures, one of a man reading, the other of a man cutting wood. One boy says the reader is playing while the woodcutter is working; the other boy says just the opposite.

The explanation is that one boy's father is a college professor who reads at work, and cuts wood on weekends for fun. The other lad's dad is a woodcutter, who reads for pleasure.

As an example of the same task being either work or play, doing the morning chores, including milking a few goats, can be a sublime experience on a balmy spring day when the plum blossoms are perfuming the air, newborn kids cavort in fresh straw, and the chickens are laying well. The same chores on a blustery winter day when the water pipes are frozen and you discover that a fox got into the henhouse overnight and a goat kicks over the full pail of milk — that's not nearly as much fun.

One of Diane's relatives told this story: In 1942 he was working with the U.S. Engineer Department in Fiji, erecting ten 50,000 gallon steel gas tanks. Native labor was needed to help the welding crews, but the local colonials said they'd never get the Fijians to work beyond the first payday. Most had their little plot of land, a bure (traditional native hut) and a vegetable garden, and fishing was easy: why work?

The canny Americans devised a plan. They erected two of the tanks at once, making a game of it. The losing crew had to throw a party for the crew that finished first. "Fijians are a happy-go-lucky people who exerted great energy as long as it was a game. They didn't have to work, just play." The plan worked.

Obviously then, leisure depends on a state of mind. Neulinger refers to this as *perceived freedom.* You choose to do something, anything, because you want to, and that's that. If you do something because you *must* do it, from a sense of duty or for any other reason, then it's work.

It's difficult to know whether a homesteader is working, or playing. In a similar vein, when talking about the difficulty of going on vacation when there are farm animals to care for, I have often asked, "Why would you want to go anywhere else when you live on a homestead?" We, and many others, have gone years without a night away from home, not simply because we "couldn't get away" but because we were having enough fun so there was no desire to go anywhere else. Like Thoreau, "I have traveled far, in Concord." If I can't identify every weed and insect on the tiny piece of the planet I inhabit, there's not much point in flying across an ocean to expand my universe: there's a universe to be explored in my own backyard.

Leisure, recreation and play

None of this is to suggest that leisure isn't necessary, or even that it's over-rated. It is, however, under-studied by the average person. While some shrug it off as mere "spare time" with "nothing to do," others see it as essential for both mental and physical health: the traditional view is that leisure is literally re-creation, or recharging the batteries — primarily to improve work performance, unfortunately. On the other hand, it can be considered an essential element of personal development, and even civilization; as such, it has come to be seen as one of the *purposes* of work.

Sorting this out requires recognizing the several aspects of leisure. The most apparent, today, is recreation, which can be defined as refreshing the mind or body with an activity that amuses or stimulates. This covers a lot of territory: it could mean solving a crossword puzzle or skydiving, touring China or tripping on recreational drugs.

"Play" is just one form of recreation, most often in reference to children but also applied to activities such as golf and "games" such as football, baseball and basketball.

It's difficult to correlate free time as being "leisure" — as in a leisurely stroll through a park — with what often occupies people's spare time. Violence has always played a role. Throwing Christians to the lions and beheading royalty during the French Revolution were considered entertainment; cockfighting was, in ancient times, and still is in some places. Today we have violent video games, and football.

While thousands of people sometimes pay hundreds of dollars to watch a football game in person, millions more watch on tv. All forms of "small screen entertainment" now account for the lion's share of American leisure time. This, of course, is a relatively recent development. In less than a hundred years, sitting in front of a computer or tv screen has replaced the dime show, medicine show, burlesque, wild west show, circus, vaudeville, variety show, musical reviews and theater, as well as activities such as barn dances. And today some kids hunched in front of a small screen think the old-timers had boring lives and "nothing to do"!

Along with the availability of small screen entertainment, leisure activities have been affected by shorter working hours. Robert William Fogel, a Nobel Prize winning economic historian, estimates that between 1880 and 1995 the amount of work per day fell nearly in half, and leisure time nearly tripled.

Most will find this incomprehensible, unbelievable, or laughable: parents in particular feel they have little or no time for themselves, but nearly everyone feels overwhelmed by the time factor. And yet, according to the U.S. Census Bureau, not only does nearly everyone over the age of 15 engage in some sort of leisure activity: women spend 5.1 hours a day watching tv, socializing or exercising, while men have 5.8 hours of free time! Watching television accounts for roughly half of that — 2.7 hours per day. Not surprisingly, individuals aged 15-19 spend six minutes per weekend day reading and 1.1 hours using a computer for games or leisure, while those over 75 spend 1.1 hours reading and 18 minutes using a computer for leisure or games.

A closer look at outdoor recreation

Given this broad view, almost any human activity can be a leisure-time activity for someone, somewhere, at some time. Tomato farmers struggle to find decent labor for the arduous and tiring task of picking tomatoes, while frail little old ladies do it for fun. Some people wouldn't jump out of an airplane if all the engines quit working and it was on fire besides; others jump out of perfectly good ones, just for fun. From ancient times, cooking was considered a lowly occupation, far beneath the dignity of hunters and warriors, and some still have that attitude. At the same time, there are popular cooking shows on tv 24/7, chefs can be celebrities, and macho men brag about their homemade breads (to say nothing of their chili and barbeque): for them, cooking is fun.

Outdoor recreation is one area with very little overlap: not many people can make a career of hiking or backpacking, camping with a tent or RV, snowmobiling or bird watching. But outdoor recreation is a $730 billion a year industry in the

U.S. It supports nearly 6.5 million jobs. It generates $88 billion in state and national tax revenue, and another $289 billion in related retail sales and services.

These figures cover equipment: boots and bicycles, kayaks and canoes, rifles and fishing rods, binoculars and boards, both surf and snow. It entails apparel, footwear and accessories, along with transportation, food and lodging, entertainment and souvenirs.

The numbers do *not* include over $30 billion spent on boats and other big-ticket items, only a small portion of the more than $14 billion in recreational vehicle sales, and none of the billions spent on leased and purchased recreational land, cabins and second homes. Outdoor recreation is big business.

According to the Outdoor Industry Foundation, more Americans owe their jobs to bicycle-related recreation than there are people employed as lawyers. More Americans owe their jobs to snow-based recreation than there are physicians and surgeons. The active outdoor recreation economy employs five times more Americans than Wal-Mart, the world's largest private employer.

However, the industry isn't exactly excited about how it's doing. One clear indication has been the decline in the use of national parks. Park visits increased steadily for 50 years, peaking in 1987 with 287 million visitors. Since then they have declined more than 25 percent. Hunting and fishing have seen even steeper declines.

Environmental and health specialists seem even more concerned than capitalists, and with good reason. No one questions the value of outdoor recreation in terms of physical, emotional and psychological well-being. Some scoff at the notion of national park visits having anything to do with these benefits. But with the majority of Americans living in towns and cities where interaction with nature is limited or nearly impossible, it's a disturbing sign. Kids who have become used to a temperature of 70 degrees, winter and summer, with no bugs, no cuts and scrapes, or even sunburn, can't be expected to confront nature like those who lead a less-protected lifestyle.

According to studies cited by O.R.W. Pergams and P.A. Zaradic in the *Journal of Environmental Management* (2006), environmentally responsible behavior results from direct contact with the environment rather than knowledge of ecology, and extended periods spent in natural areas seem to create the most environmentally responsible behavior. And then there is the importance of the role model, but with interest and involvement in the outdoors declining for a generation, those role models are unavailable to most of today's youth.

Researchers have noted a universal decline in "nature-based recreation," in such diverse areas as Spain and Japan. Most of the blame is heaped on small screen recreation, although there are many other contributing factors. However, Pergams and Zaradic point out that everybody has 24 hours in a day, seven days a week and 52 weeks a year. So it's significant that in 1987 the average American spent zero hours on the Internet, and in 2003, 174 hours (plus 90 more on video games). Including movies, the average American spent 327 *more* hours on small screen entertainment in 2003 than in 1987. With the Internet, we can assume this has increased appreciably more since then.

For years, homesteaders and organic farmers have bemoaned the fact that most city people have no idea where their food comes from, no idea of how humans are connected to Nature, and little idea of the fragility and finiteness of our planet. As a result, "saving" it has little meaning; for some it's a silly joke. When it comes to conservation and many other environmental concerns, this attitude could be suicidal.

One answer has been the creation of WebRangers, an Internet site for school children that has been operating since 2003. In 2007, a bill intended to reduce the "nature deficit" in children was introduced in Congress. It was called "No Child Left Inside." While that purports to tempt youngsters into the Great Outdoors, it pits "biophilia" against "videophilia," with the former defined as "the innately emotional affiliation of human beings to other organisms" (Wilson, 1984), the idea that we humans have an affinity for the natural world that has evolved over millennia and is part of our genes, just like our tendency to be territorial and to protect our young. Videophilia is "the new human tendency to focus on sedentary activities involving electronic media."

A 2004 Minnesota Dept. of Natural Resources Outdoor Recreation Participation Survey found that 97.5% of the decline in visits to national parks had four causes: time spent on the internet; time spent playing video games, time spent watching movies; and oil prices.

The Minnesota DNR study said, "The replacement of vigorous outdoor activities by sedentary, indoor lifestyles has far-reaching adverse consequences for our physical and mental health, for our economy, and for natural resources themselves."

It went on to note that 60% of Minnesotans are overweight or obese, 33% have high cholesterol, 22% have high blood pressure, 6% have diabetes and 26% have pre-diabetes. Obesity has tripled among teenagers, and quadrupled among 6-11-year-olds. Now there is concern that not only will today's youth be the first American generation to be worse off than their parents: they might not live as long, either. According to one paper, "public park and recreation services are becoming part of the healthcare system of the United States and are now being recognized as such."

The survey points out that the primary contributing factor to the decline in nature-based recreation is a drop in participation by young adults (ages 20-40) and their children. Projecting that generational trend into the future offers little cheer for environmentalism.

When three-fourths of our time is free...

According to some specialists who have studied trends going back to the 1800s, a generation from now over three-fourths of our time will be "free," available for doing whatever we want to. John Neulinger, in his 1974 book *The Psychology of Leisure*, goes even further: he suggests that one day a society could be *based* on leisure. What would we do with that time, and what are the implications?

> **In one sense, this is at the heart of this book: if we already have more stuff than we need, more than we ought to want, more than Planet Earth can sustainably provide, then why in the world be concerned about "creating jobs" to manufacture more?**
>
> **Concurrently, much of what most people today consider "leisure" is simply wasted time — meaning wasted lives — especially when taken to excess; creative leisure expands, improves, and polishes our humanity, making the world a better place.**
>
> **Marrying these two ideas is not an impossible utopian dream.**

A homesteader would eagerly look forward to such a prospect, not to have more time to lounge around in any of the myriad ways the capitalist society has devised, from backyard spas to ocean cruises, but for *creative* leisure.

We have seen the difficulties in pinning down a good definition of "leisure." "Creativity" is just as difficult. One general definition is "the production of novel, useful products," after which there are more than a hundred variations, including ours. Combining two such slippery words ventures into dangerous territory. But for those engaged in simple living, it's not all that complicated.

Creative leisure simply refers to free time that offers a reward, and the greater the better. Of course, that's on a sliding scale.

With the simplest kind of leisure, let's say taking a nap lying in the grass on a sunny day, the reward might be waking up feeling refreshed, which is fine. At the opposite end of the scale we might spend our leisure time in the workshop, creating a table or a chair. The reward is not only tangible and material and potentially even valuable in a pecuniary sense — the table or chair — but also in the personal satisfaction it provides — which might entail not only pride of workmanship but also the satisfaction of having mastered the art and science of making dovetail joints, and perhaps even extending to a truly creative new design.

The possibilities on this end of the continuum are obviously endless. Such leisure time could be spent in the garden, kitchen, library, anywhere you *want* to be, doing something that truly interests you to the point where you forget where you are or what time it is.

Some examples closer to the center might include bicycling, skiing, or any other form of exercise; attending a play or concert or visiting a museum or art gallery or making your own music or art; dining out or touring a new city or even a foreign country.

There is nothing wrong with just sitting, for brief periods. But no sensible human would get much satisfaction from continuous napping, and anyone who could tolerate long stretches of any other form of leisure near that end of the scale is, at the very least, missing out on *living*.

We all have to find our personal comfort zone on that scale, but the more leisure that's available, the more important it becomes to use it creatively, not only to fully live, but to avoid going nuts. We need to achieve balance.

About global warming:

Richard Wolfson, professor of physics at Middlebury College and an expert at interpreting concepts in physics, climatology and engineering for non-specialists (one of his books is *Simply Einstein: Relativity Demystified*), has recorded a series of lectures on global warming. After six hours of looking at his charts and graphs and listening to his explanations I understood that yes indeed, the globe is warming, and it's very likely anthropological (AGW), caused by human activity.

That evening I read a long letter in *The Wall Street Journal* (which does not believe in AGW) signed by no fewer than sixteen apparently eminent scientists saying, in essence, that global warming is a crock.

A few days later the same paper ran another letter, a rebuttal from an opposition group, signed by *twenty-four* scientists.

This is just a tiny sample of how ridiculous the controversy has become. The result, of course, is that nothing is decided or accomplished.

However, the real story, for us, here, is not the juvenile arguing. It's the fascinating correlation between these arguments, many of the others we're examining, and the entire theme of this book: we're in deep trouble on many fronts, and we're dithering on all of them. Will we manage to work our way out of the mess, or must we accept whatever nature hands us?

Chapter 16: Global warming: A hot topic

Many people don't let a lack of information prevent them from having strong opinions, as seen in letters to editors and certainly on the web. However, many of those involved in the AGW debate appear to be quite knowledgeable. To me, the biggest mystery about global warming is why both skeptics and believers debate it so vigorously. Why do they think it's worth the effort, and why do they have such strong feelings?

Maybe I'm just blasé. More than 50 years ago I took a class in climatology at the University of Wisconsin which covered not only the major ice ages that occurred over millions of years, but the "little ice ages" between those, and still lesser temperature variations at other times... which in geological chronology means the Earth's temperature has varied since the beginning. It was a small class; climate change was a scientific fact and an ongoing phenomenon, everyone just accepted it, and nobody really cared very much. For us students, at least, it was an adjunct to studying other Earth sciences.

To make matters worse, about 25 years ago I wrote a novel, *The Place Called Attar...* a story based on global *cooling*, which was much bandied about at the time. I don't know whether to be amused or embarrassed by that now, but it does indicate a long fascination with climate change.

The naked truth is, people like me who believe in sustainability, who regard the Earth as a sacred trust, and who embrace the concept of *enough*, are predisposed to accept AGW as fact, and why not? We're against the rape of the planet and pollution of any kind and the depletion of natural resources, whether or not any of those affect climate. If they do, then we have all the more reason to change our ways, and more ammunition to convince others to join us.

It's a near certainty that the venomous denials involve more than simple facts. Any decision made or opinion formed with inaccurate or incomplete information has only a 50-50 chance of being correct, and it's a certainty that no one has complete and accurate information on global climate. Considering webs and butterflies, probably 99% of our decisions and opinions are based on faulty data. This is undoubtedly the case with something as complex and far-reaching as climate change.

Time again for rational ignorance

Despite my studies, my knowledge of the science involved is very limited. I wouldn't attempt to explain, for example, how today's concentration of CO_2 is some 30% higher than in perhaps hundreds of thousands of years and how that concentration is accumulative, so that even the relatively minor amount we humans account for builds up over time, and has been building up since the advent of the Industrial Revolution and the widespread use of fossil fuels. Just as important, there are other "forcing agents" such as methane, and airborne particulates called aerosols (such as *sulfate aerosols* resulting primarily from coal combustion) — which are involved in *cooling,* which obviously makes everything even more complicated. And there is much, much more that the average person hasn't even heard about.

It's not just fossil fuels

Then too, while the burning of fossil fuels is usually at the center of any debate about anthropological global warming, other human activities also play a role: deforestation reduces the CO_2 ordinarily used by plants; methane is produced by sewage treatment plants, landfills, and agriculture ranging from cattle to rice paddies; even jet contrails play a role.

What mere human is going to sort this all out, and then put the pieces of the puzzle together to come up with a definitive answer? And if the people who make careers out of studying the subject can't agree, what hope is there for us ordinary blokes? Even if we study the topic, who's going to listen to what we amateurs think?

Note that there is little disagreement about global warming per se: the argument involves the influences of human involvement. But even that leaves room for differences: some people (including most economists, according to one survey) think climate change will have little or no effect on society; others foresee floods, droughts, famines, populated coastal areas under water, and even the extinction of humanity.

Anyone who is deeply interested can easily become immersed in explanations such as Prof. Wolfson's. His twelve 30-minute illustrated lectures are available on DVD at www.thegreatcourses.com. When you learn how temperatures and carbon dioxide levels of hundreds of thousands of years ago are determined and the strong correlation between the two, how anthropogenic CO_2 of the past few centuries is measured, and gain a basic classroom knowledge of many of the other pertinent factors, it becomes much easier to evaluate the masses of information, or misinformation, put out for the general public. It's actually quite interesting and intriguing, and it will certainly vault you into a new league at cocktail parties.

One reward of a course like this — and a benefit of any decent adult education — is a new understanding of and appreciation for the utterly astounding depth and breadth of knowledge acquired and studied by the "specialist experts" I often delight in skewering for their "three blind men's description of an elephant." Especially fascinating (to me) in this one was the explanation of how we can estimate temperatures from thousands and even hundreds of thousands of years ago by such means as isotope ratios (of oxygen-16 and oxygen-18) from ice cores and shell-forming marine organisms; the study of lake sediments and pollen; and other methods that can look back tens or even thousands of millions of years. Like the study of astronomy, it puts our petty human concerns into perspective: don't sweat the small stuff — and it's all small stuff.

Others can discuss and debate the causes and effects of basic climate change; they can argue about the roles the capitalist democratic System should play, if any; they can speculate on the effects of all the above on the New Normal. Let us take a different route: let's examine a few of the webs connected with global warming that are already becoming obvious to those who are attuned to such things.

Agricultural zones move north

To start out with something simple, phenologists — those who observe and record the timing of such natural events as first budburst in spring and the arrival and behaviors of specific birds, animals and insects — are well aware that the climate is warming.

The 2012 USDA release of a new growing zone map lent official credibility to the warming theory (although the Agriculture Department denies any connection to global warming: they say they just have more and better data, a cop out that conflicts with the phenology observations). The zone map shows isotherms, lines that connect locations sharing the same minimum temperatures, indicating areas where plants with known cold-hardy tolerance can be expected to survive. All of the USDA's ten growing zones have moved north in the past 15 years.

This is great for my northern garden, right? Since my garden went from a Zone 3 to a Zone 4, according to the USDA, I should be able to grow more and better fruits and vegetables, and so feeding my family will be easier than ever. And a rise in CO_2 is actually *beneficial* to plants: some growers add it to greenhouse air intentionally!

If only it were that simple.

Most people are aware, even in today's city-centric society, that farming is a risky business: floods, droughts, hail, frosts both early and late, insects and diseases, these are all forces of nature to contend with. Even the casual gardener quickly becomes aware that growing conditions can change drastically and rapidly in any given year, and that no two years are alike. All of these are affected by climate.

Climate affects bugs? Of course. One of the advantages of being a grower in the North is that many crop and garden pests that plague the South die out over winter in cold climates, which sometimes more than makes up for the shorter growing season. Many such pests are following the zone charts north. Plant diseases are similarly affected.

The zone maps refer to the lowest winter temperatures, something that primarily affects perennials, those plants that survive from one year to the next. Most farm and garden crops are annuals, that is, they are planted in spring and by fall or winter they're dead. These plants don't care how cold the winter gets: they're concerned with conditions during their growing period.

A small temperature change makes a big difference

This is a good place to be reminded that while the 0.65°C (1.17°F) global rise in temperature since the start of the 20th century doesn't sound like much, that's not the point. For one thing, when averaged over an entire planet, poles and equator, land and oceans, mountains and deserts, the variation is considerable. During the last Ice Age mile-thick ice sheets covered large portions of Europe and North America, but the average temperature then was only about 6°F lower than it is today. And perhaps most significantly, an average is the peak of a bell curve: move the average up a few degrees, and the base of the curve moves with it. Heat waves and cold spells are normal phenomena that occur at the very edges of the averages. With a higher average we can expect more severe extremes.

But back to the maps: even an unusually mild winter can be followed by too-cool temperatures at certain critical stages in the growing season.

This can become extremely complex.

Honeybees don't fly in cold, wet weather: if that's when the plants are in bloom, the flowers won't get pollinated and the crop is diminished. And honeybees pollinate at least 125 crops in North America, from apples and oranges to animal foods such as clover and alfalfa, which ultimately become milk, cheese and ice cream, and hamburger.

Corn requires heat during tasseling (each silk on an ear of corn is attached to one kernel, and each silk must be fertilized by pollen from the tassels), but crops such as lettuce will "bolt," or become bitter and go to seed, when the weather turns warm. All plants require water, of course, but when and how much they receive from nature depends on the weather. Some crops require a longer growing season than others; some are more easily damaged by wind than others, and of course hurricanes and tornados devastate everything in their paths.

All of these are affected by climate; if the climate changes, the problems change; but if we can't predict one we can't predict or prepare for the other.

And the webs continue

Climate's complexity can be seen in the increasingly common dust storms bedeviling the American Southwest.

Dust collected at a monitoring station in the San Juan Mountains of southwest Colorado was 24 times as great in 2010 as in 2005. Core samples from lakes high in the Rockies show a dramatic increase in dust level layers since 1900, when the West was swarming with activity, degrading vast swaths of a protective crust of lichen, fungi and bacterial colonies that normally hold loose soil in place.

Hydrologists have determined that dust kicked up in Arizona or Texas often drifts north on the jet stream; the dark particles cover the snow pack in the mountains, absorb sunlight, and accelerate melting, sometimes by weeks. When too much snow melts all at once there's not enough reservoir capacity to hold it all, and not enough water later for the 27 million people in seven western states and Mexico (plus farm irrigation) who depend on water from the Colorado River basin.

Officials in Indonesia are quite sure that country's devastating floods in 2011 were due in large part to deforestation. But such chains can become more complicated than the average human would care to get involved with. Case in point: bark beetles cause megafires.

A fascinating web spun by the mountain pine beetle

Literally billions of the mountain pine beetles (genus *Dendroctunus,* meaning "tree killer") have already killed millions of acres of lodgepole and ponderosa pines across the western U.S. and Canada, from New Mexico and Arizona to Alaska; more than 35 million acres in British Columbia alone. The infestation itself has many webs.

Smokey the Bear (with human help) has suppressed wildfires, one of nature's ways of controlling the beetles. Older trees are more susceptible to insect damage, and today's protected trees are older, providing the beetles with a more desirable environment. Another control was winter temperatures of -30°F to -40° for weeks at a time, but these haven't been recorded in some of those areas for decades. A decade-long drought weakened the trees, making them more susceptible to the insect damage.

Scientists at the National Atmospheric Research Center in Boulder, Colorado, say the dead and dying trees might be changing rainfall patterns, especially from Montana and Wyoming south. Healthy live trees *absorb* carbon dioxide from the atmosphere while dead trees *give off* carbon dioxide as they decompose, with a dramatic effect on local climate in particular.

In some regions the pines have been totally wiped out, creating a "kindling effect." Thus, recent wildfires in Arizona and New Mexico have been of historic proportions… *megafires.* Increased home construction in forested areas makes it worse.

Fast-moving crown fires are the main threat in living or recently-killed standing forests. After a few years, when the trees fall to the ground, burning piles of logs can be catastrophic. You have probably seen pictures of how quickly a forest recovers after a "natural" fire in a living forest, but piles of dead wood cause much more severe and long-lasting damage to soils and ecosystems.

Mudslides and silt buildups in rivers and reservoirs are only one visible result. Canadian biologists warn of flash flooding when live trees no longer hold back snow, making it melt more slowly. Such floods affect salmon and other wildlife. In Yellowstone, the beetles are killing trees that produce the fat-rich pine nuts critical to grizzly bears. And it goes on and on.

The tourism industry is worried. Many ski areas have cut down their forests because of the hazard of falling trees. Highway departments are also concerned about falling trees. Some towns like Vail and Steamboat Springs, Colorado are completely surrounded by forest. Grand County, Colorado, hosts four million visitors a year: one official wondered, "What happens if this becomes an ugly place to be?"

A freak wind blew the beetles across the Continental Divide into northern Alberta in 2006, and there is concern that the beetles will eventually reach the Great Lakes.

Where we are also awaiting invaders from the east: European ash borers, as well as gypsy moths.

We simply don't know

Examining just this one small aspect of life on our planet, it's easy to see that tracing all of the links, and all of the potential connections and consequences, is beyond our capability: we simply don't know the outcome of any specific action, because we don't even know for certain what's happening. None of this can be tested in a laboratory, and computer simulations are not perfect. The only certainty is that a changing climate, or even just concerns about a changing climate, will have an impact on capitalism, whether this involves "cap and trade" of carbon credits, reducing emissions, or continuing past levels of pollution.

If we believe the preponderance of evidence (and polls), a majority of people and scientists think global warming is real. The controversy begins when we ask if it's man-made. Then, does anybody really know whether or not changing any of our current practices would actually make any difference? Would the economic cost offset any conceivable benefits? What should we be doing now?

The answer is, nobody really knows: we might as well pursue rational ignorance on a global scale.

It goes without saying that if a significant chunk of land ice plunged into the sea, enough to raise the sea level, the world economy would be seriously affected: some of the most heavily populated and economically important areas of the world are on low-lying seacoasts. (Note that sea ice, which includes most of the Arctic, would have no effect: it has already displaced the water and melting won't change anything, just as when the ice in a highball melts the glass doesn't overflow. In reality, most of the expected rise in sea level will come from the expansion of warming ocean water.) Widespread and prolonged droughts and serious floods would certainly have effects, as would other violent weather events. More peripheral situations, like the mountain pine beetle invasion, would be far more difficult to predict, as would the economic consequences.

So, what can an individual do? Those who are convinced that they have all the answers and believe they can anticipate all the webs are likely to attempt to convince and influence others, both individuals and the capitalist democratic System. Others are being somewhat more cautious and circumspect. Thus far, the arguments and disagreements cancel each other out, again leaving the bystanders in the majority.

A word about capitalism:

Capitalism, in all its various forms found along the sliding scale of economic systems, can exist under almost any type of government: there was limited capitalism in feudalist societies, and there is a great deal of capitalism in The People's Republic of China, neither of them democratic.

On the other hand, economists tell us that a democratic political system can partner only with capitalism: all other economic systems are incompatible.

But remember that democracy also exists on a sliding scale, somewhere between pure democracy and totalitarianism.

Therefore, we have two systems — economic and political, both on a continuum — blended into one larger system — creating a third continuum. That's the basis of the capitalist democracy System that rules our lives. No wonder it's so confusing!

If you're familiar with the harmonics of, say, a guitar string, that's a helpful analogy. A string creates one tone by vibrating at a fundamental frequency, or 1st harmonic. Within that, other sections of the same string vibrate at different frequencies, creating 2nd and 3rd harmonics. To our ears they all blend together to create one pleasing harmonious tone.

Add to capitalist democracy the vibrations of all the other webs we've been talking about. If they too were in harmony the result might be wonderful music. They are not in harmony. Instead of creating a beautiful symphony the "pleasing harmony" becomes chaotic cacophony. The dissonance we're hearing now suggests that something is frightfully wrong. Even a cursory investigation suggests that part of the disharmony is coming from the democracy.

What's the status of the "democracy" part of our capitalist democracy, and what might we expect in the New Normal?

Chapter 17: Thinking about democracy

The Greeks had a word for it: *democracy* is a compound word meaning "rule by the people." And they meant it literally, as early as 508 BCE, with every citizen (meaning free men, not women or slaves) having a direct vote in all the affairs of the government.

This obviously became unwieldy with large numbers of people. In his *Republic,* Plato sets 10,000 citizens as a reasonable upper population limit. The Greeks met this challenge with their city-states. The Romans took it to another level, moving democracy along the political continuum by introducing *representative* democracy, as well as the division between nobility and commoners in the senate and assembly.

Western civilization took a hit after the Roman Empire collapsed, and by the Middle Ages feudalism was prevalent. While some democratic ideas and ideals were maintained and modified during this period, it wasn't until around 1700 that they got some serious and widespread attention, thanks to English philosopher John Locke's *Two Treatises* (1690) and French philosopher Jean Jacques Rousseau's *The Social Contract* (1762). As we have seen, capitalism was also developing at this time, and as they supported and nurtured each other, the capitalist-democracy symbiosis blossomed.

The minds behind the American Revolution were well-acquainted with what had gone before: Thomas Jefferson, Benjamin Franklin, Alexander Hamilton and many of the others knew both history and philosophy, and they didn't hesitate to mix both of those with experience, common sense, and more than a dash of creativity.

The resulting blend was something entirely new: a democratic republic, with a senate and an assembly, and three branches of government, none with absolute power. This provided a large degree of democracy but without the size limitations of the Greek model; it avoided Plato's concerns about the uneducated masses having too much control (we won't venture too far into the implications of *this* bucket of worms) and, most notably, lessened the possibility of a tyrant seizing power over the people. (But note that the people can still *elect* a tyrant if they so choose.)

How relevant is democracy today?

That's about where we are today. But plugging in all the bits of history we've looked at in connection with capitalism, it's obvious that the world today is drastically different from the worlds of ancient Greece or Rome, and even early America. How relevant is democracy in view of these changes? Perhaps even more to the point, how has the democratic republic itself changed after two centuries?

The most obvious difference is that the world is tremendously more complex than ever before. There are many more people: the old Greek limit of 10,000 citizens per democratic unit would be ludicrous, today. New York passed that limit in 1737; today more than 8 million people call that city "home." Nearly 250 American cities have populations in excess of 100,000. With such numbers, pure democracy is clearly out of the question.

Large numbers of people create complexity in many other areas, such as numbers of laws. Nobody even knows how many thousands of laws are on the books, but there are more than 4,500 *federal crimes.* Today, it's possible to be sent to a federal prison for something you didn't even realize was against the law. (*The Wall Street Journal* ran a series of investigative articles on this in 2011, including a detailed account of a hospital maintenance engineer who faced prison time because of a plugged toilet.) Interestingly, in terms of our observations of how changes have been occurring more rapidly recently, more than 450 of these crimes have been created just since 2000, and needless to say, some beggar the imagination.

Why so many laws?

One possible explanation for the proliferation of laws is that so many politicians are lawyers. Of the 100-member U.S. Senate, 60 have law degrees. ("That'd be fine if we had a lawsuit to settle," Ron Johnson said in his ad when running for the U.S. Senate in 2010, "but we have an economy to fix." Johnson is a wealthy Wisconsin plastics company executive who favors business experience over legal expertise.) Nearly half of the representatives have law degrees. Critics find two major problems with lawyer domination of legislatures:

First, by concentrating their educations, experience and efforts on such a narrow field, what qualifies these people to make important decisions regarding business, economics, nutrition, medicine, education, agriculture, and all the other matters that come before the legislatures?

Second, even though there are more than 1,100,000 lawyers in the U.S., that's less than 1% of the population. When this was pointed out on a *Wall Street Journal* blog, one comment was, "Seems to me that having so many lawyers in the Senate is clear evidence that this body is not representative of its citizens, nor is it attracting the best, brightest, and most accomplished Americans, by any stretch of the imagination."

It has been suggested, more than once, that laws are so complex because they're written by lawyers: as the only people who understand such bills, their services are required to administer them.

More than 2,000 years ago Plato proposed a special class of people, trained and nurtured from childhood on, who would be uniquely qualified to rule. Today, in America, that would go over like the proverbial lead balloon. But then, an oligarchy of any kind — rule by a privileged few — would be anathema to most Americans. Or would it be? Before we string out this interesting thread to see where it leads, let's take a brief look at how laws come to be — not according to your high school civics class, but in the real world.

Staying on top of things

No ordinary citizen could possibly hope to be well-informed about the hundreds of matters that come before Congress, such as online poker, online piracy, and school nutrition (pizza is now officially a vegetable). The question then arises, how do our elected representatives keep up-to-date on so many topics of such vital importance?

For one thing, they get a lot of help — information, ideas, advice, that sort of thing — from people who have the means to really study the details of the various questions. These people, called "lobbyists," are experts in very specific areas and they're so eager to help elected representatives make wise decisions that they spend billions of dollars doing so.

The top sector in these activities is the health field, which spent $4.752 billion from 1998-2011: $377,948,406 in 2011 alone. Finance, insurance and real estate came in a close second, with $4.738 billion. Then came communications and electronics with $3.9 billion, energy and natural resources with $3.5 billion, and transportation with $2.4 billion.

Top industry: pharmaceuticals and health products, spending $2.26 billion, 1998-2001, followed by insurance, electric utilities and business associations. Of more than passing interest, education spent $1,025,533,329, and civil servants/public officials spent $932 million.

Taking it down to individual spenders, and for just 2011, we have the U.S. Chamber of Commerce ($46 million); General Electric ($21 million); National Assn. of Realtors ($16 million); and the American Medical Assn. ($16 million). Others of interest in the top 20 include Blue Cross/Blue Shield, American Hospital Assn., AARP, Pfizer Inc., and National Assn. of Broadcasters. These are some of the groups (that is, people), who help our elected officials make the rules we all must live by.

Closely aligned with lobbyists are the Political Action Committees, or PACs. The National Association of Realtors was active here too, but their $1,351,150 in 2011was topped by the $1,440,500 from National Beer Wholesalers Assn. Make a note of this for later reference: American Crystal Sugar is number nine on the list, with a contribution of $991,500.

Why so much money? For one thing, getting elected is expensive. The old days of travelling from town to town, getting up on a stump and giving a speech, are long gone. The 2008 presidential election cost $5.3 billion; the 2012 version is projected to hit $6 billion; some even predict $8 billion, including house and senate races. President Obama alone is on target to spend $1 billion. ($8 billion equals the median $50,000 a year income of 16,000 American families.)

Campaign spending surged after the U.S. Supreme Court's ruling in the Citizens United case, which stated that, "restrictions on corporate independent expenditures are invalid." In other words, corporations are considered people, and although they can't vote, they can influence voters by spending as much as they care to allocate to the cause. If we ask the question, "Why would they?" the most obvious answer is not that they're eager to participate in the democratic process, but that they hope or even expect to benefit from their contributions.

Sometimes, even winning an election isn't enough. In Wisconsin in 2012, the move to recall the newly-elected governor and several other high officials (legitimately voted in in elections costing millions) was projected to cost in excess of $9 million more. And then there was another election, costing additional millions. Poor people don't run for public office.

And that brings us back to oligarchy... and perhaps even what some Americans suspect borders on kleptocracy, (literally "rule by thieves.")

Rule by a few

We have seen that 60% of the U.S. Senate and more than half of most other legislative bodies consist of lawyers, who account for less than 1% of the total U.S. populace. That could logically be considered a form of "rule by a few," but there's more. There is also the question of *money.*

This need not be confined to the wealth of individuals in any legislature (although there are more millionaires than lawyers in the Senate, and nearly half of the Representatives are millionaires.) As we have just seen, spending on elections, and lobbying, now accounts for billions and billions of dollars, dollars that make nothing, provide no shelter or clothing, and feed no one, aside from the trickle-through of those billions (newspapers and tv stations that sell campaign ads employ people who pay mortgages and buy groceries). We can be assured that most of these billions are not coming from the worker who supports a family on $35,000 or even $50,000 a year.

There has been a great deal of talk about "the 1%" recently; that small segment of the population that makes and controls an enormously outsized proportion of the economy. We won't debate their effect on government and legislative matters right now, but this gives rise to an important question: can a true democracy exist where there is vast disparity in wealth?

U.S. Supreme Court Justice Louis Brandeis thought not. "We may have democracy," he said, "or we may have wealth concentrated in the hands of a few, but we can't have both." That we now have wealth concentrated in the hands of a few is an undisputable fact.

As this is being written, the 2012 presidential election is just getting revved up, and money is looming large as a sticking point. Mitt Romney is being criticized for paying only 15% tax on his $21.6 million in income, and Newt Gingrich is under fire for being bankrolled, in a "super PAC", to the tune of $10 million by billionaire Sheldon Adelson.

Threads of webs: **Adelson's fortune came from casinos in Las Vegas, Singapore, and Macau. He has been charged with bribery in Macau and anti-union activity in Las Vegas. He also owns a newspaper in Israel that opposes any peace settlement with the Palestinians... and Gingrich recently stirred up a controversy when he called the Palestinians "an invented people."**

Politics is full of odd coincidences.

As of late 2011, the Congressional Budget Office reported that more than half of total U.S. income goes to those in the top 20 percentile. And it's getting worse: incomes in the middle and lower levels have been declining since the Crash, while those at the top have been increasing. According to an earlier report, those at the very top (0.1 percent) saw their incomes soar more than 400 percent between 1979 and 2005.

Economist and *New York Times* columnist Paul Krugman called it a stark reality: "We have a society in which money is increasingly concentrated in the hands of a few people, and in which that concentration of income and wealth threatens to make us a democracy in name only."

It is not true, as some claim, that we are still an upper-middle-class society where educated, skilled or trained workers are doing very well. They're doing better than lower-class uneducated unskilled workers, but according to the Budget Office report, their economic gains as a group have been nil since 2000, while the very top tiers prospered. There might be reasons, rooted in economics: The very rich have different investment portfolios than the rest of us, and were less affected by the Crash. Most of their income is from investments, which are taxed at a lower rate than wages and salaries, which means they not only get more than most of us but they also get to *keep* more of it. Whatever the reasons, the income gap is enormous, it's growing, and it affects democracy.

It was big news when it came out that General Electric, a worldwide conglomerate with $14.2 billion in profits in 2010, not only didn't pay a cent in taxes that year: it claimed a tax credit of $3.2 billion. But maybe it shouldn't have been a shock, according to the Citizens for Tax Justice and the Institute on Taxation and Economic Policy. Those watchdog groups say that of the 280 most profitable companies in America, 30 paid "less than zero" in taxes in the previous three years, and 78 didn't pay any federal income tax in at least one of the three years. It was all perfectly legal of course, under the current tax code.

Pork barrel legislation

Lobbying is a fact of life in American politics. So are subsidies, and pork. Subsidies are interesting enough, and a

big enough topic somewhat more connected to capitalism than
to democracy, so we'll examine that in another chapter. Pork,
on the other hand, is a direct result of the democratic process,
in some cases an integral part of that process.

Getting elected is strenuous, and expensive. Getting re-
elected is almost as bad... except. If the incumbent has "done a
good job," getting re-elected can be relatively easy. In most
cases "doing a good job" means sending money from
Washington back to the home district, in the form of pork
barrel projects.

(The term "pork barrel" dates back to just after the Civil
War, and refers to Southern planters doling out pork — from
the salted pork barrel — to slaves, as an occasional treat.)

Pork barrel legislation refers to appropriations of public
funds, usually by Congress, for projects that are of little or no
importance to the nation as a whole but which are vigorously
promoted by a legislator or legislators to pump money from
Washington to their home districts. Pork often becomes trivia
news when it involves something like spending $107,000 to
study the sex life of the Japanese quail or $150,000 to study the
Hatfield-McCoy feud; only somewhat less frequently does it
engender outrage, as with the $50,000,000 indoor rainforest in
Iowa; or the infamous "Bridge to Nowhere", a $398 million
project to link mainland Alaska to Gravina Island, population
50.

The best-known of these legislators was "The Pork King,"
Sen. Robert C. Byrd (D-W.Va.; b.1917-d.2010), who was also
referred to as West Virginia's one-man billion-dollar industry.
After securing $97 million in fiscal 1999, Byrd became the first
person in history to obtain more than $1 billion for his state,
according to the Citizens Against Government Waste
Congressional Pig Book.

And he wasn't very modest: more than 30 of these projects
include his name: The Robert C. Byrd Highway, High School,
Center for Hospitality and Tourism, Locks and Dam, Green
Bank Telescope, Federal Correctional Institution, and on and
on. There was also a statue of him in the state capitol while he
was still alive... even though state law prohibits statues of

government officials until they have been dead for at least 50 years.

Elected to the U.S. House of Representatives in 1952, and to the Senate in 1958, he held that office until his death in 2010, making him the longest-serving member in the history of the U.S. Congress. (And yes, he had a law degree — but not until after he was already a senator. Prior to his first election he was a gas station attendant, grocery store clerk, shipyard welder and a butcher — as well as the *Exalted Cyclops* of the local Ku Klux Klan, a group he disavowed when running for public office, although he did participate in the 83-day filibuster against the Civil Rights Act of 1964, which he also said later he regretted.)

As part of the economic web it's noteworthy that many people have observed that despite all this largesse, West Virginia is still a "poor" state, while a few miles away, the Raleigh-Durham "Triangle" area of North Carolina has a booming economy based on capitalist enterprise, not pork. West Virginia per capita income is $29,534, ranking it 49th among the 50 states, ahead of only Mississippi. (Although Congress appropriated $500,000 for a new building for a teapot museum in Sparta, North Carolina, the project was cancelled before any money was spent; the museum, with more than 6,000 teapots, closed in 2010.)

Austerity of government has become a hot topic since the Crash, but pork has been little affected — except that now the term "earmarks" is preferred, the earmarks are supposed to be more transparent, and they can't be named after sitting members of the House. But the *2010 Congressional Pig Book* still listed 9,048 requested projects worth $10 billion and 81 anonymous projects worth $6.5 billion.

When this money flows into a region some local promoters get giddy: "This project didn't cost anything: the money came from Washington!" They forget where Washington gets its money: not from producing anything, of value or otherwise. And when Washington gets a dollar, it never, ever returns 100 cents.

The question of class

America has been hailed as a classless society almost from the beginning, and for nearly as long, almost everyone has known that's a crock of baloney... especially the poor, the uneducated, the minorities, the many who are all three and know full well they're not in the upper middle class. This might even be expanded: the sick and infirm, gays, single mothers, those in certain occupations, even the obese and smokers might feel discriminated against today. The explanation or apology is that "equality" refers to things like opportunity, not to class distinctions.

Even though class might not be based on wealth, the lower classes seldom have much money. However, that has not been a very strong common bond, compared with the other factors.

But since the Crash of '08, the number of people who are struggling financially has increased dramatically: America is no longer dominated by a middle class, much less an upper middle class. And the new "lower class" no longer consists exclusively of the traditionally downtrodden. This contrast with the arguably obscene wealth at the very top of the heap is a warning sign, if not already an imminent disaster for democracy. But there are other differences, and definitions, of class.

The "duh" in democracy: ignorant voters

American ignorance of government is legendary. Polls routinely report that most voters can't identify their congressional representatives... and that the average voter can name more of the seven dwarves than justices on the Supreme Court. But ignorance goes far beyond those kinds of trivia questions. (As a practical matter, what does knowing the name of a judge have to do with the state of the union? Many, if not most, other details of government are likewise simply not worth our time or effort; we have more important uses for our time, and the information wouldn't offer any real benefits anyway. Economists call this "rational ignorance.")

If a college professor has no clue as to why his car is acting funny, a doctor no concept of how a meal appears on her dinner plate, or a banker has no recourse but to call a professional when his electric garage door opener doesn't work — and those with even more advanced degrees in even narrower specialties have even greater difficulty with anything outside their specialties — then what's to be expected of us common folk? The only people among us who are qualified to be leaders, so it's said, are too smart to run for office.

And such a person probably would have almost no chance of being elected because even when they're not ignorant, the majority of voters are uninformed, misinformed, short-sighted, or voting their own self-interest.

Laura Penny (in *More Money Than Brains*) wrote "We have really put the 'duh' in democracy, creating a perverse equality" by allowing, even demanding, that everyone vote, no matter how ill-informed.

Elections are, for the most part, popularity contests, as much as voting for high school class officers. The millions and billions of dollars spent on advertising are seldom meant to inform; like food advertising, they sell the sizzle, not the steak.

This often includes one or two hot-button issues. Voters are routinely focused on a single issue that's important to them, personally, whether as a purse-string or some other self-interest matter or one of philosophy or religion or just plain principle. The candidate who's on their side in this gets their vote, no matter how many of perhaps dozens of other issues they might *disagree* on.

Candidates are often shortsighted, looking no further ahead than the next election. It's called "kicking the can down the road." They know balancing a budget will require sacrifices from their constituents, who will blame the lawmaker for those sacrifices. Better to kick the can down the road and get re-elected, preferably as long as possible, when someone else will take the blame. Obviously, voters share that frame of mind.

"I'd never vote for anyone stupid enough to run for public office"

Those who even bother to vote, that is. In the 2008 presidential election, which was clearly a history-making event, only 64 percent of eligible voters cast a ballot. Of interest in terms of looking to the New Normal, this overall rate was about equal to the 2004 election… but voting by young people, blacks and Hispanics increased, while turnout among other demographic groups was stagnant, or decreased.

To some people, this is tragic, and another sign of democracy's decline. To others, it's the logical result of the two-party system, where the choice is, as Helen Keller observed, between Tweedledum and Tweedledee, or two peas in a pod. (Incidentally, many people aren't aware that Helen Keller, lauded as a heroic example of overcoming adversity in childhood, was a socialist. Ultra-patriots generally whitewash this aspect of her life to preserve her heroine status.)

Or, take P. J. O'Rourke's satirical advice (and the title of his 2010 book): "Don't vote; it just encourages the bastards." Libertarians and anarchists certainly agree: voting for Tweedledum or Tweedledee merely legitimizes the farce; voting for "none of the above," even if such write-ins were counted, would accomplish nothing. Even voting for candidates not sanctioned by either of the two controlling parties is pretty much a wasted ballot. Why bother… and why pretend that the system is working?

But such is democracy. In an earlier book (*A Parliament of Whores,* 1991) O'Rourke wrote, "Imagine if all of life were determined by majority rule. Every meal would be a pizza. Every pair of pants, even those in a Brooks Brothers suit, would be stone-washed denim. Celebrity diet and exercise books would be the only things on the shelves at the library. And — since women are a majority of the population — we'd all be married to Mel Gibson."

Another somewhat more serious and arguably more apt description of democracy (often misattributed to Benjamin

Franklin) is, "democracy is two wolves and a lamb voting on what to have for lunch."

And although former U.K. Prime Minister Winston Churchill reportedly said, "The best argument against democracy is a five-minute conversation with the average voter," he also usually gets in the last word: "Democracy is the worst form of government, except for all those other forms that have been tried from time to time."

Like capitalism, democracy has changed considerably since the Constitution was written; science, technology and knowledge have changed; the nation has changed. Is democracy working better now than when the Constitution was signed in 1787, or worse?

It would be naive to assume that democracy won't undergo even further transformation in any New Normal. What that will involve remains to be seen.

A word about food:

At some point in 2010, an estimated 17 million Americans experienced difficulty feeding everyone in the family. With as many as 20 million people out of work, around six million unemployed for at least six months, food banks across the country became strained.

For anyone in the 99%, food is a major component in the family budget. On average, food takes 13% of a family's income, but the less money you have the higher that percentage: for some, it reaches 50%. And food prices keep rising.

With the industrialization of food, in addition to the vagaries of weather and other natural causes of famine in the past, it wouldn't take much to disrupt the long supply lines from field to table.

To cost and availability, add safety and moral considerations, and food deserves a special section in any discussion of the New Normal.

Chapter 18:
The industrialization of food
A capitalist's dream

A reminder: To the well-ordered mind accustomed to linear thinking, this book − and certainly this chapter − might appear to be unorganized chaos. That's because it reflects life, underlining the webs and tangents and indeed, the chaos of the real world. It stresses that nothing is all black or all white, everything is on a sliding scale, and most of all, there are no simple questions where the answers don't have implications and consequences often far beyond what mere humans can envision. We must allow for that, and seek harmony and balance. *Nowhere is that clearer than in the food industry.*

"The neat thing about food is, everybody uses it, every day, and only once."

As a commodity that's absolutely essential, used several times a day, and literally *consumed* so the supply needs to be constantly replenished, food fulfills a capitalist's fondest dreams. Food is a huge part of the economy, and a major component of the family budget.

Despite that, most of us with farm or garden backgrounds don't normally think of food in connection with industry: "industry" suggests grimy steel mills and automobile factories and belching smokestacks, while "agriculture" brings to mind fresh green fields, blue skies, white fences and red barns, an image marketers of even the most over-processed products of industrial agriculture like to nurture. "Farm" and "fresh" go together naturally. Who wants to eat food that comes from a test tube or a factory?

But that's a rather recent phenomenon. Industrialism was well advanced in many other areas before turning to food. The reason was simple: up to and during the feudal period virtually all food was locally grown and distributed. Any "surplus" went to royalty and the landed gentry, the warrior and leisure classes. There was little reason, or opportunity, for capitalism to get involved.

Capitalism began to replace feudalism in the 16th century. This paved the way for the Renaissance, the Reformation, and the scientific progress of the 17th century which brought even more drastic changes, and faster. Those changes included new crops, such as maize and potatoes from the New World, and new ways of growing even the old crops. As the capitalist society slowly took shape, entrepreneurs saw opportunities in some of the more time-consuming and specialized traditional household tasks — making butter and cheese, or wine and beer.

Preserving food through drying and salting (and smoking, although technically that isn't a preservative) was known since Neolithic times. It wasn't until 1809, after many years of experimenting, that Frenchman Nicolas Appert discovered a way to preserve food by sterilization in a vacuum, with his well-known peas in a wine bottle for Napoleon's troops. More than 50 years passed before the first preserve factory or "cannery" was established, in 1860, but after that, new developments came rapidly.

Louis Pasteur described pasteurization in 1862; Nestlé invented condensed milk, Liebig's contribution was beef extracts and dry concentrated soups, and Mege-Mouriés developed margarine. These ideas of preservation, concentration, extraction and substitution — in forms not well-suited to the domestic hearth — soon became the backbone of an industrialized food industry which began to replace the self-sufficient subsistence family homestead.

And as one thing quickly leads to another with capitalism, in less than a century we had spray drying, freeze drying, and freezing; cans (and a choice of more than a dozen types of can openers), along with preservatives such as sodium benzoate, sorbates, sulfur dioxide, nitrites and nitrates, phenolase inhibitors such as ascorbic acid, metal-chelating agents such as ethylenediamine tetraacetic acid, antioxidants such as butylated hydroxyanisole and many others; and of course artificial sweeteners and coloring agents, not to mention complete frozen ready-to-eat tv dinners. Although anyone could survive on a handful of basic foods — in a pinch you could *survive* on potatoes — the average 2010 supermarket offered 38,718 different items.

The Native Americans' "three sisters" — corn, squash and beans — is often cited not only as a decent diet, but an example of sustainable agriculture. American sharecroppers had the three Ms: meat (salt pork), molasses, and meal (cornmeal). Well into the 20th century the mainstays of the American diet were meat, potatoes and flour. As recently as 1941 the USDA kept track of 18 food commodities and by 1961, 53. Today the data cover several hundred commodities.

Refined sugar is an industrial product with close ties to capitalism. At one time it was called "white gold:" the cost was around $100 a pound, and its production methods a closely-guarded secret. In 1700 the average consumption was about 4 pounds per year. Today we consume about 66 pounds per person a year... along with a nearly equal amount of high fructose corn syrup, glucose syrup and dextrose, as well as other sweeteners contributed by the food industry branch of capitalism... and 1.3 pounds of honey. Some reports claim that more than 50 percent of Americans consume ½ pound of sugar a day, and 32% are obese. (Refined sugar is blamed for many other health problems as well.) And, as one of the most heavily subsidized agricultural products in the world, sugar also plays an important role in government and politics. (See Chapter 21.)

Effects of capitalism on food

One benefit of capitalism is its supposed efficiency. Mass production — substituting machines (and capital) for human labor, using conveyor belt production lines to robotize that labor into mind-numbing zombie-ism, buying in bulk, standardization, cutting corners, and above all, placing profits above any considerations of human health, welfare and satisfaction — did indeed usher in an era of ever-lower food prices for the consumer, as well as variety, and in some cases, improved safety and nutrition (although most of this was imposed by democracy, not a free offering from capitalism).

These industrial techniques were only the tip of the iceberg. Food processed in a factory rather than the home kitchen requires much larger quantities, which involves different varieties of crops (e.g. cultivars that ripen all at the same time to facilitate machine harvesting, and tougher varieties that can *withstand* machine harvesting), and a different kind of farming, which eventually affects manufacturers of farm machinery, fertilizers, and many other products. Food factories require packaging, and shipping, and grocery stores.

But the industrialization of food went far beyond that. It invaded the kitchen itself. Not content with preparing the tomatoes, seasoning and cooking the sauce, and canning it, or by cleaning and canning or freezing the peas and carrots and beans, industry also peels the potatoes, cuts them into strips, fries them, freezes them and packages them. All the "cook" has to do is reheat them. And frozen French fries fill only a small portion of the supermarket space allotted to pre-prepared potatoes. There are also complete ready-to-eat meals… and fast food.

Dining outside the home, once mainly the province of travelers and businessmen, went through a series of ups and downs in early America. Now, according to the Economic Research Service/USDA, almost three-quarters of the people surveyed eat out at least once a week — and 10% eat out almost every day. Today the average household spends $2,700 a year on dining out, and $3,700 on home cooking. Roughly half of the dining out involves "fast food," which takes both capitalism and industrialization to the hilt.

McDonald's was not the first drive-in or fast food establishment: Dairy Queen, A&W and others preceded it. But McDonald's became the most famous and successful, and their story is well-known.

Brothers Richard and Maurice McDonald owned and operated a drive-in restaurant in southern California since 1940. By 1948, they were tired of recruiting new carhops and short order cooks, who were in great demand in the drive-in restaurant business after the war. They were fed up with the teenage boys the cute carhops attracted and sick of replacing the tableware those young customers broke and stole. They devised a plan that would change the world.

From *The Complete Idiot's Guide to Self-Sufficient Living:* "They tore up the old menu and started over from scratch. Nothing on the new menu required a knife, fork, or spoon. Burgers were the only sandwiches. They replaced breakable dishes and glassware with paper and came up with the assembly line kitchen. Grilling the hamburger, dressing and wrapping it, fixing the fries, making the milk-shake, and running the cash register were all separate jobs. They simplified the training, and because no skill was required, they slashed the payroll."

They were bought out by Ray Kroc, a milk-shake machine salesman who had been partnering with them, and by 1959 there were more than 100 McDonald's restaurants in operation. Ten years later there were more than 1,000. By the end of 2010 they had 32,737 locations.

In number of locations, McDonald's was passed by Subway, with 33,749 restaurants worldwide in 2010. Both are still growing.

A 1955 survey of Chicago restaurants revealed that kitchen labor had been reduced 25% in just five years because of "prefabricated meats, frozen foods, pre-pared potatoes and commercial pies and cakes."

There are approximately 28,000 what the U.S. Bureau of Labor Statistics calls "food manufacturing" establishments in the U.S., although not one of them could manufacture an apple or an egg.

The availability of fats and oils grew from 36 pounds per person in 1909 to 87 pounds in 2008. The increase is related to the rise in popularity of French fries in fast food restaurants.

Industrial vs. organic food production

The increased quantities and variety and lower prices did not come without costs, some of which have been pointed out by organic farmers and gardeners for more than 50 years. Often ridiculed by the capitalist and academic communities, largely ignored by the masses, a small core of die-hard organic agriculturists hung on... and eventually made their point. Their vindication came when capitalist industrial agribusiness started to take notice of the market share it was losing and took steps to not only backtrack on their criticism, but to develop ways to get in on the action. This can only involve smoke and mirrors or outright chicanery, because industrial agriculture, by definition, is in opposition to organic agriculture, by definition. This is most easily explained by non-food examples.

Manufactured products were made by hand (*manu:* hand; *factus:* make) until the Industrial Revolution's introduction of jigs and machine tools that allowed the production of interchangeable parts which were required for conveyor belt assembly lines. These were all in use long before Henry Ford perfected them to the point of having a Model T roll off the production line every 93 minutes.

This industrial template calls for *specialization, simplification, routinization,* and *mechanization.* These have been applied to agriculture (thus eliminating the "culture," according to some, which is why we use that term as little as possible in the context of industrial food production).

Agribusinesses *specialize* in milk cows or beef cattle, pigs or chickens, or corn or wheat: in monoculture. In contrast, organic farms are diversified, as is nature. The reasons are many, and important, but for city people, a few examples will suffice:

An industrial hog farm can house as many as 500,000 animals: Smithfield Foods, Inc. has one in Utah. In terms of logistics — food in, waste out, health care, maintenance, etc. — this is equivalent to a large city. Close confinement is associated with disease and other problems, and you can probably imagine the challenges of manure disposal. Chicken concentration camps face similar problems, and are even better known and more widespread. Organic production eliminates these "factories," and their attendant problems.

Agribusiness is *simplified*; organic farming is complex. The Extension agent (parroting experts working in labs) recommends 10-10-10 NPK fertilizer, which the farmer buys and applies. Simple. Voluntary serfs who toil for the vertically integrated poultry and swine industries — capitalist enterprises that provide the animals, the feed, everything but the grunt labor — do as they are told by the specialist field reps. They aren't allowed to think for themselves or experiment: the gospel is handed down from corporate headquarters, which in turn gets it from accredited government-run universities. It's part of the capitalist-democracy symbiosis; part of the System. It's simple.

The organic farmer pays attention to NPK, but also monitors trace elements, humus content, soil life and much more, most of it by personal observation and involvement. Science is not ignored, but it's tempered with thinking and good sense. A specialist very often has no idea what's going on in another area of the web, or how one thing might be connected to something else; the hands-on farmer is very much aware of the whole picture.

Agribusiness is *routine.* There are now farms, even here in backwoods small-farm northern Wisconsin, where workers do nothing but milk cows for an entire 8-hour shift. Organic farmers don't punch time clocks, and every day is different, just like nature.

Agribusiness views life as a *mechanical* process, to be manipulated through chemistry and genetics and such management techniques as cutting the tails off pigs and cows and the beaks off chickens — who have no use for them anyway in those small wire-floored cages, and debeaking prevents them from pecking each other to death out of stress and boredom. Organic farming sees life as a biological process, mysterious and wonderful, and something to be respected. Industrial farming regards nature as something to be overcome; organic farming cooperates with nature.

Obviously, many people approve of this industrial system of food production: in the parlance of economists, the benefits outweigh the costs. But as we have seen, capitalists and economists don't look at costs (or benefits) the way some people such as homesteaders and organic farmers and gardeners do.

The case for organic agriculture

J. I. Rodale (1898-1971) was a man of many interests but he's best-known as the godfather of organic agriculture in America, starting with *Organic Gardening & Farming* magazine (1942). Failing to attract commercial farmers but having broad appeal to backyard gardeners, it was later renamed *Organic Gardening,* and in 1950 was joined by an even more successful popular magazine, *Prevention.*

Rodale considered agriculture and health inseparable, and held that human health required eating healthful foods, which could only come from healthy soil, which required organic matter to support the biological life that constituted a healthy soil — plus an absence of the forms of pesticides and fertilizers that would destroy that living soil. (Many of his ideas came from Sir Albert Howard [English botanist, 1873-1947] and Lady Eve Balfour [English farmer & educator, 1899-1990].) Academics scoffed, and argued with his use of "organic" to describe this form of sustainable agriculture, but eventually the term caught on, as did organic foods in general.

As an amusing aside on the argument about terminology, not many people are aware that one of Rodale's accomplishments was *The Synonym Finder,* the hands-down best thesaurus available anywhere, in my humble opinion. He also wrote plays, and published a quirky little magazine that printed the same stories in four languages. He knew exactly what "organic" meant!

Rodale never created the buzz he had hoped for among commercial farmers, which of course would have been essential for his goal of improving the diet of the entire country. His *New Farm* magazine was not very successful, and his research farm attracted little attention from capitalist farmers. He did dabble in homesteading, publishing such books as *Homesteader's Handbook to Raising Small Livestock* and *Raising the Homestead Hog*, both written by J. D. Belanger (full disclosure: that's me). Although both of these would have been best sellers by New York Times standards (they sold thousands of copies, but not fast enough to make the best seller list), Rodale Press found a more lucrative niche… most notably with *The South Beach Diet*, by Dr. Arthur Agatston, which became a national phenomenon. Capitalism must go with what works.

A few farmers were not fazed by the lack of establishment support for organic agriculture. They not only believed in it: they practiced it, gathered empirical data on their success, and the most vocal of them wrote and spoke about it to spread the word. One of these is Joel Salatin, well-known as a working farmer due to his writing and extensive lecturing; he was, in fact, a newspaper writer before trying his hand at full-time farming. He is, in his own words, a "Christian-libertarian-environmentalist-capitalist-lunatic-farmer." He considers his farming a ministry.

His 550-acre Polyface Farm in Virginia is based on grass, which beef cattle graze on a rotational basis. After the cattle have eaten the grass down to a predetermined level they are moved to a fresh pasture and chickens in portable shelters take over, distributing the cattle manure with their scratching and consuming fly larva. Diversification is important: rabbits, sheep, pigs and turkeys are also involved. Another key part of his philosophy is localization, including on-site butchering.

In 2009 Salatin was a recipient of a $100,000 Heinz Award, presented by the Heinz Family Foundation in memory of the late Senator John Heinz, "for creating alternative, environmentally friendly farming techniques, spawning a movement towards local, sustainable agriculture that has been replicated by family farms around the country."

Teresa Heinz, chairman of the Heinz Family Foundation, said, "Joel Salatin is more than the 'high priest of the pasture;' he's a brilliant farmer. He is brilliant because he keeps it simple… The big corporate farms can no longer tell us that pollution will always come with farming. Mr. Salatin's work shows us that this is not true because on his lands, farming is no longer part of the problem; it is part of the solution to a better environment."

Earl Butz, Secretary of Agriculture under Presidents Nixon and Ford, dismissed 1970s environmentalists by saying, "Before we go back to organic agriculture, somebody is going to have to decide what 50 million people we are going to let starve."

Joel Salatin obviously isn't letting anybody starve. But neither is he "going back" to organic agriculture. He has plucked good ideas from thither and yon, and melded them into his own ideas and observations on how to maximize production in an integrated system on a holistic farm.

It would interest the late Mr. Butz, and many others today, to know that Polyface Farm nets in excess of $150,000 annually.

Food advertising & marketing

Perhaps strangest of all for a commodity that everyone requires on a daily basis, industrialized food requires *advertising*. Of course, it's not strange at all when we consider that agribusiness is a part of capitalism and therefore requires constant growth… and that capitalists are in constant competition with one another. It's not the food itself that's being advertised, but the capitalist enterprise behind it.

Food and candy rank number six among advertising categories, with an annual expenditure of $6,672,300,000 a year (2010). This does not include restaurants, which add another $5,652.8 million.

The Federal Trade Commission estimates that major food and beverage corporations spend at least $1.6 billion a year to convince kids to eat foods that health experts say they shouldn't eat. And as the web fans out… obesity costs the country $147 billion a year… and since being overweight is the number one reason military *recruits are rejected, some military leaders have pointed out that it also affects national security.*

Some groups are using ads to fight ads, which seems strange to anyone who is in favor of simplification and economy. Snickers, alone, spends about eight times as much as the entire "5 a Day" California and federal programs promoting fruits and vegetables. (Many will find it hard to believe Snickers needs advertising at all to compete with broccoli.)

This whole idea of the right hand conflicting with the left brings up the question of how much economic activity is essentially useless, wasted, by two sides canceling each other out. It's bad enough in normal competition (such as advertising any product or political candidate) but when the same government is both promoting *and* discouraging such things as tobacco, sugar, and other foods, at the same time, it certainly seems inefficient, if not hypocritical.

The agribusiness cheerleaders delight in reminding us that "food is cheap." Maybe so, but if billions of what we spend on food goes for advertising something we all need every day anyway, doesn't it seem like it should be even cheaper?

Fact: The farmer gets less than 20¢ of every dollar spent on food eaten at home. And "the farmer" no longer means a self-employed guy in bib overalls and a straw hat: it's more likely to be a corporation using vast sums of capital for automation, peons just a notch above slave labor, or both.

Fact: A box of oatmeal can sell for more than 40 times as much as the farmer gets for the oats.

Fact: At least 2,500 items in the typical grocery store use corn in some form during production or processing, frequently in the form of high-fructose corn syrup. So when the price of corn goes up because it's in demand as the raw product of ethanol, the price of food increases as well.

Fact: When corn costs $2.28 per bushel (the 20-year average) the corn in a box of corn flakes costs about 3.3 cents.

News bulletin: **In July, 2012, corn hit $8 a bushel, a 50% increase in a month, due to the worst drought in half a century.**

"Marketing" is more than just advertising

In the world of capitalism and advertising, food marketing isn't confined to those ubiquitous newspaper inserts or full-page ads or tv spots. "Marketing" is much broader than just advertising.

Most consumers are more aware now than they were a generation ago about the psychological manipulation they're faced with in the supermarket. But supermarkets keep piling it on. Too many people caught on to the fact that the package often costs more than what's inside, which is why "family size" and "super size" containers were usually bargains. Recently, we've seen an increase in the larger sizes actually costing *more* per unit, meaning you have to stay on your toes. The "giant economy pack" might be big, but it isn't necessarily the most economical, nowadays.

Milk is placed in the back of the store so when you pop in — just for a jug of milk, you know — you're forced down the snack aisle. Higher profit items are placed at eye level, and at the ends of aisles. Produce is associated with "fresh," so we're finding more and more non-produce in that section to take advantage of our perceptions. Misting produce has nothing to do with freshness, but it makes vegetables look better, as does lighting. Ever wonder why there are so many different kinds of cereal? Pure capitalism. Coupons, "buy two, get one free!," the list seems endless.

Food budgets are far more flexible than most people realize. In 2009, people making $40,000-$50,000 spent $5,560 of it on food. People making more than $125,000 spent $12,655 on food. They didn't eat twice as much: they just spent more.

The extremes: in Texas, the average Austin household spent $12,447 on food ($6,301 on dining out), while the average in Detroit, Michigan was $2,246 ($871 on dining out).

Supermarkets are hawking "new" products every week, but the law of diminishing returns is becoming apparent: it's getting harder and harder for the food industry to come up with something "new and improved."

But is nut butter really new just because it's Justin's Natural Maple Almond Butter Squeeze Pack? What about potato chips fully loaded with sour cream, green onion, cheddar cheese *plus* a hint of smoke flavor? And do we really need 36.5 proof alcoholic whipped cream (…er, dairy product)?

What's next? How about "cultured meat"? Experts claim that this product could feed the world, spare the lives of millions of animals, save the environment, and maybe the whole planet. Yes, it's made in the factory equivalent of a Petri dish, but no, it's not "imitation" meat or a vegetarian meat substitute like soy protein. It's made from stem cells left over from waste in slaughterhouses, which are cultured and nurtured. In late 2011 Mark Post, a vascular biologist at the University of Maastricht in the Netherlands, said he believes he can show it's possible within a year.

But there's no need to wait, if you want "chicken nuggets" made from mycoprotein (fungus). Quorn chicken nuggets have been available in Europe for more than 20 years, they're available in the U.S. now — and they're making people with a certain type of allergy quite sick.

Note: Neither of these have any connection with "pink slime" that made headlines after the above was written.

Some foods touted as "new" aren't even merely re-engineered old ones: chia seeds, for example, or spelt, quinoa or brown tomatoes are better described as neglected age-old foods that have only recently been discovered to have market potential. In the recent past, marketers changed the name of Chinese gooseberries to kiwi fruit, and they sell more slimehead fish by calling it orange roughy.

In the 1980s, "low erucic acid rapeseed oil" became "canola oil," and sales improved. The FDA now allows "prunes" to be called "dried plums." Recently there has been a move to call high-fructose corn syrup "corn sugar."

There is always the danger of falling into the trap of limited vision, like the fellow who suggested closing the patent office because "everything worthwhile has already been invented"... back in the days of Abraham Lincoln. And yet, in the realm of food, where there are already more choices than any one person could even sample, and where the "improvements" added by the system are cosmetic at best (and almost always more expensive), maybe we really have reached the point of "enough." One indication of this might be the increased interest in and emphasis on "old-fashioned" foods, recipes, and kitchen tools, and less interest in new products that still trickle into the market. The organic and slow food movements are just a small part of this trend. What they bode for the New Normal remains to be seen.

A new (and better) way of being a picky eater

We could consider the time line of food, not to suggest going back to a certain period when the system made more sense — such a period never existed — but as an exercise to see how diet has changed over the generations. Then we might pick and choose those elements that make the most sense, for us, now, in terms of our physical, economic and planetary health, as well as the pleasures of fine dining, however we might choose to define that. I was always intrigued to read that the early French voyageurs traversed the North American wilderness supplied with nothing more than flour and lard, until I realized that the bread I bake (and consider delicious) is made with only flour, water, oil (or lard), yeast and a pinch of salt. And according to Charles Pack, whom we'll meet in the next chapter, as recently as 1917 bread still constituted more than half of the French diet. Our picking and choosing would involve better nutrition and less boredom, but with no need for thousands and thousands of choices.

The list of benefits realized due to the industrialization of agriculture is long, and the truth is, not even the most rugged ascetics among us would care to forego very many of them. But the processing and over-processing can seldom be considered a benefit when there's an alternative. That's also true of the convenience factor.

Here we're crediting capitalism not only with the benefits bestowed by science, but by other parts of the system such as transportation. Not everyone is in favor of food preserved with *tert*-butylhydroquinone, or even pasteurized milk (that's a big issue in Wisconsin and elsewhere), but what banana lover would argue with the availability of bananas throughout the country, and throughout the year? Tasteless giant strawberries in the north in February aren't on every must-have list, but what's a Greek salad (or a martini) without olives, or a day without an orange or its juice?

Oops — today's news is that "not from concentrate" orange juice is not what we thought it was. And Coca Cola (you do know that Coke makes Minute Maid orange juice and Pepsi makes Tropicana, don't you?) has found an unapproved fungicide in orange juice produced in Brazil, where most OJ sold in the U.S. comes from.

Actually, this came out back in 2009 with *Squeezed: What You Don't Know About Orange Juice*, by Alissa Hamilton. OJ is often a heavily processed product. In the pasteurization process, it's heated, stripped of oxygen and flavor chemicals, then put in huge storage vats for up to a year. When it's ready for packaging, flavor derived from orange essence and oils is added to make it taste fresh. Each company has its own special flavor pack, but to call it "natural" at this point is a real stretch, she said.

When talking about food in the context of capitalism it can be hard to know how or where to separate the comestible itself from preservation, processing and preparation. Very few supermarket foods nowadays can avoid industrial manipulation.

And then we open a whole new can of capitalistic worms if we introduce home refrigerators and freezers (which most homesteaders say they'd be loathe to do without), microwave ovens, pressure canners and a host of other tools that save time and effort or simply do a better job than any alternative. But here again, overkill is evident in the stores and catalogs.

Now the nagging questions are not only when do we know how much is enough and how do we know when we have overstepped the bounds, but how do we pick and choose what truly adds to our lives, ignoring the rest? Capitalism prefers that we act like unthinking robots; the New Normal encourages us to act like intelligent beings. That's much more difficult, but a lot more fun.

The drawbacks of industrialized food

The benefits of industrialized foods are not without accompanying drawbacks, many of which have become well-known in recent years as organic foods and nutritional information have been in the spotlight, along with slow food and eating locally.

Some studies suggest that organically grown foods contain higher levels of nutrition. Processing can affect nutritional density; most people are aware that heat destroys vitamin C in canned fruits. The widespread use of food additives concerns many consumers. Sugar and salt content are often criticized, but so are artificial sweeteners, preservatives and stabilizers as well as food coloring (whether made from insects or petroleum)… and even the linings of cans. (Some health experts are concerned about levels of hormone-disrupting chemicals such as bisphenol A (BPA) used in the linings of tin cans. But as of now, there is no substitute.) Industrially produced ingredients, such as partially hydrogenated vegetable oils, have come in for sharp criticism. So has fat content, resulting in a call for baking potato chips instead of deep-frying them, for example.

But here we get into trap territory again: many people think fried chips and double cheeseburgers with bacon simply taste better than any alternatives, and nutrition be damned!

Democracy isn't going to restrict freedom of choice… theoretically, at least, although some people find the sliding scale moving uncomfortably farther away from the democratic side, and closer to the "Big Brother" side. And of course, capitalism certainly isn't going to argue about any of it. They have PR to show that they really are concerned about people's health. And they are, insofar as it affects business. But the bottom line issue isn't nutrition, it's profit. If profit depends on the consumer's demand for nutrition, then of course capitalism is in favor of nutrition too. And if it uses some of its profits to protect the people's right to choose by lobbying against onerous labeling and outright bans on certain products, well, that's just democracy.

And then, in spite of the much-ballyhooed safety of American food and the food inspection system, recalls — as well as food-borne illnesses, and even deaths — are commonplace. Lettuce and ground beef, melons and chicken livers, peppers and eggs, all these and more have been implicated.

Modern slavery in the food industry

Some drawbacks associated with the progress of food technology might be considered subjective, such as flavor, although not many will argue that a Florida tomato tastes anything like a homegrown one, and NFC orange juice consistently loses out in taste tests with fresh-squeezed.

Other drawbacks are more disturbing. Although many Americans are at least dimly aware that child labor is used in some parts of the world for, say, manufacturing clothing, not many associate the food on their tables with what can only be called "slavery. "

One of the more notorious examples is the bonded labor used in Southeast Asia's shrimping industry, which provides more shrimp to the U.S. than any other country. In Honduras, divers are dying from harvesting "red gold" —lobster, sold in the U.S. But we can find many examples closer to home.

If you're not familiar with the use of forced labor in Florida tomato fields, check out Barry Eastabrook's expostulatory book, *Tomatoland.* The flavorless fruits will leave a taste in your mouth that's even worse than the cardboard they're often compared to.

Some exploitation of human labor isn't quite so blatant,
although still disturbing. In 2011 Alabama put into effect a law
that requires police to question people they suspect might be
in the U.S. illegally and punishes businesses that hire them. Its
intent was to eliminate undocumented workers, but it also
drove off untold thousands of legal immigrants who feared
harassment. Most of these were connected with agribusiness
— field hands picking apples or tomatoes, workers in poultry
processing plants butchering chickens, cutting up catfish.

Some said the undocumented workers were taking jobs from
Americans. But even in areas where the unemployment rate
was 18%, twice the national average at the time, American-
born workers didn't want those jobs: the work was too hard,
the pay too low.

The question then is, is slave labor all black and white, or
does it come in degrees? Is being paid $2 to fill a 25-pound
basket, working 11 hours a day, a fair wage? A good worker
can make $60 a day stooped over in the Alabama heat, but
very few non-immigrants are "good workers." Most new hires
don't last a day.

(I was one of them in the 1950s. A buddy and I picked beans
in California. At the end of the day we hadn't made enough to
buy a peanut butter sandwich. He returned to Wisconsin. I
joined the Marine Corps. Boot camp was easier, and we got
fed.)

The farmers and food factory owners say they can't afford to
pay more, because they're already losing business to other
countries where the pay is even less. In some ways, this strikes
at the heart of the homesteaders' argument: if the stoop labor
employed in the food industry (and there is a lot of it) were
paid a "fair" wage (whatever that might be), the price of food
to the consumer would increase, making industrialized
agriculture look like less of a bargain. Include subsidies, the
costs to the commons, and other hidden expenses we've been
looking at, and it becomes very likely that "growing your
own" is not nearly the whacko idea so many perceive it to be.
In other words, if we strip the faulty accounting out of the

capitalist food system, homesteading could, should, and for most cash-strapped people *would* be the standard lifestyle!

In any event, the true cost of food is much higher than we're paying, today. How long this convoluted accounting can continue is debatable, but we must certainly plug this information into any assessment of the New Normal.

Questioning capitalism

Questioning capitalism's effects on civilization is nothing new: some thinkers have criticized its impact, real or imagined, on local cultures and society since the beginning, when it displaced the guilds. Its current influence on the economic system in general, and industrial agriculture in particular, would blow the minds of some of those early critics, but today hardly anyone notices.

And hardly anyone questions "The Green Revolution." Making two stalks of wheat grow where only one grew before represents wonderful progress, and supposedly feeds more people, but it doesn't come without side effects and a price, only one of which is the shredding of local, regional and even national cultures. The required fertilizers and pesticides — products of capitalism — can destroy age-old local methods, cultures and economies. Worst of all, those agribusiness methods are not sustainable.

Industrial agribusiness destroyed small family farms in the U.S.A. People forced off the land left the countryside for factory jobs in the cities. As a result, the nearby small towns with their feed mills and hardware stores, car dealers and coffee shops, grocers and bankers and movie houses, went out of business, one-by-one. Schools and churches closed, and the towns died. (The local post office appears to be among the last to go, thanks to its ties to government and labor unions; capitalists would have dealt with this mess decades ago.)

The webs become even more complex when we speak of the impact of industrial agriculture per se on the planet. Here we could talk about the detrimental effects of monoculture on the biosphere, lowering water tables through widespread irrigation, and the devastation of the rain forests to grow more food "more cheaply."

Then consider the state of the oceans, and fishing. Nets the size of football fields and GPS locators undoubtedly improve production and "efficiency," but what happens when there are no more fish? (I have seen cod for $17 a pound; at that price, for us, there are already "no more fish.")

Much has been written about all of this — the book on tomatoes and slavery just mentioned, many on migrant farm labor, and even more on the environmental effects of chemical use. The bottom line is that our much-vaunted "cheap food" comes at a price. It is not cheap. Farm subsidies, which we have yet to discuss, are no secret, and subsidies of various kinds to food industries are nothing new, but food prices are also kept artificially low by exploiting labor, and living off the capital of the Earth.

Those who want to avoid all this must produce their own, but that involves working for wages bordering on slavery. Capitalism sees to that. Our question is, as all the webs come together and perceptions change, might there be a different method of accounting in the New Normal? Could this possibly cause yet another revolution — a revolution to overthrow industrial agriculture — not from a socialist uprising but based on the capitalist principle of creative destruction?

There are webs of another kind. British researchers at the London School of Hygiene and Tropical Medicine wondered what would happen if the English heeded the World Health Organization's guidelines for a healthy diet, meaning less meat and dairy and more fruits and vegetables. They estimated that some 70,000 would live a little longer by avoiding such diet-related problems as heart disease and cancer.

However, in Brazil, diet-related illnesses are not nearly as common as in the U.K. At the same time, Brazil's economy is heavily dependent on the export of beef. The WHO diet wouldn't make Brazilians much healthier, but it could make them a great deal poorer.

Such are the ways the webs work.

The Roundup Story

Any discussion of industrial vs. organic agriculture could go on forever, but let's cut it off with one last little story.

Most Americans are city people with no connection to the land: mention an herbicide (weed killer) and they can't imagine how that might affect them, except maybe on the golf course or their lawns. There's a much bigger story.

Roundup herbicide (active ingredient: glyphosate), developed by Monsanto, went on the market in 1973. Its capitalistic role was to eliminate the need (time, labor, fuel) for using mechanical tillage to kill weeds, which reduce crop yields due to competition for sun, water and nutrients. It was an improvement on older, more potent herbicides because of a technological breakthrough that made it "as safe as table salt," according to the manufacturer (and that was before table salt got such a bad rap from nutritionists).

There are many twists and turns to the story including charges of false advertising and scientific fraud, but for our purposes here the important details include these:

Monsanto developed "Roundup Ready" soybeans and corn, which could be sprayed without being damaged, making the herbicide even more useful. This was accomplished using genetic modification, which itself is a controversial technology, creating what are sometimes referred to as "Frankenfoods," But follow the money: Not only was this a profitable combination from the beginning: it provided insurance for after the patents ran out, as they did in 2000.

From the beginning, some organic farmers and others expressed concerns about weeds developing resistance to Roundup — much like the corn and soybeans developed through genetic engineering, and as had been observed with other herbicides earlier. Assurances were given that this was not a problem.

However, as of the 2011 crop season farmers reported 103 biotypes of herbicide-resistant weeds within 63 species — 15 confirmed as resistant to glyphosate.

Which means farmers go back to mechanical cultivation… or in the tradition of capitalistic enterprise, someone comes up with an even more powerful herbicide. The latter is ironic: company making money creates problem; company makes even more money by "solving" problem. This is another version of the capitalist technique of "developing a cure for which there is no disease."

All of the perhaps seemingly unconnected snippets in this chapter could be multiplied and expanded… and in the real world, they are, daily. (We'll also examine some of them more closely in coming chapters.) The world isn't nearly as simple as the System has lulled us to believe. As parts of that System begin to fray, will we discover the truth, that despite our technological advances, nature really is still in charge? Or will enough people cry, "enough!"?

Chapter 19:
One thing just leads to another...

A book review gone wild?

Some readers might think this long chapter should be an afterword, or an appendix, or Book II... or, heaven forbid, deleted. I include it as a chapter because although at first reading it might seem disconnected and off the track, the truth is that it embodies all that has gone before and much that is yet to come. It's not just a book review that got out of hand.

It begins, however, as a book review, albeit one with a narrow purpose: it demonstrates that it's possible to feed a nation, or a significant part of a nation, utilizing "waste" land and spare-time labor... without capitalism and its industrial agribusiness. That raises the question, what are the implications of that for today?

Little webs that spin off from the main premise suggest that even with the high unemployment and stories of hungry and underfed people today, such gardens aren't likely to become widespread, even though they could solve a myriad of problems. The world is a different place than it was 100 years ago, and people are different, too. Part of our quest is to discover how, and why. The stories that follow are not presented as mere history: compare them with what you see today, and they will be a key to understanding the New Normal.

This chapter also lays bare the continuum, the sliding scale, the shades of grey that are never black or white. It shows the interplay of people, government, and capitalism, and how shifting balances can change lives, and the world.

It demonstrates the necessity of thinking for yourself: unlike a totalitarian socialistic system where the masses are told what to think and do, a capitalist democracy demands a certain amount of skepticism and a great deal of evaluation, both of which require knowledge and information. And we must remember that much of today's noise is not information; much of today's education is not knowledge.

We'll note that relevance depends on purpose: Park and Swenson biographers (two men we'll be talking about) don't even mention war gardens; that aspect of their lives was deemed insignificant to such historians, while for us, the gardens are the only reason we heard about these men and are talking about them here.

And again there are those webs — the inescapable economic fact that no thing is one thing, there are many, they're all connected, and all events have unanticipated consequences. The book we're reviewing raises questions that led to studying USDA Yearbooks which led to investigating the growing influence of socialists in that period which led to the Green Corn Rebellion which had implications for the McCarthy era of the 1950s with a backlash lasting into the present... where we face the New Normal.

And then there's the fascinating story of Magnus Swenson and the American Dream... which admittedly is only peripherally connected with War Gardens but that's how we learned about him and where else would this story fit any better? A story we can relate only in a barebones outline, which is more than we can tell about thousands of similar people (including Patrick O'Brien whom we met in Chapter 1) because their lives were less dramatic. But could his experience be repeated today? Is the American Dream still valid at all? What does this tell us about immigration today?

No, this is not an appendix, nor is it off the track. Although the past is prologue, this doesn't tell us what we might expect in the New Normal: nevertheless, it will give us some clues.

The War Garden Victorious;
Yes, we can feed ourselves

One of the most inspiring books on gardening I have ever read says nothing at all about tilling the soil, fertilization or irrigation, seed selection or plant spacing; instead, it talks about railroads and industries, schools and chambers of commerce, and above all, war, and its effects on the economics of food and the spirits of nations.

It's inspiring because it's an upbeat description of an entire nation busily engaged in home food production, suggesting that even if we couldn't feed the whole country with backyard gardening in our spare time, we could come darn close — and we'd be happier and better off in the process! As such, its appeal to a homesteader is obvious, but it should be of widespread interest today when so many have more time than money.

The War Garden Victorious, by Charles Lathrop Pack, was published in 1919 by the National War Garden Commission. It describes, in glowing terms, how American civilians helped win WWI by producing food in backyards and vacant lots and by implication, what one facet of a New Normal could look like.

Charles Lathrop Pack was no homesteader, nor even a gardener. He was said to be one of the five richest men in America, and is much better known as a stamp collector and a philanthropist than for his involvement in home food production. His father and grandfather had made fortunes in the Michigan lumber industry; he expanded that with savvy investments in southern forestland and banking. In this small book, one of several he wrote on the subject, he describes how the National War Garden Commission came into being:

"The author, wishing, as every patriot wished, to do a war work which was actually necessary, which was essentially practical, and which would most certainly aid in making the war successful, conceived the idea in March, 1917, of inspiring the people of the United States to plant war gardens in order to increase the supply of food without the use of land already cultivated, of labor already engaged in agricultural work, of time devoted to other necessary occupations, and of transportation facilities which were already inadequate to the demands made upon them. In March, therefore, some weeks before the United States entered the war, he organized for this work a commission known as the National War Garden Commission."

This could be considered a good description of homesteading, and it could certainly apply to the world today. But Pack goes on to describe the situation as it was in 1917: There was a worldwide lack of food, and only the United States could prevent world starvation. That was exceptionalism, but in 1917 it was the truth.

That was because "when the drums sounded the call to colors in the summer of 1914, three million Frenchmen shouldered their rifles, the majority of them leaving their small farms idle. Russia, almost totally agricultural, armed eight million. All men of fighting age were drafted in Belgium; England armed five million, Germany, Austria, Bulgaria, Turkey… in all, perhaps 20-30 million men were involved, and most had been farmers." (In the U.S., close to 30 workers out of a hundred were farmers at that time.)

In addition, crops were "maturing or already ripe for the sickle." And to make matters worse, those millions of soldiers swept over the fields, "trampling, burning and destroying vast stores of food."

So in just a few short weeks the year's food supply was greatly diminished; vast areas of farmland in Belgium and France on the western front as well as Hungary, East Prussia and Russia on the east were rendered unproductive; the overwhelming majority of farmers in those regions were in uniform; and the global food supply was entirely out of kilter.

Pack takes care to describe this balance in terms of capitalism: "Ordinarily the food-supply system was as nicely adjusted as a watch. Production was balanced against consumption. Given markets were supplied from given sources. So unfailing was this system that each of the belligerent nations absolutely depended upon other nations for certain parts of its food, and had received its expected supply as unfailingly as our daily milk and newspapers are delivered to our doors."

(Later we learn, from other sources, that not all American farm laborers shared this viewpoint.)

Before the war, England had produced about 20 percent of its food needs, France, 50%, Italy, about 66%. "If the

120,000,000 people of the entente nations were to have food, if they were to procure enough to keep them from actual starvation, that food must come from the nearest markets."

That meant the United States. "Whether we wished to undertake the task or not, Fate had saddled the burden upon our backs." American exceptionalism was imposed by Fate.

Meatless Mondays, Wheatless Wednesdays

Accumulated stores helped avoid worldwide famine for a while. But 1916 was disastrous for agriculture. Crops failed everywhere, including in the United States. Since the U.S. had pooled its food resources with Europe, nations on both sides of the Atlantic were living hand-to-mouth. Pack reported that European peasants (i.e., most of the people) existed largely on wheat, even in good times: he claimed that bread constituted nearly 52 percent of the French diet. The bread ration was lowered until it reached seven ounces a day per capita. In Italy, macaroni was entirely prohibited in some districts, and the bread ration reduced to eight ounces a day. The fighting men were included in this rationing.

Meatless days were established, milk production decreased by 60 percent, sugar consumption in England was reduced by nearly 75 percent. Rationing simply set allowable maximums: there was no guarantee that even that much, or anything at all, would be obtainable.

The U.S. too had meatless and wheatless days, but the high prices of butter, eggs and milk served as another form of rationing: they were unaffordable for many, and consumption plummeted.

It would be years before the war-torn farmlands of Europe would produce anything again. In the U.S., the problem was labor. For at least a decade before America entered the war there had been an exodus from farm to city as farmers were lured by the high wages in towns and factories. The war hastened that, not only by forging plowshares into swords and farmers into soldiers, but by expanding the factory production of munitions and other war materiel.

In a burst of patriotism Pack wrote, "In the lexicon of the typical American there is no such word as 'cannot'. Keen-eyed Americans who saw the situation as it really was, decided that if the mountain would not go to Mahomet, they would see that Mahomet went to the mountain. The mountain in this case was labor, and Mahomet the space necessary for the production of food. These men, with that vision without which the people perish, possessed imagination. They saw little fountains of foodstuffs springing up everywhere, and the products of these tiny fountains, like rain-drops in a watershed, uniting to form rushing streams which would fill the great reservoirs built for their compounding. The tiny fountains were innumerable backyard and vacant-lot gardens. The problem was to create these fountains.

"Those 'fountains' could only be created by the systematic education of the people, the one hundred million people of the United States. Such a huge educational campaign could be carried out only through the customary channels of publicity — the daily press, the periodicals, the bulletin-boards and other usual avenues. Oddly enough, it is usually hardest to influence man for his own benefit. The matter of home food production was no exception to the rule. Before the people would spring to the hoe, as they instinctively sprang to the rifle, they had to be shown, and shown conclusively, that the bearing of one implement was as patriotic a duty as the carrying of the other."

One of the "keen-eyed Americans who saw the situation as it really was," one of the men with that vision without which the people would perish, one of the men who possessed imagination, was obviously none other than Pack himself. After consulting with other men eager to do their duty, he "conceived and organized the Commission."

Not surprisingly, considering his nearly perfect description of how a capitalist might like to see himself, the men (and one woman, Mrs. John Dickenson, whose husband was on the Chicago Board of Trade) he recruited were captains of industry: bankers, lawyers, a railroad president. The exceptions were a congressman and the legendary plantsman Luther Burbank.

"The sole aim of the National War Garden Commission was to arouse the patriots of America to the importance of putting all idle land to work, to teach them how to do it. And to educate them to conserve by canning and drying all food they could not use while fresh. The idea of 'city farmer' came into being."

Growing food in a backyard or vacant lots — "slacker land" that was "as useless as the human loafer" — not only increased food production: it was food "FOB the Kitchen Door," avoiding the problems of transportation and distribution normally associated with the agricultural system.

It was quite literally another aspect of the war. First, recruits were needed, and the volunteer army required volunteer enlistment, leading to (among other things) a wide range of recruiting posters calculated to whip up patriotism. In the days before television, eye-catching posters were widely used in advertising, and some of those commissioned by the War Garden Commission became very popular. One showed a dreamily stern young female version of Uncle Sam, clothed in a flowing American flag and sowing seeds from a basket, with the headline, "Will You Have a Part in Victory?" and a subhead, "Every Garden a Munition Factory!" Another was headed, "We Can Can Vegetables Fruit and the Kaiser too!" Another urged patriots to "Sow the Seeds of Victory." These were displayed wherever people congregated: in railway stations, libraries, stores, banks, factory entrances and clubs, as well as appearing in newspapers and magazines.

Peer pressure was enlisted. Window hangers, printed in green, were "proudly displayed in the front windows of several million homes," so even gardens hidden in back yards would not go unnoticed. Similar window hangers were later available to households who preserved food by canning and drying. (Freezing was not an option in 1919.)

The amount of "useless" idle acreage in most American towns and cities was astounding. A survey in Minneapolis showed more than 5,000 acres in vacant lots; greater New

York was estimated to have 186,000 vacant lots in 1917. The National War Commission urged Americans to "put the slacker land to work," and they did. In 1917 an estimated 3,000,000 pieces of previously uncultivated land were put into production; that increased in 1918. After a "careful survey," the estimated number reached 5,285,000.

Food, FOB the kitchen door

Again, Pack pointed out that the gardens affected more than food. He claimed that a million soldiers required at least 4,250,000 pounds of food a day, and the U.S. was planning to raise an army of 4-5 million. Taking that from the ordinary channels of trade would mean that civilians would be forced to pay ruinous prices for what remained. War gardening helped avoid this. *(Note: I don't understand this: even had those soldiers remained civilians, they would have eaten.)*

It also made labor go further, Pack reasoned, by releasing men who would have otherwise been necessary on farms to produce "cannon and shells and rifles and uniforms and innumerable other articles demanded in incomprehensible quantities."

He expanded on the idea of "Food FOB the Kitchen Door" by reiterating that even in 1917, commercial foods passed through many hands before reaching the consumer. Food produced in the backyard is handled only by those who eat it.

Let us suppose, he said, that the average backyard garden produces only a hundred pounds of food, which is a ridiculous estimate: the actual yield was many times greater. But even a hundred pounds in each of the 5,285,000 1918 gardens would be 528,285,000 pounds of food — which called for hardly a single public carrier of goods, freeing up many thousands of men for other work. Writing that today, he certainly would have included the savings in energy and pollution, although he did mention the conservation of coal and steam-power, and the prevention of wear and tear on railroad tracks and equipment. When every freight car in the country was urgently needed to haul war goods, war gardens helped.

Garden propaganda

The linchpin of the whole operation was education, which Pack wasn't afraid to call propaganda. Articles and feature stories dealing with gardening and designed to stimulate the movement appeared in periodicals throughout the country, and "war gardens sprang up as if by magic. Gardening came to be the thing."

Planting a garden was only the start. Many new recruits of the war garden army had never handled a hoe, even though most people in 1918 were not far removed from the farm. So daily garden lessons were prepared for the newspapers. They were short, simple, non-technical, and written by experts, and "lacking in nothing essential." Booklets were prepared, explaining how to plant and care for different vegetables. Millions of copies were printed, and distributed through libraries, chambers of commerce, trade groups, women's clubs, banks, and manufacturing concerns.

It worked. So much food was produced that attention was turned to preserving the harvest. Information on canning and drying soon supplemented that on growing, through the same distribution channels. In 1917 an estimated $350,000,000 worth of food was produced in war gardens; in 1918 the value reached $525,000,000. In 1917 500,000,000 quarts of canned fruits and vegetables were stored on pantry shelves; in 1918, 1,450,000,000.

Among the records collected by the National War Garden Commission was the journal of a Pennsylvania gardener with a plot measuring 40x40 feet. The list included exact quantities of beets, radishes, carrots, rutabagas, peas, potatoes, cabbage, cauliflower, tomatoes, green beans, dry beans, peppers, cucumbers, celery, rhubarb, onions, and even more — including "parsley, used freely" and "horseradish, all desired." Pack estimated that if even one-half of the families in America had a garden like this, they would produce as much food as we shipped to Europe before the war.

Marion, Indiana, held the record for the number of war gardens.
With a population of 20,000, it counted 14,081 vegetable plots.

Community gardens

Not all war gardens were backyard or family plots. Pack
wrote, "Instead of allowing each gardener to till his own land,
it was better, where possible, to have a large area properly
plowed and harrowed and then allow the gardener to care for
his individual plot... The land was uniformly and properly
prepared and at small expense. Community gardening made
for both better gardens and better communities, for the spirit
of emulation at once led each gardener to do his best, while
common toil for a common end made for better understanding
and better acquaintanceship; and sympathetic understanding
is the rock upon which democracy is founded."

Note that community gardens are pretty far along the
sliding scale to socialism, and it's somewhat at odds with
capitalism, but it all ends up bolstering democracy.

Capitalism did play a role, however: many community
gardens were provided by factories, with the result that bosses
often worked alongside secretaries and common laborers.
There were times when a worker with farm experience was
able to tutor his foreman, in the company garden, establishing
rapport and furthering democracy. Pack seemed to relish these
side effects almost as much as the provender produced,
saying, "Unquestionably, community gardening will continue.
It will be the peacetime descendant of the war garden."

If only that were true! Capitalism's gravitational pull was
too strong, and while home food production, renamed Victory
Gardens, reappeared in WWII, home gardening in general
remained a hobby, enjoyed by comparatively few. Of all the
community gardens of WWII only two survived into the 21st
century: Fenway Community in Boston, and Dowling
Community in Minneapolis.

Camp Dix, N.J., was the first war garden at an army base, if 400
acres can even be called a garden. After extolling that effort, which
included harvesting 5,000 bushels of potatoes, Pack said, "Thus, in

teeming army camps and on isolated mountain-tops, on the wide reaches of the prairies and in sun-splashed openings in the dusky forests; beside roaring factories and in sequestered nooks on which deer and bear peer shyly from near-by leafy coverts, there have sprung up innumerable war gardens. In riding across the country one sees them beside the railroad right-of-way, in back yards, small and great, on lawns and in open fields, in every conceivable place that tell, as truly as the tiny Liberty Loan button on the coat-lapel, where the owner stands and what he stands for, because a war garden is a service badge of living green." War gardens were definitely a proud part of American exceptionalism in 1917-19.

This book was not for sale and was not widely distributed, so it's extremely rare. But it's worth checking out, if only for the illustrations of the posters. You can find the complete *The War Garden Victorious* at http://digital.library.wisc.edu/1711.dl/HumanEcol.WarGard Vic

Shades of grey and spreading webs

The nature of both capitalism and democracy have conditioned us to be suspicious, even skeptical; when something is presented as either all black or all white, without even a nod to that omnipresent sliding scale, we should at the very least be curious.

The War Garden struck me as painting a picture that was just a little too perfect; something seemed to be missing. It struck me that Charles Lathrop Pack took a little too much credit. For one thing, in such a massive undertaking, where was the U.S. Department of Agriculture? I looked into the United States Department of Agriculture Yearbooks to gain another perspective.

Reading the "Report of the Secretary" for 1917, 1918 and 1919 was instructive. For one thing, although gardens were mentioned, there was nary a word about any "National War Garden Commission." On the contrary, Secretary of Agriculture David Franklin Houston claims as much glory for his department as Park did for the commission. In 1917 Houston wrote:

"Special attention was directed to the importance of home gardens in all parts of the nation. A series of 27 brief popular articles containing instructions for the preparation of soil, for garden planting, and for the care of vegetables was prepared and distributed. A special Farmers' Bulletin, *The Small Vegetable Garden,* was quickly printed and more than a million copies were promptly distributed. Throughout the growing season the Department continued to supply the press regularly with practical timely information designed to encourage a second and even third crop of vegetables. This campaign, supported by the efforts of county agents, other field workers of the Department, the staffs of the agricultural colleges, and private workers, stimulated, it is estimated, the planting of from two hundred to three hundred percent more gardens than had ever before produced food in the united States in one season. This was particularly true in the South."

Outright rivalry between the department and the commission seems unlikely, but there is no sign, anywhere, of any cooperation, either. Nevertheless, if we are to take the two accounts at face value, both groups were active in the same fields. Houston continues:

"The home-demonstration activities were immediately intensified. Early in the summer all home economics extension workers turned aside from their regular activities and aided in special campaigns for food conservation. Canning, drying, salting and storing were emphasized in every state and special stress was laid upon the importance of using perishable products in such a way that the home might support itself and make as little demand as possible on the transportation facilities for supplies from other sections of the country."

One sentence on "the response of farmers" is quite interesting: "Imbued with patriotic motives, influenced by favorable market prices, and falling in with the suggestions of the Department of Agriculture and of State agricultural agencies, the farmers of the nation manifested much interest in the campaign for increased production and displayed efficient activity in reference both to plant and animal foodstuffs and feedstuffs." The weather helped, too, he noted, but patriotism, the profit motive, and the "suggestions of the Department" were paramount. And again without mentioning profit specifically, he concludes by saying that farmers "will not permit her (Germany) to impose illegal restrictions on their privilege of going freely to any part of the world where they have a legal right to go or of sending their products into the open markets of the world." Government was clearly on the side of capitalism.

Nowhere does Houston write with the verve and élan of Park, but the 1918 report starts out on a particularly strange note: "The part of the millions of men, women, boys, and girls on the farms and the organized agricultural agencies assisting them, including the Federal Department of Agriculture, the State colleges and departments of agriculture, and farmers' organizations, played during the war in sustaining this Nation and those with which we are associated is striking but altogether too little known and appreciated... The proper utilization of available foods is one thing; the increase of production along economic lines is quite a different thing... The work of the agricultural agencies is not much in the public eye. There is little of the dramatic about it... To the great urban population it is comparatively unknown."

If this is sour grapes, it gets worse. He claims that in terms of personnel, financial support and effectiveness, the ag agencies of the U.S. "excel those of any other three nations combined." Again, in 1918 that was undoubtedly true. But then in stark contrast to Park's bubbly reports of daily front page gardening tips from the Commission, Houston whines that, "very many urban people are unaware of such institutions. These people have seen the windows of cities placarded and papers filled with pleas for conservation, for investment in bonds, and for subscriptions to the Red Cross. They have wondered why they have not seen any similar evidence of activity in the field of agriculture."

This could lead a skeptic to suspect that Pack and his Commission really did outdo Houston and the Department...

which is probably immaterial, except to those who favor volunteerism over big government... such as Herbert Hoover, who was head of the United States Food Administration and who, after becoming president, still favored volunteerism during the Crash of 1929, much to his chagrin. But that's not just a web: that's another story.

Only much later, after talking about pink bollworm of cotton, citrus canker and seed-grain loans in drouth (sic) areas, does Houston get to "information and publication work." While this centers on furnishing information to farmers, "the Department has found it wise to present to people of the cities accurate statements of its recommendations and advice on the distribution and saving of food materials; and the work of the Department was enlarged to this end. An illustrated weekly news service is now furnished on request to... a total of 7,450 publications... A home-garden series and a canning-drying series were distributed in much the same manner." Once again we get a very different picture from that presented by Park.

Which one is most accurate? Which reporter can we trust? Even being informed doesn't guarantee being *educated,* in small matters like this that don't make any difference, as well as in situations of earth-shaking importance. It doesn't pay to get too cocky.

This reminds me of my experiences as an editor dealing with small scale ("laughable") and organic ("horrors!") agriculture in the 1960s and '70s. Extension agents and university people were entirely condescending. But a few years later, when both organics and small-scale farming became popular with the masses, these same people had so much advice to offer you'd think they'd *invented* both of them.

Magnus Swenson and the American Dream

Meanwhile, even before the Federal Government took action on the impending food crisis, several states got involved. Wisconsin was the first to organize both state and county-level Councils of Defense whose mission included addressing the food problem that was developing in 1917. The head of the

Wisconsin Council was Magnus Swenson, a well-known and highly versatile businessman, then in his sixties, who was also active in public affairs.

Swenson, who counted engineer and inventor among his accomplishments, came up with several innovative ideas including the cultivation of home gardens and the institution of meatless and wheatless days. President Woodrow Wilson named Herbert Hoover to lead the new United States Food Administration; Hoover adopted many of Swenson's policies, appointed him Wisconsin State Food Administrator, and later, food relief administrator to the Baltic countries of Europe.

That was his role in the war garden movement, but it couldn't have happened had he not aspired to The American Dream, which is a much longer, more entwined, complicated and fascinating — and inspiring story. To truly appreciate it we must go back much further, to his birth in Langesand, Norway, April 12, 1854.

His mother died when he was two. His father remarried, and Magnus became an abused and neglected stepchild. When his father's rope factory burned down, leaving the family destitute, Magnus set out for the land of opportunity, America. He was 14 years old.

He made passage on a small ship with a list of 60 passengers, each one required to bring enough food for the six-week crossing. Bad weather stretched that out to eight weeks, and 22 of the passengers died.

The little ship sailed up the St. Lawrence in July, 1868. Young Magnus went from Canada to Detroit to Chicago to Janesville, Wisconsin, where he had an uncle, a foreman in the blacksmith shop of the Northwestern Railroad. Too weak from the journey to work, he spent his first year in America in school learning English. A year later he became a blacksmith's helper in the railroad shops, but was soon promoted to mechanic. Being curious and a quick learner, he decided to become an engineer, and in 1875 he entered the University of Wisconsin.

In one of many amusing little asides that make the man human, a biographer notes that the Norwegian immigrant showed up to register in June, and was surprised to learn that English is a very odd language: classes didn't *commence* on *commencement* day, and he had to wait another three months!

He matriculated in the department of mining and metallurgy, which was part of the college of engineering, in a university with a total enrollment of 350. There was no college of agriculture, and chemical engineering wasn't even a field at that time: he was to play important roles in both of these, later.

Another humanizing story: During the summer vacation of 1878 he was employed as a surveyor for a proposed roadbed for the Northwestern Railroad through the Dakotas, for a wage of $35 a month. It soon became apparent that he and his partner covered more distance than any other crew, and for their proficiency in laying out track, their wages were increased to $100 a month. It wasn't until 50 years later, when Swenson was invited to Chicago to attend the railroad's anniversary celebration, that the truth emerged:

Magnus noted that the mule carrying their equipment walked a straight path with an even, steady pace. Using his surveyor's chain to measure that pace, he found that it hardly varied an inch in a hundred yards. So instead of measuring distances by chain, the two boys took turns riding the mule and counting its paces as it followed the line of stakes. Many years later when the roadbed was resurveyed, the measurements by mule proved to be amazingly accurate.

The next summer he colored maps for the U.S. Geological Survey and spent part of the summer in mineral identification for the geological survey of Wisconsin, using the recently developed petrographic microscope and involving an understanding of crystallography, the intricate behavior of light passing through crystals, and a fine sense of color discrimination. He sketched the mineral sections, and with watercolors, painted the beautiful polarization colors of minerals as they appear when observed between crossed nicols (prisms used to produce and analyze polarized light). Both of these summer jobs required artistic abilities. Later, painting became a hobby.

In his senior year his interests turned to analytical chemistry. His thesis was "The Chemical Analysis of Madison Well Waters," a dramatic subject at that time since the germ theory of disease had only recently been proposed by Pasteur and Koch and it wasn't widely accepted. So when Swenson announced that nearly all the water in Madison was polluted by sewage — each family had its own well and cesspool — his opinion that Madison's drinking water was fit only as liquid fertilizer was not well received. No one connected the water with the prevalence of typhoid, scarlet fever, and diphtheria in the city.

He was able to persuade Madison physicians, however, and a chemical laboratory was opened in the basement of the capitol, although at one point he had to ask for an escort of two policemen when he collected water samples. Eventually, Madison acquired a central water supply from deep wells, and cesspools were replaced by a central sewage system. Swenson graduated in mining and metallurgy in 1880, but was granted special honors for his work on the well waters of Madison. The laboratory established by Swenson is now the State Laboratory of Hygiene, which analyzes more than 100,000 samples yearly from around the state.

That same year the University of Wisconsin College of Agriculture was created, with a faculty of Prof. W.A. Henry — and Magnus Swenson, a research assistant whose salary of $1,200 a year was $200 more than the professor's. (There were also only two students.) Their first research project involved sugar, an expensive commodity, most of which was imported from Cuba. Sugar cane didn't grow in Wisconsin: Swenson proposed to experiment with sugar extracted from sorghum cane. In the process the mining engineer also became involved in agronomy, botany and horticulture; the design and operation of machinery; and he became a chemical engineer 25 years before that field was recognized as a profession.

All of this led to a lucrative position on a sugar plantation in Texas — at the astounding salary of $10,000 a year. But Swenson didn't care for Texas, or how the plantation and mill were run, operating as they did "with negro convicts, who were treated as beasts." So a year later he was in Kansas, employed by a group of Boston capitalists hoping to develop the refining of sugar from sorghum cane.

According to biographer Olaf Hougen of the American-Norwegian Historical Association, "It was characteristic of his alert and active mind to direct his interests to new creative efforts, to new products and inventions. Whenever a factory, or machine, or institution was perfected and could be entrusted to others, he willingly made the transfer with little regard for further credit or recognition or even adequate compensation." Accordingly, his inventive genius spread to many other activities, including the invention of a cylindrical cotton baler, manufacturing, and mining, his college major.

He retired in 1902, in Madison, where he was instrumental in establishing the department of chemical engineering, one of the first in the nation. He also had a hand in the first hydroelectric plants on the Wisconsin River, which became "the hardest working river in the world."

The last 25 years of his life were spent as "an administrator and executive in undertaking great civic duties for his city, state and nation. These latter duties... have nearly eclipsed his early technical achievements."

Swenson was exceptionally versatile and extremely practical. To him, life was a constantly interesting adventure. And again, from Olaf Hougen: "He cared little for the rewards of his labor or for credit. Outside of his patents he transferred little of his developments to writing. He contributed to no scientific journals. He was interested in theory only in so far as it could be applied to practical uses. He spent no time in mathematical formulations but was able to cut a path straight through all the complex and intricate variables of chemical and mechanical processes to attain a reasonable and economical solution of the problem with the least expenditure of time."

Magnus Swenson was one of more than 15 million immigrants of that period. You probably never heard of him. How many more, like him, have you not heard about? Many "Americans" (that is, descendents of earlier immigrants) were against this inflow of foreigners in part because they took jobs away from workers already here. Yet, what would the American Dream, and American exceptionalism, have been without people like Magnus Swenson?

According to Hougen, Swenson could say, "I never spent a dull hour in my life." And no one could say he did not achieve the American Dream, or didn't contribute to American exceptionalism.

One wonders where and how he would fit in today.

Chapter 20:
The Ultimate in Eating In:
Food FOB the Kitchen Door

In *The War Garden Victorious* Charles Lathrop Pack often used the term "food FOB the kitchen door," the "freight on board" (or variously, free on board) being a reference to the transportation costs saved by home gardens, an important consideration during the war. That commercial term wouldn't be widely recognized today. One that would resonate with many more people would be "eating in." Dining at home, once the norm for most families, is becoming common again, frequently as a belt-tightening measure even when it involves take-out rather than home-cooked.

Home-cooked meals made from scratch with food FOB the kitchen door would be the *ultimate* in eating in. But how practical would that be? How many modern Americans would even consider it?

As of today, not many. The industrial agribusiness sector of capitalism works so smoothly and effortlessly that most Americans don't even bother thinking about their food, where it comes from, how it's grown or how it reaches their plates. Like all the other sectors of capitalism, it's so complex and intertwined that few people understand how it works, or even feel the need to think about it.

This does not mean most people aren't aware of the controversy between "conventional" and "organic" farming; however, awareness is a long way from understanding. Pitting capitalism and what passes for modern science against environmentalists who sometimes seem stuck in the past doesn't help. (Incidentally, "environmentalists" are customarily described as extremists or freaks of one kind or another. I can think of several reasons: one is that *nobody* wants to live in an ugly, denuded, polluted unsustainable world, not even the greediest capitalists who can board their private jets and enjoy the few unspoiled areas still remaining on the planet. To that end we're all concerned about the environment, at least in our own backyards. But the people who take this seriously and *do* something about it, and then apply it to the entire planet, even if it threatens some aspect of capitalism, must be nut cases, and therefore can only be described as environmentalists with certain adjectives.)

The cheerleaders of conventional farming

Conventional farming obviously has many proponents, supporters and cheerleaders, including many in highly influential positions in capitalism. (Crazed environmentalists tend to not be associated with the same kind of capitalism… dare I say "crazed capitalism?"… and thus lack power and credibility among the rationally ignorant masses.) Among these, one stands out as a patron saint of industrial agribusiness, and is often called the father of the so-called Green Revolution: Norman Borlaug.

Born in Iowa in 1914, Borlaug studied forestry, then plant pathology, and became involved in a Rockefeller Foundation project to boost wheat productivity, largely through genetics, which required chemical fertilization. As a result, he was said to have kept a billion people from starving, and he was awarded the Nobel Peace Prize in 1970.

He taught at Texas A&M, which in 2000 named a new agricultural biotechnology center after him. At the dedication ceremony he declared that, "We have to have this new technology if we are to meet the growing food needs for the next 25 years." He feared that without biotechnology, famine would become widespread.

When asked what he thought of organic farming and the claim that it's better for human health and the environment, he told an interviewer "That's ridiculous. This shouldn't even be a debate. Even if you used all the organic material that you have — the animal manures, the human waste, the plant residues — and get them back on the soil, you couldn't feed more than 4 billion people. In addition, if all agriculture were organic, you would have to increase cropland dramatically, spreading out into marginal areas and cutting down millions of acres of forests." *(Ronald Bailey in* Reason, *April 2000.)*

There was a lot more in this vein: Borlaug was obviously exasperated by "environmental extremists" who, he admitted, jeopardized his funding, among other problems, and who were responsible for stupid moves like banning DDT.

Once again us poor common folk are left scratching our heads and wondering what to believe and who the extremists really are. While Borlaug undoubtedly knew biotechnology, some of his ideas about organic farming seem quaintly naïve, if not totally off-base, especially when balanced against the real-world experience of people like Joel Salatin. But how are we to decide?

Borlaug died in 2009.

Another controversy

Two blind men trying to describe an elephant by touching it, one perhaps encountering the massive side and the other a ropey tail, couldn't be any further apart than two people discussing farming, blinded by their convictions and, perhaps, personal experiences. Tunnel vision, the over-specialization we have been so cautious of, is as evident in agriculture as anywhere else.

It shouldn't surprise anyone that the "conventional" farm supporters are much more likely to wear blinders than the organic variety: conventional implies, correctly, that it's the norm, the standard taught in schools and workshops, by advisors and consultants, covered in newspapers and magazines and the establishment, and courted by marketers; it's hard to ignore or avoid, and it's taken for granted as the norm.

Organic, on the other hand, involves either sound bites from those who consider all organic farmers environmental extremists, or the loudest environmental extremists themselves… or it requires making a conscious and concerted effort to understand what it's all about. Because so few people even care, few are actually familiar with either side, with the

Norman Borlaugs or the Joel Salatins. How can such uninformed people decide which is the *real* Green Revolution?

The origins of French Intensive Gardening

To remedy that in at least a very minor way, let us turn once again to our custom of starting at the beginning, to see how we arrived at where we are today. We begin with gardening as practiced in France in the 1800s. While this involved several methods and ideas, some going back perhaps thousands of years, the best description we have today can be found in *French Market Gardening: including practical details of "intensive cultivation" for English growers,* by John Weathers.

Published in 1909, this book describes gardens of 40 years earlier, when market gardens around Paris supplied much of Europe (including England) with winter and early spring salads and vegetables. Quite unlike Pack's book (that merely described gardens without any how-to advice) this one is more than 200 pages of step-by-step instructions, or "practical details for English growers." The whys and wherefores are set out in the introduction:

"There is no contrast in the farm or garden world more striking than that between the market-gardens of London and Paris: about London broad sweeps in the Thames valley, wind-swept, shelterless, well farmed; about Paris close gardens, walled in, richly cultivated, and verdant with crops, even at the most inclement time of the year, and with not an inch of space wasted with paths. And this is not owing to the differences of climate, although people say, whenever one speaks of it, "It is a question of climate." I do not know a worse climate in winter than that of Paris, the season when the gardeners get their most profitable results. For all green things our climate is, if anything, a shade better than theirs. The very fact of the little cloche covering acres proves that the climate of Paris is not so good. The late M. Henri de Vilmorin used to tell me that his father had much considered the market-gardens of the two capitals, and estimated that the French grower of vegetables got at least four times the quantity obtained in the larger and broader cultures round London. Be it noted here that this book concerns the limited culture of the Paris market- gardens, for around Paris, as around London, there is the large field culture of vegetables. There is good soil round Paris in the Seine valley, and we cannot complain of the soil in the valley of the Thames, but it is a totally different system and plan we have to look to."

The basics of the system included very deep cultivation (24 inches, now referred to as "double-digging") with generous amounts of horse manure and bedding (readily available in Paris at that time) incorporated, both contributing to growing beds raised above the natural soil level. These beds were never walked on or compacted by machinery. Then plants were spaced much closer together than was the custom in other areas, resulting in less weeding and more efficient watering, as well as a great increase in production per acre, or per square foot.

Weathers wrote that the system he described was not new, but declared that it was almost exclusively French, if not entirely Parisian. He believed that the first great proponent of it was Claude Mollet (1601-1643), the first gardener to Louis XIII. Another French gardener, La Quintinye (1626-1688) wrote *Instruction pour les jardins fruitiers et potagers*, telling how he was able to furnish the kitchen of Louis XIV with asparagus and sorrel in December, radishes, lettuce and mushrooms in January, cauliflowers in March, strawberries in early April, peas in May and melons in June. From this Weathers concludes that the art of intensive cultivation was by no means in its infancy, even in the 17th century. "Frames were already in use, and long before them cloches were common." Heat was provided by the composting manure.

Between 1600 and 1800 "great progress seems to have been made," and inevitably, much experience gained, despite the French Revolution and wars. The combination of much higher yields — up to four times those of English gardeners — plus the ability to produce fresh food out of season, made the

French gardens the salad bowl of Europe. (One wonders how much these gardens affected French cuisine... or was it the other way around?)

"In 1844, according to Courtois-Gerard, about 1,500 acres of land were devoted to intensive cultivation in Paris. This area was in the hands of 1,125 growers, so that each had an average of not much more than an acre." After that, railroads, boulevards and other "improvements" made the land around Paris too valuable for food production (in the capitalist sense), and even more devastating, the horseless carriage greatly diminished the ready supply of manure so abundant in a large city of the time, and so essential to the success of the gardening method.

Nevertheless, Weathers asserts that even in the early 1900s "about 1,300 growers practise the intensive system of cultivation on about 3,000 acres of land. These growers have about 460,000 lights (glass frames), and from 5,000,000 to 6,000,000 bell-glasses or cloches among them. The largest number of lights used by a single individual is said to be 1,400, and the smallest 60; while the greatest number of cloches used by one man is said to be 5,000, the lowest number being 100. The produce grown by these market-gardeners is considered to be worth over half a million sterling yearly giving an average of about 400 to each grower."

Consequently, continued urbanization, mechanization, and more wars took their toll on large-scale intensive growing, although *potagers* or kitchen gardens are both common and intensively cultivated even today.

The links: Steiner and Chadwick

One of the links between then and now was Rudolf Steiner (1861-1925), an Austrian philosopher of many interests including biodynamic agriculture. Far from being a specialist with tunnel vision, he veered off in the other direction, actively engaging in medicine, visual arts, performing arts, architecture, and education, and the Theosophical Society (and after splitting with that, the Anthroposophical Society). After studying mathematics, physics, chemistry, botany, biology, and literature, he earned a doctorate in philosophy.

If truth be told, his connections to spiritual movements such as anthroposophy and his attempts to find a synthesis between science and mysticism might well be responsible for some of the ridicule organic farmers and gardeners still encounter today: the biodynamic agriculture he developed and promoted incorporated the application of natural materials prepared in specific ways in order to engage non-physical beings and elemental forces, and timing farming tasks to utilize the influences of the moon and planets, ideas that do not sit well with those of modern scientific bent who see nothing odd about genetic modification or using poisonous chemicals on edible food.

However, his central thesis — that the farm is an organism, a whole, and should therefore be self-sustaining — remains an important plank in most versions of organic farming, and is arguably one of his most important contributions to mainstream organic methods.

Steiner overlaps with Alan Chadwick (1909-1980), an English aristocrat who was introduced to Steiner's ideas by his mother. Like Steiner, Chadwick was a renaissance man, if not a polymath: he was an expert skier and skater, a professional painter, a violinist, a British naval officer in World War II, and a Shakespearean actor, as well as a master gardener. He learned from Steiner, personally, and combined that with French Intensive gardening, developing his own unique method, which landed him an invitation to establish the Student Garden Project at the University of California, Santa Cruz in 1967.

The project bloomed under his direction, becoming (in 1993) The Center for Agroecology and Sustainable Food Systems (CASFS) at the University of California, Santa Cruz. This has become a world-renowned research center most Americans have never heard of, devoted to helping Third World farmers harvest high yields of food in small spaces with a minimal use of chemicals. To this end it has trained hundreds of gardeners and future teachers in an innovative and well-known apprentice program. (Note that it has not received the accolades accorded the work of Norman Borlaug, with the same Third World small farmers, even though Borlaug's methods require continuing applications of petroleum-based chemical fertilizers and pesticides, as well as machinery, all requiring extraction, manufacture, and transportation.)

John Jeavons

One of Chadwick's students was John Jeavons. Now in his 70s, Jeavons has practiced, researched and promoted small-scale sustainable agriculture for more than 40 years. Although he operates the nonprofit educational center Ecology Action near Willits, California which he formed in 1972, and lectures widely, he is best-known as the author of the oft-updated *How to Grow More Vegetables Than You Ever Thought Possible on Less Land Than You Can Imagine,* one of those rare books with a title that's completely and honestly descriptive.

He points out that conventional farming uses 15,000-30,000 square feet of land to provide one person with the average American diet. He has slimmed that down to 4,000 square feet. Starting with the methods and concepts of Chadwick and his predecessors, Jeavons tested and tinkered with ideas of his own until in 1999 his system had become so unique he trademarked its name: the Grow Biointensive method.

One of its hallmarks is the closed-system concept pioneered by Steiner, developed to a high degree on a practical level. In stark contrast to Borlaug's assertion that there isn't enough organic material to enable organic farming to feed the world, Jeavons claims that his method builds up to 20 pounds of farmable soil for every pound of food eaten. What's more, in contrast with Borlaug's claim that organic farming would require far more arable land, Jeavons uses from one-fourth to one-seventh as much… and all without outside inputs, including chemical fertilizers, herbicides and other pesticides, or fossil fuel, either for the actual tillage or manufacturing and transportation.

An important element of the closed system is the production of "carbon crops," such as corn, wheat and millet. While important as food, they are equally valuable for the carbon they contribute to the compost bins. Not to be ignored is the fact that they produce far greater yields in an intensive setting than on highly mechanized farms: there are definitely diseconomies of scale in agriculture. Roughly half of the garden is devoted to these crops.

About a third is devoted to high-calorie root crops: potatoes, carrots, turnips, beets and parsnips. These produce a lot of calories in a small space, but are also important because they can be stored for long periods without laborious or expensive processing such as canning or freezing.

That leaves only about 1/6th of the space for what most people would call their "garden": tomatoes, peppers, lettuce and the like. But never fear: you can grow more vegetables than you ever thought possible on less land than you can imagine! One secret is to plant exactly as much of each crop as you want or need, based on Jeavons' years of experimenting and record-keeping. He can tell you precisely how many seeds to plant in order to produce a given amount of a specific vegetable, how much space to allot, the protein and calorie content of the edible portion and the proportion of waste that will be composted and returned to the soil.

Experienced gardeners can be excused if they're a tad skeptical (especially if they're not from California) and neophytes are well-advised to exercise caution: a first-time gardener has much to learn, including the sad reality that no two years are the same: as they say about stocks and mutual funds, "past performance is no guarantee of future results." Conventional farmers with thousands of acres face the same risks and gambles. However, recorded as bona fide results over many years in a real-life situation, these numbers can't be dismissed. They certainly can't be ignored as easily as the Norman Borlaugs of the world seem to think.

John Jeavons has distilled Biointensive Gardening down to eight steps:

1. Double-dug raised beds, dating back to 17th century France

2. Composting, popularized and improved by Sir Albert Howard, Lady Eve Balfour, J.I. Rodale and many others

3. Intensive planting, again credited to early French gardeners, updated and popularized by Mel Bartholomew's "square foot gardening"

4. Companion planting: a technique traced to the Native American "three sisters" (corn, squash and beans) and even earlier in other cultures

5. Carbon farming, to feed the compost pile

6. Calorie farming, essential for a year-round food supply

7. Open-pollinated seeds instead of hybrids, for self-sufficiency

8. Treat all the parts as a whole; use the entire system

John Jeavons' book has been translated into seven languages, and his Ecology Action Grow Biointensive workshops have trained hundreds, who have put that knowledge into practice in more than 130 countries around the globe. They claim that their methods make it possible to grow food using 67% to 88% less water; 50% to 100% less fertilizer; and 99% less energy than commercial agriculture, while using a fraction of the resources.

What's more, these techniques, properly used, can produce 2-6 times more food, build up the soil up to 60 times faster than nature, and reduce the amount of land required to feed a family by 50% or more. Again, none of this attracts much attention in the general press, which continues to idolize anyone who makes two stalks of wheat grow where one grew before… as long as they use biotechnology and chemicals.

This isn't the end of the line for organics. From the 17th century gardens of French royalty to modern composting techniques, others have gone even further, incorporating fish into the biocycle, or poultry and rabbits, or earthworms, or all of these and more.

So now, when we compare these claims with the assertions of Norman Borlaug (and countless others) that organic farming is "ridiculous," "there shouldn't even be a debate," and "if all agriculture were organic you would have to

increase cropland dramatically," we obviously have a
dilemma: who's right, what are we supposed to believe, and in
which direction is the world headed?

Here are my personal thoughts:

1. Capitalism's investment in industrial agribusiness is
immense; as we have observed in many other areas of human
activity discussed in previous chapters, that involvement will
be fiercely defended, not only by corporations, capitalists, and
governments but perhaps even more stoutly by consumers,
meaning the entire democratic capitalist System. Under these
conditions, changes will not result from logic or rational
decisions: only a major upheaval (such as the World Wars
provided in the last century) can dislodge such firmly rooted
conventions. Conceivable potential upheavals might include
climate change, energy shortages, global economic disruption,
war... and expert doomsayers can add many more.

2. We have also noted that while science and technology
have made tremendous strides, particularly in the past 300
years, people themselves have changed but little; nevertheless,
the wealth of different *cultures* evident in the human race
amply demonstrates what we're capable of; what's more,
cultures can and do evolve very rapidly (witness the
popularity of Mexican and oriental food in the U.S., or the
cultures spawned by the Internet and cell phones or the
Americanization of... well, most of the world). The current
and growing interest in home cooking, organic and locally-
grown foods, and even home gardening might not be enough
to change the entire culture from agribusiness to
homesteading, but rational logic suggests that it could make
the transition much more likely and easier; it could occur even
with an upheaval that isn't so "major," because many
consumers are primed for it.

3. The usual agribusiness argument that organic farming
could not feed the world is probably true... if they're talking
about *industrial* farms adopting organic methods and ignoring
the holistic nature of the entire organic system, which of
course they are: they show no indication of even being aware
of such a system because "it shouldn't even be a debate," so

they don't even bother looking into it. How scientific is that? In our scenario we don't need "them" and their industry to feed the world; we can feed ourselves!

Instead of the extremely economically inefficient use of capital and human labor to produce yet another private jet to add to the 10,000 already in use, or another pair of shoes to add to the 2,700 pairs the Imelda Marcoses of the world already have, or the innumerable gewgaws and gadgets that clutter up so many stores and homes, or the well over 400 different choices of breakfast cereal, we propose devoting some of the labor saved to food production on a small and local scale.

It's hard to see how most wealthy modern people can view meaningful, enjoyable employment in personal food production as demeaning subsistence farming, and yet consider repetitive brain-dulling work on a production line (at a pace mandated by a conveyor belt) working for money to *buy* food as somehow noble and uplifting. Something's wrong with this picture.

Summary

The previous chapter gave us not only a good indication of the possibilities, but an account of actual results during two World Wars. This chapter has updated that, making home food production even easier and more attractive, suggesting that if we had the desire or need, we could go a long way toward feeding ourselves without industrial agribusiness. While the very idea might seem insane to anyone but the Amish or homesteaders, it deserves consideration in light of the New Normal. Even today, many people go hungry, unnecessarily, in the U.S. as well as in Third World countries. Capitalistic industrial agribusiness is very likely to be unsustainable, or at least become a serious concern in the future. It's good to know that a ready, waiting, surprisingly simple, (and despite the ignorance of many, *proven*) alternative is available.

Already, several trends indicate that a cultural evolution is taking place and a cultural revolution isn't out of the question.

Among the more obvious and generally recognized trends are the new attitudes towards eating, and food itself. A generation ago, who could have foreseen a tv network devoted exclusively to food, along with cooking shows on other channels as well as periodicals devoted to the subject (with no decrease in coverage in more general publications) and a plethora of new cookbooks, without even considering the web, cooking classes and demonstrations, "professional" cookware and kitchens, and more?

The webs here include "new" and unusual foods, ethnic and adventurous foods, organic foods, heirloom and locally grown foods. Organic foods have gone from being a hippie fad, to a niche market, to winning valuable shelf space at Wal-Mart and other mainstream mass marketers. Health foods have spread far beyond yogurt and sprouts, granola and meusli. There is continuing and increasing pressure to reduce fat, salt and sugar, contributing to even more awareness of the benefits of good nutrition. This has led to increased interest in growing your own, and while it hasn't yet blossomed as some had hoped or expected, home gardening has become more respectable. This involves yet another set of webs.

Have you noticed the interest in entomophagy lately? Although eating insects is common in many cultures, and chocolate-covered ants and fried grasshoppers have long been a novelty in America, there is increasing talk about the food value and environmental ramifications of adding bugs to the human diet. In a hungry world this could be a very serious and real possibility.

As an aside on this, the uproar about Starbucks using food coloring made from cochineal insects is somewhat amusing. The extract was used by Aztecs and Mayans in the 15th century. Its use was diminished after the introduction of synthetic dyes, but was revived after more recent concerns about artificial food additives. Most red and pink foods use either the extract (listed as carmine), or Red Dye #40 — made from petroleum. Take your pick.

Most importantly, while few non-gardeners are aware of it — and many active gardeners unfamiliar with either historical gardening or the latest methodology don't realize it either —

the art and science of home food production has made amazing progress in the past century. If food FOB the kitchen door was a realized possibility in 1918, how much easier, more efficient, and more rewarding must it be today?

There's the entire concept of organic gardening: soil improvement through compost, integrated pest management, companion planting. There are new or more commonly used techniques that greatly increase production: square foot gardening, vertical gardening, container gardening, four-season gardening, drip irrigation, raised beds and even edible landscaping. There are new technologies involving greenhouses and cold frames, hot frames and hoop houses, lighting and ventilation and even holistic systems melding vegetables, chickens, worms and fish involving everything from organic matter to oxygen levels. Hydroponics, or "soil-less" gardening, is making gains. Today's home food production system is not your grandmother's vegetable garden.

Replacing Grandma's old-time wisdom and experience are the new gardening gurus who base their thinking on Grandma's ways, but then go far beyond, proving that increased efficiency is possible without becoming enmeshed in industrial agribusiness.

What's keeping so many people from making use of all of this, or conversely, what would it take to convince them?

An increase in home food production (primarily vegetable gardening, although poultry and rabbits have also been involved historically), has been common in depressed economies, and the Great Recession was no exception: major seed companies reported sales increase of as much as 40 percent in 2009, and according to the National Gardening Association, participation in food gardening increased by 14 percent, or five million households, in 2010.

Yet, this totals only 41 million gardens in a nation of roughly 114 million households, and we don't know how many of these had only a few tomato or pepper plants, or a row of lettuce and a few radishes. In any event, there's a great deal of uncultivated ground out there.

Would an even deeper recession, or a depression, do the job? Could something else effect a cultural change that would suddenly make home food production attractive?

Or maybe the organic and environmental hippies will end up being right, and industrial agribusiness will simply sink of its own weight… by destroying the Earth.

We now know we can expect the unexpected, and that anything is possible.

Chapter 21: How sweet it is — not; The bitter story of sugar

Food is essential for the life of any animal; consequently, nature has equipped all to obtain what they need whether with talons, claws, fangs — or beaks uniquely suited to cracking seeds, catching fish or tearing flesh.

Domesticated or captive animals have it easier: family dogs and cats have their bowls of manufactured kibble; the cow in a stall, a manger for preserved silage; the pig, a trough with prepared feed that's scientifically formulated and amended to promote faster growth. These, of course, are dependent on the solicitude and dependability, as well as the wealth, knowledge and wisdom, of the caretaker.

Human animals that could easily gather their own food likewise depend on the wisdom and benevolence of outside sources, on "caretakers" — namely, on capitalist industrial agribusiness. How industrialized peoples are fed is a marvelous story of complexity that is so far removed from the simple process of *eating* that few can even follow the webs.

One of the more interesting and important strands deals with agricultural subsidies, and one of the more interesting crops involved in that — plus its involvement with industrialization and capitalism in general — is worth examining as a microcosm of the much bigger picture. That crop is sugar.

When you ask "How much sugar is enough?" the answer would seem to be that almost any amount is too much for human health... but the capitalist democratic System can never get enough, of anything.

Sugar is not an essential food: on the contrary, some watchdogs of public health have proposed that sugar be regulated like alcohol or tobacco: not only is it not a food, it's a health hazard. Its dispensability is amply demonstrated by the fact that sugar was unknown to most of the world before the 12th century, and by the 18th it was still an unaffordable luxury for most. We can obviously live without it.

But we don't. The average American consumes 150 pounds of sugar a year; 6-1/2 ounces a day. Some people far exceed that.

Such a controversial product must be examined carefully, from many angles, but when we look at sugar's history, chemistry, effects on health, and relationships to capitalism, colonialism (and slavery), industry and technology, and government subsidies… well, we're looking at a very complex picture. And it all started with an early human chewing on a blade of grass.

Sugarcane is native to New Guinea, tropical South Asia and Southeast India. Originally, the only way to extract the sweetness was by chewing on the raw cane (as one large sugar company's advertising depicted happy young boys doing on their Hawaiian plantations not too long ago). About 500 BCE, according to those who study such things, the cane juice was boiled down into a syrup, the syrup was cooled, and the result was sugar crystals. (The crystals were called *khanda,* which accounts for our word *candy.*)

Indian sailors and itinerant Buddhist monks spread the crystals throughout the region, but not until the Crusades did the "sweet salt" reach Europe, where it was available, in very limited quantities, only to the very wealthy. As we have seen in so many other cases, what was once virtually unheard of except in a very small area became an obscene luxury elsewhere, then a necessary nicety, and finally, an everyday necessity for even the lowest classes, worldwide. This seems to be a pattern of human nature, even without capitalism.

Before sugar, the only sweetener was honey, and in North America, maple syrup.

But this proliferation required technology and industry as well as commerce and trade. Production techniques involving crushing or grinding the cane and condensing the juice, leaving sugary solids, originated in India, then spread to the Arab Empire where plantations, sugar mills and refineries proved lucrative as far west as the Mediterranean region.

Sugar was expensive because it was highly labor-intensive. The weight and volume of the cane made it difficult to harvest, transport and process. It was hard work, and time-consuming: local peasants occupied in producing their own food had no desire or incentive to get involved in sugar. The solution was slave labor.

By the 1400s improved presses doubled the amount of juice obtained from the cane and early capitalists provided money for mills and ships. By the 1500s there were thousands of plantations and mills in the New World, from Brazil to Cuba and Jamaica.

These thousands of mills required not only slaves and ships but also machines, meaning cast iron gears, levers, axels and other components. Much of the European technology incorporating mold-making and iron casting, important components in the early stages of the Industrial Revolution in the early 17th century, can be attributed to sugar.

Sugar's role in the European colonization of the Americas was likewise enormous: it was the original incentive for European expansion and colonization, as well as the foundation of the trans-Atlantic slave trade, and in some small way, it contributed to the establishment of the United States of America.

The Caribbean produced sugar at unheard-of low cost, and became the world's leading source. By 1750 the largest sugar producer in the world was a French colony, Saint-Domingue, (now Haiti). That same year sugar surpassed grain as the most valuable commodity in European trade, accounting for 20% of all imports. British sugar consumption went from four pounds per person in 1700 to 18 pounds in 1800, 36 pounds by 1850 and more than 100 pounds by 1900. The human "necessary" diet now included sweetened tea, cocoa, jam, and confections and chocolates.

As what farmers call "a heavy feeder," sugar cane quickly depleted the soil, resulting in many experiments with manures and artificial manures. (Sir Albert Howard, the father of organic farming, became famous for improving on the Indore method of composting, Indore being a location in India where sugar was first grown as a crop, and composting being necessary to maintain soil fertility.) There were several varieties of *Saccharum officinarum*, making it relatively simple for plant breeders to develop new strains with higher sugar content. In these ways, sugar had an influence on general agriculture.

Making sugar in a laboratory: the story of beet sugar

Cane sugar was "discovered" when somebody chewed on a stem of grass and found it tasty. Technology progresses: beet sugar was discovered by a German chemist, in a laboratory. That was in 1747, but the first sugar beet factory didn't go into operation until 1801. In 1813, Napoleon banned imports of sugar — a rather empty gesture, since France was cut off from Caribbean trade by a British blockade anyway during the Napoleonic Wars — which provided a boost to beet sugar. Sugar cane requires tropical growing conditions; sugar beets can tolerate a much more temperate climate, and therefore have a wider range. Today, beet sugar accounts for roughly 30% of world production.

In the U.S., cane sugar production is concentrated in Florida, Louisiana, Texas, Hawaii and Puerto Rico. Sugar beets are produced in the Red River Valley (eastern North Dakota and adjacent Minnesota), the Great Lakes region (Michigan and Ohio), Upper Great Plains (Montana, northwestern Wyoming, western North Dakota), Central Great Plains (Colorado, Nebraska, southern Wyoming), the Northwest (Idaho, Washington, eastern Oregon) and the far west (California, central Oregon). The

production cost of beet sugar is much higher than cane sugar. Less than one-half of one percent of all U.S. farms grow sugar.

However, much cane and beet sugar (sucrose) has been replaced by high-fructose corn syrup, although the process by which this is produced was developed only in 1957. (Technology progresses faster and faster.) This sweetener is the overwhelming choice of food and beverage manufacturers (fabricators), including Coca-Cola and Pepsi. But here the webs fan out in nearly bewildering profusion.

We could get into the sometimes combative debates about the health effects of high fructose corn syrup, the many ripple effects of growing corn for its sugar... which includes ethanol, which of course is another can of worms entirely... but then what about the sugar cane Brazil converts into ethanol? We can't cover all of this in one book, but since these are actual facts, they have to be accounted for in the real world.

Since high fructose corn syrup was introduced, other sweeteners have been developed and marketed, with checkered results. Between 2000 and 2004, 3,920 new products containing artificial sweeteners hit the market, not only in diet sodas, cereals and sugar-free desserts, ketchup and yogurt, but in such products as toothpaste... and even some misleadingly-labeled "maple syrup."

Once touted by organic foodists, the natural sweetener stevia was banned in the U.S. by the FDA on the grounds that it hadn't been approved as a food additive. That ban was withdrawn in 2008. In 1965 aspartame was discovered, in a lab, by accident, by a scientist at the G. D. Searle company (later purchased by Monsanto, the maker of Roundup herbicide and other nonfood products). That patent expired in 1992. Splenda (sucralose) is notable mainly because the Sugar Association (comprised of American sugar cane and beet growers) filed five false advertising claims against its manufacturer, just one indication of the in-fighting among various classes of sweeteners.

Advertising also comes under fire from a number of health groups that oppose the blatant marketing of sugar-laden foods to children, in particular. While the main target is beverages, and breakfast cereals are notorious for their sugar content, the concerns include anything containing excessive amount of sugar (or salt, or fat).

Childhood obesity is the principle rallying point, but diabetes, cardiovascular diseases, Alzheimer's, as well as macular degeneration and tooth decay have been connected with sugar. More recently this has been extended to altered hormones, metabolism and blood pressure, along with "significant damage to the liver."

In 2012, University of California-San Francisco researchers said worldwide sugar consumption doubled in the last 50 years and is now contributing to 35 million deaths a year. In an article in *Nature,* they suggested that sugar come under government control, just like alcohol and tobacco.

The capitalist/democracy connection with sugar

The truth is, government already plays a large role in sugar… but not to restrict its use. We can go back even further, to before there even was a United States of America and the British involvement with sugar in America (and European governments had their fingers in the sugar bowl long before that). In fact, it might be said that sugar had a hand in instigating the American Revolution that resulted in the formation of the new republic.

Protesting the Sugar Act

New England's shipping trade depending on slaves, molasses and rum was well established by 1733 when, at the insistence of large sugar plantation owners in the British West Indies, the British Parliament passed the Molasses Act, imposing a prohibitively high tax of six pence per gallon on molasses imported from the French, Dutch and Spanish West Indian colonies. Had it been collected, the tax would have shut down the New England rum industry. It was not collected. Smuggling and bribery were easy, and cheaper.

The French and Indian War substantially increased the British national debt. When the war ended, in 1763, the British maintained a standing army of 10,000 in the colonies. Paying for these troops in addition to servicing the national debt posed a problem. It was felt that Americans should be paying at least a portion of the expense of defending the colonies, but the largely ineffective 30-year-old molasses tax wasn't producing much revenue, and besides, it was scheduled to expire that very same year.

That tax was replaced by the Sugar Act of 1764 — also known as the American Revenue Act. Although the tax was cut in half, it promised stricter enforcement, and included other restrictions on trade. Smuggling became more dangerous, and New England ports suffered. Protests against the Sugar Act were led by Samuel Adams and James Otis. Fifty Boston merchants agreed to boycott British luxury goods, and colonial manufacturing increased to avoid imports and to offset the decrease in the shipping trade. The Sugar Act was only a prelude to the Stamp Act, taxation without representation became a popular concern, and the colonists declared their independence.

One way the new American government raised money was with a tariff on, ironically, sugar. Starting with the very first American revenue bill in 1789, sugar has had a constant presence in the Congress of the United States.

"Protectionism" is a blanket term describing any governmental policy designed primarily to protect specific industries from foreign competition, for reasons ranging from cultural identity to national security, and of course, to cynics, to enrich those industries and their lobbyists. These policies include not only tariffs, but quotas on imports, and subsidies, both direct and indirect. All of them generate controversy, whether dealing with dairy products, steel, wheat, or sugar.

The original 1789 sugar tariff was meant to raise revenue: there was little or no domestic production to protect until the Louisiana Purchase in 1803. That remained in effect until 1890, when the McKinley Tariff Act raised protective tariff rates on many imports, but not sugar. Instead, the fledgling domestic sugar industry was *subsidized* at 2¢ per pound. Just four years later this was scuttled, and an *ad valorem* tariff on sugar added

40 percent to the cost of imported sugar. Although the tax was lowered in 1897, it remained otherwise unchanged until 1934. Then it became more complicated.

The country, indeed, the world, was in the Great Depression. The U.S. sugar industry was overproducing. The Sugar Act of 1934 required the Secretary of Agriculture to determine the annual consumption of sugar, and then assign production quotas to both foreign and domestic producers. Other provisions included minimum wages for field workers, child labor, acreage restrictions, and benefit payments to growers. (We're glossing over such details as the processing tax, which the Supreme Court held unconstitutional in 1936, when Congress okayed a new but almost identical Sugar Act, swapping out the processing tax for an excise tax; also the temporary suspension of the quota system during WWII.)

When the latest version of the act expired in 1974, world sugar prices were high, and appeared to be stable, meaning price supports were no longer needed. But prices fell, supports were reinstituted in 1977, and the system has changed but little since then.

Sugar subsidies... that aren't

Although the distinctions might seem blurry, sugar is supported by a combination of price support loans, marketing allotments, and import quotas, not subsidies. (Even 2012 presidential candidates didn't make the distinction, much to the chagrin of the sugar lobby; for us, here, this will also be a topic of rational ignorance, except for a brief mention later.)

The sugar lobby is rich, and powerful, and it has been successful in bolstering prices, which of course are paid by consumers. In fact, this particular lobby has been used as an example of how the process works:

Virtually everybody uses sugar, but the bulk of that is hidden in manufactured food products; the rest is so minimal no one worries about a few cents per pound. Consumers who use 6-7 ounces of the product a day, most without even realizing it, aren't going to organize, or spend money, to protest sugar prices.

The major producers, however, number only a handful, and for them large sums of money are at stake. It's relatively easy for them to exert influence on any form of legislation, such as restricting the sugar trade.

But — don't let this surprise you — it gets complicated. One web is the Sweetener Users Association, representing industries using sugar, which now comes in many different forms. This group argues that liberalizing trade in sugar would benefit the U.S. economy through lower prices, it would *keep food manufacturing jobs in the United States* as well as maintaining a U.S. sugar refinery industry *with its well-paid union jobs* (emphases mine; it's always about "jobs"), as well as stimulating demand, encouraging product innovation, etc. etc. And it gets even more interesting.

Chicago is (or was) the nation's candy store, producing more than any other locality. Illinois is the leading producer of high fructose corn syrup, the lower-cost sugar substitute used in many products — but not in candy. Although not directly involved, those downstate Illinois farmers and agribusiness interests back the federal price support program for cane and beet sugar growers and producers, because that makes U.S. sugar at least twice as expensive as it is in other countries. (Some sources say the price is tripled.) Expensive sugar props up the demand for and the price of corn syrup.

Critics (including then-Mayor Richard Daly) claimed that artificial price inflation was unfair to both consumers and to Chicago candy makers, whose jobs went from 13,000 to 10,000 in just five years. And the giant Brach's factory had just announced that it was closing, eliminating another 1,100 jobs. Brach's moved its operation to Mexico, and a few years later Fannie May also left Chicago. Kraft moved its Lifesavers factory from Michigan to Canada, and Hershey relocated plants from Pennsylvania, Colorado and California to Canada, where sugar costs were lower.

Illinois Senator Richard Durbin said, "it's a difficult vote in Illinois because you have important people on both sides of the issue." (The significance of "important people" in this context isn't quite clear… but it doesn't appear to refer to consumers of Brach's or Fannie May candies. We'll have to use our imaginations.)

At that time the government bought more than a million tons of sugar in a year for $435 million, and paid $1.4 million a month just to store it. The U.S. General Accounting Office estimated that Americans paid an extra $1.9 billion in 1998 because of supports. (Sugar makes up as much as 50 percent of some types of candy.)

Sugar's critics also point to the role "Big Sugar" plays in setting nutritional guidelines, such as those promulgated by the World Health Organization and the Food and Agriculture Organization of the United Nations. They also accuse sugar interests of hiding nutritional information on food and drink packaging: when the Center for Science in the Public Interest petitioned the FDA to require food manufacturers to clearly label the amount of added sugar in a package or serving — instead of camouflaging that information with terms like dextrose, glucose, fructose, lactose, corn syrup, maple syrup, honey, invert sugar, and malt. The petition was opposed by the sugar interests, and it failed.

There was also controversy over the wording of the government dietary guidelines on sugar: instead of "limiting" sugar intake, consumers are asked to use "moderation."

And it doesn't end there. As one result of artificially high sugar prices, large areas of the Florida Everglades have been transformed into sugar plantations, resulting in ecological damage related to drainage, wildlife habitat, and fertilizer runoff.

More webs... and money

Speaking of Florida, have you heard of the Fanjul family? Dating back to the early days of sugar in Cuba, they left that country after the Castro takeover. (Their Havana residence, and its art collection, is now the Museo Nacional de Bellas Artes de Cuba.) After abandoning their Cuban home and fortune, they quickly recovered and now own Domino sugar, Florida Crystals, and other sugar operations in six countries.

According to a Wikileaks document uncovered by the *Palm Beach Post* in 2012, the State Department accused members of the family of opposing the Central American Free Trade Agreement, a priority of the George W. Bush administration… while making substantial contributions to Bush. Florida Crystals spent $520,000 on lobbying in the first three quarters of 2011. Domino Sugar is also a registered lobby client. The lobbying included tariffs, tax credits, foreign trade… and biofuels, which has become a side business as sugar cane "waste" is used to produce electricity.

Here's another strange twist of the webs: In August of 2011 American Crystal Sugar locked out more than 1,300 union workers in North Dakota, Minnesota and Iowa, in a contract dispute. In January, 2012, the union representing the workers said it planned to lobby *against* the federal sugar program, breaking a long-standing tradition of siding with the farmers and refiners. The farmers and refiners said the unionists were biting the hand that feeds them.

Also as of January, 2012, responding to a question posed during the Republican presidential debate in Florida, both Newt Gingrich and Mitt Romney called for an end to federal sugar subsidies. They were immediately rebuffed by sugar industry supporters, including Sen. Kent Conrad (D-ND), Rep. Rick Berg (R-ND) and Sen. Al Franken (D-MN), who accused the candidates of "spreading misinformation about a vital program that does not subsidize the sugar industry." Berg's statement said the sugar industry generates nearly $10 billion a year for the U.S. economy, including $1 billion and 13,000 jobs in North Dakota. (In Florida, sugar cane production and processing accounts for $3.1 billion and more than 25,000 direct jobs.)

Gingrich said he tried to reform agriculture when Speaker of the House (1995-1999) but it was impossible because of "the capacity of the agricultural groups to defend themselves." In an ideal world, he said, the sugar industry would operate in an open market, but it's "very hard to imagine how you're going to get there. Cane sugar hides behind beet sugar, and there are just too many beet sugar districts in the United

States. It's an amazing side story about how interest groups operate."

And Romney agreed.

Conrad, on the other hand, was "taken aback" by the candidates' comments because they were calling for the elimination of a program that helps provide thousands of jobs in the country. "I think it reflects the media elite bias against rural America, which is very pronounced and repeated over and over," he said. "To have two presidential candidates so woefully ignorant was so striking and disappointing."

Lobbies

We haven't gotten into the numbers of former congressional people who now work as lobbyists and in similar capacities, and many other troublesome concerns. But we've seen enough to wonder, which side is right? Whom do we believe? And what difference does any of it make? So far we can come up with these takeaway points:

• Lobbying interferes with capitalism by introducing government intervention into the marketing function;

• Lobbying interferes with democracy by exerting undue influence on lawmakers, based on money and clout, not on what is right, or moral, or best for the people or the country;

• There is no way lobbying can be ended, because *it works.* It's entrenched.

Sugar has been used as a case study, but it's only a microcosm of the vast and complex system: sugar is only a bit player. The negative health aspects of sugar, along with its long history of government support combined with its impact on colonization, slavery, industrial technology both mechanical and chemical, helps demonstrate the chaotic complexity of the webs and the sheer hopelessness of reforms.

But milk could provide another and in some ways even better example. Here we have marketing orders and a price support program (to prop up prices), income support program (to push prices down), trade barriers (to keep domestic prices artificially high) and export subsidies (to encourage exports by compensating for the other programs that keep domestic prices above world prices).

Cheese, peanuts, cotton, orange juice, and rice, as well as beef, pork, chicken and turkey, are all involved. One watchdog group counted 10,720 pages of rules for the USDA to enforce.

Federal marketing orders are used for milk, fruits, vegetables and other farm products. The stated purpose is to "enforce product quality standards, regulate the flow of product to the market, standardize packages and containers, create reserve pools for storable commodities, and authorize production and marketing research and advertising." They're also designed to improve returns to producers, which translates into higher prices for consumers.

Humans are "kept" animals...

Like all animals, humans are endowed by nature with everything required to feed themselves. Today's "civilized, domesticated" humans are kept-animals that, instead of relying on nature and their natural gifts, depend on merchants, chemists, bankers, a bit of slavery, a lot of government boondoggling, lawyers and lobbyists, and many other keepers, to place food before them every day. Total self-sufficiency is impossible, but few even try, and the masses don't even have any idea what's involved.

It's hard to imagine all of this going on with a product we don't even need, and which might even be dangerous. So much science, technology, greed, political intrigue, suffering — and money — and for what? Imagine what alternatives could have been accomplished with the same resources, had we just said, "Enough!"

Chapter 22: The New Normal

In one sense, every generation faces a "new normal." Events and situations, whether dramatic (wars, plagues, migrations) or relatively unimportant (the introduction of tv, computers or cell phones), change the way each generation lives and thinks.

Unarguably, technological changes have ushered in "new ages:" the loom, the steam engine, the automobile, electricity. Some have had monumental impacts on civilization, literally changing the world.

One example is the printing press, or more accurately, as we have seen, Gutenberg's printing *system* consisting of moveable metal type, oil-based ink, and the press itself. Historians who can draw out webs and threads credit printing with the development of literacy and education in general; capitalism in the form of paper, ink and press manufacturers; mercantilism, art, engineering, and you-name-it; the printing press quite literally changed the face of the Earth and the course of civilization.

Historians estimate that in the first 50 years of printing more than two million books were produced, an absolutely astounding number given the population of Europe at that time (after the Black Death) and the fact that perhaps less than five percent of those people were literate.

Now we have semiconductor-based microelectronic technology — and the Internet. It's no longer unusual for something to "go viral" and reach millions of people around the world within days. If the printing press changed the world so drastically, what might we expect of the Internet?

There are differences. One in particular stands out. The first presses disseminated copies of the ancient Greek and Roman philosophers, and the Bible — books that had been perpetuated by scribes. Later, books on significant topics, written specifically for the new press, were penned by educated, thoughtful people.

Compare that with the bulk of what appears on the Internet, and certainly with the material that goes viral. Some days I feel as if the Internet is one giant supermarket tabloid. It seems likely that the Internet will affect civilization as much as the printing press did, but in what ways and to what end? It's not a comforting thought. This is one of the more disturbing puzzles shrouding the New Normal.

The significant factor is cultural. The printing press revolution involved knowledge, science and philosophy and technology. The Internet revolution involves these too of course, but the king is entertainment and commerce. More than $3,000 is spent on Internet pornography — every second. Global e-commerce sales will top $1.25 trillion by 2013.

Cultural changes accompany material changes

The changes that have taken place in the last century have set the stage for a New Normal of Earth-shaking proportions; changes that have challenged the way we think and act, alter the very fiber of society, and the Earth itself. Those of a certain age who were raised with strict standards of morals and behavior in an era of scarcity and frugality, with unbreakable rules of conduct and very strong convictions about many matters both large and small, have seen most of their beliefs and assumptions shattered in the space of a lifetime.

For many pages now we've been discussing the obsession with material possessions; the changes in our homes, clothes, transportation, food and entertainment, most associated with excess and greed.

Other changes have been less materialistic. Changes in the family, for example. Seventy-five years ago divorce was something scandalous, associated only with movie stars — some people wouldn't even attend movies featuring depraved, divorced stars. Most people never considered divorce, with the Jack Benny mantra, "Murder, yes; divorce, never!" (Don't even think of joking about murder today, much less bombs on airplanes... but political correctness is a whole 'nother topic.)

Divorce soared after 1940, dropped back in 1960, peaked in 1981, and fell off again, but overall, today roughly one in five adults has been divorced at least once. Children with divorced parents were once pitied, like orphans; today they're the norm, in some cases, literally: The other day a newspaper photo of a mother-daughter event pictured five pairs, only one of which identified the mother and daughter as having the same last name. Either these children suffer severe emotional handicaps, or everything we learned 60-70 years ago was wrong; either one heralds a New Normal as surely as the coming of the railroad or the telegraph.

And why are divorce rates falling now? Aside from the fact that they decreased somewhat as a result of the recession — single people couldn't afford to marry, and married people couldn't afford to divorce — there simply aren't as many married people. Couples who cohabit "without benefit of clergy" don't get divorced, they just split! The number of couples living together without marrying increased ten-fold between 1960 and 2007; at one time, it was virtually unheard of, at least in small-town Middle America. Today it's the New Normal.

Concurrently, it was recently revealed that unmarried women under 30 now account for one-half of all births in that age group. That was once unthinkable. For some, it still is. But it's the New Normal.

Just as unthinkable was same-sex marriage, but that entire topic was unmentionable long before it got to that point: it was a mortal sin, not even to be discussed.

Cultural changes of this magnitude can't help but rock the very foundation of a belief system: "If this is what I've been taught and how I've been brought up and what all my mentors and peers have adhered to... and now, suddenly it's not only politically incorrect but *wrong* and perhaps even illegal... what else do I 'know' or believe that isn't true, or taken another way, what are we being told to believe today that will be politically incorrect, wrong and illegal tomorrow? Who can we trust, and what *can* we believe?"

In the 1940s we had only a very limited form of gym class, but even without sweating we were required to take salt tablets: can you imagine feeding kids *salt* in school, today? Eggs and whole milk were very good for you — and later, they were not. And the list goes on.

Today, average prom costs top $1,000 per teen, more than many weddings used to cost. (Today the average wedding is $27,000+… and more than $65,000 in New York City.) A high school reportedly handed out free condoms on prom night.

Then there are tattoos, piercings, and music, which are easily dismissed as mere generational differences, although the language, gestures, and attitudes inherent in today's youth culture seem far removed from anything of the past. Language once encountered only in tough dockside bars can now be heard among young girls in suburban malls.

The three-year-old son of the unmarried daughter of a has-been Alaskan politician uttered a swear word on a televised "reality" show which was reported in the media and is now being repeated here in a book, while critically important information passes into history unnoticed by the masses: how sick is that?

By now it should be obvious that I'm comparing today with my own teenage years, more than 60 years ago, and what's the point of that? What does the long-ago past have to do with today? And what will the old coot come up with next, that the downfall of America can be traced to the introduction of rock and roll? (The prospects are tempting.)

One point is that in comparing life — not only the daily routines and amenities but the hopes and promises and dreams — of 60 years ago with those same components today presents some stark contrasts, not only in the physical details but in what might be called "spiritual" terms, including patriotism and a general outlook on life. Undeniably, we are much "wealthier" now than we were then, and we enjoy many more creature comforts and conveniences. And yes, that includes even those classified as "poor."

But are we any better off? Are we healthier? Happier? More fulfilled?

These are questions that demand answers — not from politicians, not from capitalists, but from real, human people, who have spawned capitalists and politicians for their own benefit, and now that they have taken over, can rein them in, also for their own benefit.

The problem is that almost no one is asking the questions. The capitalist-democracy System has us so sedated we have ceased to question the real meaning of existence.

When will we say, "Enough!"?

Even if there were new normals in the past, there has never, in the entire history of the human race, loomed a transition like the one we face today. In terms of technology, in terms of know-how and information, in terms of morals and customs and cultures and ways of thinking, the world — literally the entire planet — has been transformed into an unrecognizable alien place in just a few generations.

This includes the forests cut down and bulldozed to build more houses, shopping centers, roads and airports; the soil, that umbilical that ties us to life, utterly destroyed by those same forces as well as others ranging from plowing and biocides to off-road vehicles and salinization caused by irrigation; the air made unbreathable; the destruction of water, extending even to the vast oceans which it turns out are not bottomless after all; the destruction of many forms of life, as well as encouraging others in the wrong places (starlings, lamprey eels, fire ants, kudzu, zebra mussels, European ash borers, etc. etc.), upsetting the delicate balance of nature, with who-knows-what long-term consequences. Even a study of the world's great rivers is depressing: many are filled with effluent, and so much water has been taken out of many others they no longer reach the sea: the Rio Grand, the sacred Yamuna in India, the River Jordan, and China's Yellow River.

Because of greed, and the inability to say *"Enough!"*

Because of pride, and the notion that Man is not a part of nature but is somehow above Nature and can, and should, control it.

Because of ignorance and stupidity, fostered largely by the soporific effects of a capitalistic democracy that enshrines ease, entitlement, shallow thinking and no thinking at all; because of brainwashing to mold humans to the needs of the System, a brainwashing welcomed by most because it promises an easier life, although not a *better* life.

Yes, even if this New Normal is different from the others, mankind will probably muddle through— if the Earth remains habitable, which certainly isn't guaranteed.

But survival isn't my concern. What I want to know is why we can't take inventory today, right now, to determine where we are, how we got here, where we want to go and how we're going to get there. Even the brief and feeble attempt to take a step in that direction with this book strongly suggests that the current capitalist democracy and its mores and technology offer little hope in elevating mankind from its current level — which has changed little in thousands of years — to something more in keeping with the immense untapped potential of the species. More "stuff" simply gets in the way, and the endless pursuit of that stuff perpetuates the System that holds us back.

Instead of merely muddling through, let's take the bull by the horns and reclaim our destiny from the invisible hands and mindless forces that have gotten us where we now stand.

It's time to shout, loudly and in unison, *"Enough!"*

I am not a nut: I know it's not going to happen like that. There is no way the future can unfold according to the old American Dream. That's all the more reason to ask what *is* going to happen?

Chapter 23: The crisis

Times of crisis demand creative unconventional thinking and bold action. Are we living in a time of crisis?

While some people are unable to see the world beyond their coddled existence and immediate personal experiences, most have a better grasp of reality. They are very aware of the intense difficulties and dangers that face us, and realize that important but difficult decisions must be made, two ideas that define "crisis."

They might be the elderly couple we have so often mentioned, who had carefully planned to survive their last years with interest earned on their modest but hard-won savings, and who have seen that income, their lifeline, eliminated by the Federal Reserve... as a means of goosing the "recovery." Not theirs, of course: they'll never recover. They are in a crisis.

Or it might be the young college graduates who recently had high but reasonable hopes and expectations but who now have only thousands of dollars of debt and no jobs. They are in a crisis.

There are the families with underwater mortgages whose plans and future financial security are now in question, as well as many others who have already lost their homes and equity to foreclosure.

Fewer Americans are working today than in 2000, but the pool of available workers has increased by more than 11 million. How could enough new jobs be created to sop up that surplus?

The average American family's net worth has plunged more than 40% since 2007. How can they possibly recover that in a sick economy, and how will this affect their retirement years?

Eighty-one percent of Americans say they are dissatisfied with their government, and three-quarters believe the country is on the wrong track. Federal Reserve Chairman Ben Bernanke has told Congress that the economy is "stuck in the mud" since the theoretical ending of the so-called recession in 2009. For the 80% of Americans born after World War II, it's not a recession: it's their Great Depression.

And it keeps getting worse.

Then the environment...

Then there are environmental crises. Observant people who are attuned to the natural world can cite dozens of them, which combined pose overwhelming dangers to not only economies, but to the survival of civilization.

Yes, people who live padded lives, insulated from nature and inextricably bound to the producer-consumer society, who rarely know where their food and other needs come from or how they got there, are often oblivious to the thin umbilical cord that connects their lives to the Earth. They can be cavalier about such concerns, ignoring them or attributing them to crazed tree-huggers. This constitutes an ominous crisis in itself. They are fiddling while Rome burns, but in their defense, what else can they do? Their ignorance of the natural world and overdependence on the System paralyzes them, and they're unable to act rationally.

Finally, in the usual compartmentalized mode of thinking, we find people concerned about many other crises: moral, political, social, health, education — take your pick.

Multiple crises, one priority

Considering all these concerns, no informed, reasonable person could possibly deny that we live not only in a time of crisis, but in a time of *many* crises. This presents another problem: how would it be possible to tackle all of them at once or, as an alternative, how might we prioritize them to pick off one at a time?

The evidence we have been examining strongly suggests that the consumer society is choking on its overindulgence and will likely gasp its last breath. A plan to deal with that near certainty should be a priority.

Pollyannas adamantly maintain that air and water pollution don't matter, that oil wells will never run dry and if they do we'll find some other source of energy to keep the machines running, that science will continue to increase food production and if all else fails, we'll simply find another planet. That's not a plan, that's just crossing your fingers.

Even if the technologists prevail and society manages to continue producing and consuming and somehow survive, is that the best course? Or is right now, in a time of crisis when important decisions must be made, a good chance to take inventory and perhaps make some valuable improvements?

There won't be any political solutions. When government attempts to limit the production and consumption of even such goods as soda pop, sugars and fats, drugs and cigarettes, the capitalist and consumer legs of the stool resist in no uncertain terms.

A utopian approach

There are two other possibilities. One is utopian, the other much more realistic, but much less desirable.

Ideas of utopias, or ideal civilizations, date back at least as far as Plato's *Republic* in ancient Greece, around 380 BC. The word comes from Sir Thomas More's *Utopia*, written in 1516. Francis Bacon came along with *New Atlantis* in 1629, with numerous others after that, including many imaginative versions from writers of science fiction and perhaps most significantly, B. F. Skinner's 1948 book *Walden Two*.

Historically, utopias have been the brainchildren of philosophers, not economists. Usually communes of one kind or another, most eschewed capitalism and even private ownership. Almost invariably they were agrarian, but there never appears to be a shortage of manufactured goods.

Although not based on economics, one of their outstanding characteristics is economic equality. According to More, in Utopia no one can want for anything, no one is poor, "and though no man has anything, yet they are all rich."

Utopia is an apt word, derived from the Greek "no place." However, *eutopia*, which is pronounced the same, means "good place." Some scholars surmise that More's book is a

satiric commentary on 16th century England, not a blueprint
for an ideal society: "No place" is a "good place."

This hasn't kept some people from trying to establish
utopias, with somewhat more modest goals. Religious utopian
communities were widespread in the U.S. in the 1800s. Later
utopias became communes. Now they are more likely to be
called intentional communities. All were or are attempts to
improve on the System.

Intentional communities for tribal animals

In the early 1970s there were reportedly 20,000-50,000
communes in the United States. Most people will be surprised
to hear that today there are still an estimated 10,000, and new
ones are formed every year. And today, they're not for
hippies.

The underlying motivation can be religious, economic,
environmental sustainability, a desire to recapture the values
of living in a tightly-knit neighborhood, or simply a longing to
get back to the Earth.

While some members were born and raised in communities
where they now rear their own children, others don't last long.
Apparently, the chains of the capitalist democracy are too
strong for some to cast off.

It's interesting to see how the basic idea of an ideal society
has lingered and intrigued people for more than 2,000 years,
and how that ideal shuns personal wealth in favor of
nonmaterial values as well as embracing nature. Even though
the ideal doesn't exist, humans apparently have an innate
yearning, perhaps involving a racial memory or possibly a
prophetic dream, for a communal lifestyle that is decidedly
different from their actual experience. We are tribal animals,
and Facebook isn't filling the gap.

At the same time, few can stomach communism, or even
socialism, unless it's voluntary, as with some of the communes
and intentional communities. Capitalism's grip on every
aspect of our lives is too strong.

But what if capitalism were to fail? What would replace it?
How?

Saying that's impossible is folly. This is a time of crisis, and anything is possible. Being prepared involves being aware of the possibilities.

We can concede that the voluntary intentional community movement isn't likely to gain widespread favor, but it's intriguing to note the trend in that direction with the development of village-like neighborhoods in many cities today. When people live, work and play in a locale with a high walkability score and the green spaces our animal nature craves (often including community gardens) with an emphasis on sustainability — well, that's getting much closer to the idea than most people could even imagine today.

Not by edict, not entirely by economics, but by a tectonic shift in the culture.

Frank Lloyd Wright grand plan

In the 1930s architect Frank Lloyd Wright designed Broadacre City. Wright believed every man deserved an acre of land, with a garden for growing his own food and a root cellar for storing it so he could be self-sufficient. He noted that on his own land, a man could "never be unemployed or a slave to anyone."

The cities — it was actually a development plan for the whole country, not site-specific — included community gardens, walking trails, parks and green spaces. Each town would be self-sufficient, with growth limited by the water supply and tillable land. The inhabitants (Wright called them homesteaders) would have the time and skills to be part-time farmers, part-time mechanics (workers), and part-time intellectuals, providing a healthy daily mix of physical and mental labor. (This mix is a surprisingly common goal for those who have had enough of the System, such as prominent back-to-the-landers Scott and Helen Nearing.)

Small factories, owned by entrepreneurs or the workers themselves, were an integral part of the city, as was the Roadside Market. With restaurants and cafés, workshops and classrooms, and public spaces no doubt landscaped and ornamented with fountains and statuary, it would be a social, business and educational center reminiscent of ancient Greece.

In that setting it's easy to envision stimulating conversations, lectures and debates replacing shopping and video games as primary attractions.

Many architects and others have wondered why so few of the ideas of "the greatest architect who ever lived" took root. His Usonian homes made use of passive solar heat, natural cooling and light, radiant heating, and an L-shaped floor plan embracing a garden terrace in the early 1900s. But except for the living room and carport, the open design concept, and in a stretch his prophetic view of suburbs and shopping malls long before they were built, his legacy has lagged far behind his stature.

One possible reason is that legendary FBI Director J. Edgar Hoover considered Wright a socialist, and he had no use for socialists or communists. He used his considerable clout to see that the greatest architect who ever lived never got a single government contract, not even during the height of the Public Works Administration.

While Wright did have a socialist bent, capitalism is largely responsible for user-friendly neighborhoods sprouting in many cities today. That means we can consider the possibility that capitalism might simply be reinvented, reducing or eliminating its shortcomings. Again, anything is possible.

A more realistic scenario?

Given the current state of affairs, including widespread inertia and almost total disagreement on virtually all topics of major importance, a more realistic scenario involves the entire establishment sitting on its hands — or every faction running off in a different direction, which would have the same results. That would be more of the same, but being accumulative, much worse.

Americans are marking time — or marching backward — in what is being called a "lost decade." They are living from payday to payday, if they still have a payday. They struggle to pay bills; some reportedly take out payday loans at usurious interest rates to buy groceries. They are frightened now, and are even more frightened about the future. Government is ineffectual, the Federal Reserve is out of ammunition, capitalists are retrenching; no change is in sight; no one even seems to have any solid ideas about what to do. So nothing happens.

Meanwhile, dreams, hopes, and even ambitions fade; lives are put on hold, or destroyed; the environment continues to deteriorate.

How long can this continue? What could possibly turn it around? The answers are unknowable, but the possibilities are frightening.

The average American is already much worse off than a decade ago. A long, slow, steady decline in economic activity would only make it worse, perhaps eventually relegating the U.S. to the status of a Third World country.

Thus ends the American Dream.

Chapter 24: Now it's your turn

I started writing this book more than 40 years ago by clipping newspaper and magazine articles that seemed pertinent to the topic: the increasing body of evidence that the democratic capitalist System wasn't truly improving humanity and was, in fact, a roadblock to the real progress the world needed, and was in decline. I had boxes and boxes of "proof," or at least what I considered strong indications, that something was wrong and that sooner or later the dam would burst and we'd be washed out.

In other words, this book could easily have several thousand pages, and new material could be added daily. And that's exactly what I'd like you to do.

You encounter new information every day, data that should, logically, be plugged in to your personal life: what to eat, how to spend or invest your money, how to improve your health, what to expect from the goings-on in Iran or North Korea or anywhere else, and so on. That's the ostensible purpose of news, anyway.

In any event, I invite you to try to evaluate this data within the framework of *Enough!* What ripple effect might this new information, situation or event have on the future? Does it strengthen or diminish the bonds between capitalism, democracy and the people? How does it affect sustainability?

Here are a few examples as of this writing. This is a short list, but take my word for it: there will be more in the news tomorrow, next week, and next year. Watch for it. Interpret it in the light of "enough." Then decide for yourself what to do about it.

Trying to make sense of the tumult

Retired journalist Bill Moyers, upon his return to work with a Sunday morning television talk show in early 2012: "I'm coming back because in tumultuous times like these I relish the company of people who try to make sense of the tumult.

"Journalism has long been for me a continuing course in adult education. Given what's happening in this country, it's time to sign up for more classes. The lack of civility and common sense that has paralyzed our democracy, the vast economic and social inequality that sends both left and right raging into the streets, the corrosive influence of money in politics — we're in a tailspin with little hope for a course correction from our elected leadership or corporate-dominated media. The need for voices of reason, simple and eloquent, has rarely been stronger."

We've been trying to "make sense of the tumult" for the past 23 chapters, but mostly in the context of "enough." That hardly begins to cover the concerns.

What about school and workplace shootings and sexual assaults (including children)? What about the greed inherent in Enron, the Madoff and other pyramid schemes, the numerous examples of malfeasance in the top echelons of business and government in the U.S. and throughout the world? What about terrorism and its fallout, the continuing economic, social and psychological costs?

There is the problem of the shrinking planet: population growth of humans and their energy slaves (which we haven't discussed at all), as well as increased appetites for material goods with the same amount of resources that are already under siege with a far smaller population, must by definition result in lower standards of living. There are problems with dangerously increasing inequality, and conflict and dissension on topics of widespread importance, including those leading to wars and revolutions. There is a decided lack of civility.

The Disunited States of America?

In 2008 Americans became aware of the prediction of an obscure Russian academic (and former KGB analyst) that an economic and moral collapse in the United States would trigger a civil war and eventual breakup of the union. Americans laughed. But Prof. Igor Panarin was serious... and he was no kook. The dean of the Russian Foreign Ministry's academy for future diplomats, he lectured, published books, attended Kremlin receptions, and was sought by the media as an expert on U.S.-Russia relations. He has a doctorate in political science, and has studied economics.

In 1998 he attended an international conference on information warfare where he revealed his theory to 400 delegates, suggesting that the disintegration would occur by 2010. He didn't attract much attention until the Great Recession, when he often gave two interviews a day, appearing on Russian tv which cut between his comments and film clips of American homeless people and lines at soup kitchens. His forecasts were "all the rage" in Moscow, according to news reports. At a White House press conference in December, 2008, when a reporter asked about White House reaction to the prediction, "I'll have to decline to comment," spokeswoman Dana Perino said, to much laughter. Prof. Panarin took that as an indication that "my views are being listened to very carefully."

He wrote that Americans hoped President-elect Barrack Obama could work miracles, "but when spring comes, it will be clear that there are no miracles."

There were no miracles, and no breakup. But Panarin had pointed out that previous forecasts of similar cataclysms had been correct, such as French political scientist Emmanuel Todd's forecast of the demise of the Soviet Union, 15 years beforehand.

Has anything improved, have any changes occurred that would make the union stronger, since 2010? What most quickly comes to mind are the Occupy Wall Street protests, the Tea Party movement (and politics in general by 2012, from local dissension in Wisconsin to the national level), the continuing housing market and unemployment, and...

"Patriot" groups explode

The Southern Poverty Law Center (SPLC) reports that militias and "patriot" groups in the U.S. went from 149 when Barrack Obama took office (and Panarin's predictions attracted attention) to more than 1,200 in early 2012, with an estimated 300,000 Americans involved. Members of the "sovereign citizen" movement claim they don't have to pay federal taxes or follow most laws; this group expanded greatly as a result of the 2008 recession. The paramilitary branch goes further; both see the federal government as their primary enemy. The FBI doesn't track such groups unless they become involved in violent or extremist activity, which has happened several times in recent years.

The movement surged after the deadly confrontations at Ruby Ridge, Idaho in 1992 and Waco, Texas in 1993, where anti-government groups clashed with federal authorities. Membership dropped during the Bush administration, but rebounded with the Obama election. Many of these people believe an Obama re-election will mean the end of the republic, the rise of socialism, and "November 7, 2012 will be the start of the next civil war." The FBI has warned that as these groups increase in size, the chances of contact with law enforcement increase, along with the chances that some incidents will end in violence which, like Ruby Ridge and Waco, could result in still more violence.

"Bad" news is much more common than "good" news. Here are some headlines from my in-basket as of today:
• "How Big Food won the childhood obesity war" examines the effects of lobbyists on efforts to curb childhood obesity: 24 states and five cities considered "soda taxes" to discourage consumption of sugary drinks — all were dropped or defeated. Four federal agencies proposed a plan to reduce sugar, salt and fat in food marketed to children: Congress (and lobbyists) killed it. After aggressive lobbying, Congress failed to eliminate pizza from a nutritional overhaul of the school lunch program by declaring it a vegetable.
• Trustees of the Social Security system said the fund will run out in 2033, three years sooner than they projected last year.
• The World Economic Forum declared that the U.S. has tumbled further down a global ranking of the world's most

competitive economies, landing at fifth place because of its huge deficits and declining public faith in government.

• Highland Park, Michigan, with $58 million in debt and a population of 12,000 (half the level of 20 years ago) reduced its $60,000 a month electric bill by ripping out 1,000 streetlights, bulbs, poles and all. Other cities have simply turned off the lights, and many others have cut back on trash collection and street maintenance, closed libraries, and reduced police forces.

On the "good" side we hear that an office building designed to last 250 years, and with no electricity or water bills, is being built in Seattle, Washington. Designing, building, and living in sustainable cities (another important topic we haven't covered here) presents untold possibilities for a new American Dream. Good news does exist, but it can be hard to find.

Along with the good and the bad, there is much that's merely... shall we say "interesting;" stuff that proves that the world is truly changing. In this category:

• "Products that Gen Y will not buy." Newspapers, of course. Beer. *Cars!* That's very interesting: there is hope, after all. But they don't use e-mail because it's too slow, too formal, too old-fashioned? Time spent on e-mail by the 12-to-17-year-old age group dropped 59% from December 2009 to December 2010; goodness only knows what it might be now. (For comparison purposes: among those 65 and older, it increased 28%.)

• Three of ten adults ages 25-34 are living with their parents — and 78% say they're okay with that. (The Pew survey didn't ask the parents what they thought.)

• The five largest employers of Gen-Yers (aged 18-29) are 1, Armed Forces; 2, Wal-Mart; 3, Starbucks; 4, Target; 5, Best Buy. McDonald's is #6.

• "Gross National Product has long been the yardstick by which economies and politicians have been measured," noted United Nations Secretary-General Ban Ki-moon at a U.N. meeting called *Happiness and Well-being: Defining a New Economic Paradigm.* "Yet," he said, "it fails to take into account the social and environmental costs of so-called progress," concluding that the world needs a new economic model based on "gross global happiness" instead of making money.

• The latest item about the state of the world to catch my attention is particularly apt because it's seemingly as far off the subject as any other delightful side trip we've taken so far; it encompasses capitalism, democracy, environmental health, culture, and almost everything else we've been discussing; and it demonstrates how pervasive the webs and butterfly wings have become. It's a book review of *Breasts: A Natural and Unnatural History*, by Florence Williams.

Science journalist Williams informs us that mammary glands are enormously mutable, growing and shrinking according to all kinds of hormonal and environmental cues. They build and dissolve the machinery of feeding, manufacture milk and adjust its quantity and composition, adding lipids and unique immune-boosting substances an infant requires. And they are extremely sensitive to estrogen-mimicking chemicals such as DDT and other "endocrine disruptors."

Scientists have so far identified 73 endocrine disruptors in everyday household products that are increasingly suspected as the reason half of American girls now reach puberty and sport breasts by age 10, raising the lifelong risk of breast cancer. "Avoid the exposure of young girls to these compounds," one scientist warned her.

She tried, enrolling herself and her 7-year-old daughter in a study evaluating household chemicals implicated in endocrine disruption. Urine tests showed that their chemical levels were far higher than expected.

After avoiding pleather, plastic-wrapped foods, scented deodorant and even bike helmets, there was some improvement, but not enough, especially in the daughter. "It's hard to keep little girls away from bubble bath and toenail polish, much less the vinyl seats of a school bus." True. It's hard to keep *anyone* away from dangers they aren't even aware of, and couldn't avoid in any event if they want to participate in the modern world.

"In fact, the whole prospect of trying to individually safeguard one's family from silent endocrine disruptors feels like a folly." It simply can't be done in any meaningful way without government intervention, she says. But we know how the capitalist-democracy convergence works. The system is the problem, not the solution.

What makes this particularly intriguing is that now we have moved beyond the American Dream: the webs have spread to the destiny of the entire human race.

Stories like these have been appearing for years, and new ones pop up every day. Combined with the other pieces of the mosaic, they tell a cautionary tale that is vastly different from the business-as-usual people, and those who are waiting for the old normal to return.

It cannot. The American Dream of the 19th and 20th centuries no longer exists, and it couldn't be fulfilled even if it did.

Younger generations might feel embittered because their legacy has been squandered by their parents and grandparents, but that's not exactly true, or fair, if we acknowledge the role of the capitalist democracy. Yes, mistakes have been made, many of them lamented from the beginning by those who believe in simple and self-sufficient living, by those who believe in "enough," or for that matter, by anyone who believes in leaving the world a better place than they found it.

But although it would be nice to leave a legacy, no generation actually owes the next one anything; there is no such thing as a free lunch, and no matter what the heritage, every generation has to make its own way with whatever resources are available.

However, there's a huge difference between not getting an inheritance and inheriting *debts* of more than $138,000 per citizen (the current amount, which is increasing every second)… as well as a world befouled and depleted by the insane desire to get more than enough. This is the tragedy.

Today, the opportunities lie in recognizing the mistakes and failures of the past and moving beyond them; in acknowledging the current state of the world and dealing with it; in forging new goals and ideals and working toward them.

The old American Dream is dead. Now the challenge is forming and working toward realizing a new one.

Epilogue

We have been looking at the webs that connect everything to everything else in enough detail to make it clear that untangling the threads and going back to where we got off the track is well nigh impossible. It would be like changing the design in a tapestry by undoing the warp and the woof and then trying to create a new pattern from the frazzled threads.

Most significantly, we have seen how closely and how well capitalism, democracy and producer-consumers work together to create a formidable *system*. Like a three-legged stool, each one needs the other two; a change to one will affect the others; and all three would fight any changes that would endanger the status quo. *Remember, the System is concerned with its own survival, not with the welfare of humanity or the planet.*

Yet the most basic problem remains: if there can be no infinite growth on a finite planet, but the System as it now stands cannot survive without infinite growth, what solutions are even possible?

Matching demand to supply

The one we have been strongly suggesting has been reducing the demands of the producer-consumers to a level the planet can provide for on a sustainable basis. And although we have taken great pains to point out that such voluntary simplicity could actually enhance human life, the recent uprisings — from Greece to Wisconsin to Spain — against various forms of "austerity" are clear indications that a move toward simplicity would require a tectonic shift in cultural attitudes. Apparently civilization isn't ready yet for its next giant leap forward.

An alternative would be to adopt a new system, perhaps reining in capitalism, democracy, or both, which would be anathema to many and even more disruptive.

Clearly, we have created a mess from which there is no easy or clean way out. Either the demand for growth will deplete and destroy the planet, or one of the three legs will collapse because the level of "enough" it requires will be unattainable: capitalism will run out of the consumers required to feed it (consumers will run out of money to support capitalism); democracy will fail to deliver what either consumers or capitalism deem to be "enough" (e.g. the "austerity" protests); and/or consumers will rebel against both capitalism and democracy for being deficient in providing what they consider to be enough.

None of these would provide a good choice... if we had a choice. We don't.

The solution is to adjust wants and needs to what the planet can provide on a sustainable basis — and ignoring pie-in-the-sky projections of future abundance of energy and other resources. This should have been done long ago. Now that so much damage has already been done it will be much more difficult, and shocking. But if we don't do it on our own, sooner or later nature will do it for us.

And this is one case where we can do something better than nature can: her methods will not be gentle.

Appendix: What next?

If you concur with some (or heaven forbid, all) of the conclusions I've drawn, you might be wondering what comes next. What can you do to protect yourself and your loved ones, how can you prepare for any of the possible eventualities?

Preparedness takes many forms, depending on your present assortment and level of skills and resources, your current situation and prospects for the immediate future, your level of concern and resultant commitment, and many others, including your age and physical condition. It can range from nothing more than having enough canned and dried food and a little cash on hand to see you through a few weeks of hard times to learning to garden to a full-fledged homestead with goats, chickens and rabbits, all the way to a full-bore survival shelter incorporating wind and solar power, water filters, gold and silver coins, complete with guns and ammo.

But if this is all new to you, start simple, and at the beginning.

By now we are very aware that in our consumer-oriented society, convenience is paramount. Most supermarkets carry less than a week's supply of food, most homes store only a few days' worth, and most cooks have no idea what's for supper before 4 P.M. This is part of our dependency on the System.

However, the can of beans you'll pick up at the grocery for tonight's meal didn't just appear on that shelf this morning: it was grown, harvested, canned, warehoused and transported by capitalist enterprises, very likely starting well over a year ago.

To be self-sufficient, a homesteader must plan ahead like a capitalist. At the most basic level, you need at least a few weeks' worth of basic food.

What's basic? Whatever you ordinarily eat that will store well. Don't make the mistake of stocking "survival foods" family members won't eat: something that doesn't appeal to you today won't taste any better when you really need it.

One easy way to get started is to simply add an extra can or two to your regular purchase of baked beans, Spam, soup or whatever, especially when they're on sale. After a few shopping trips your pantry will be filling up, and unless money is really tight, your budget will hardly notice.

Note that this is in no way escaping from the System! Doing your own warehousing is merely a first step in protecting yourself against unforeseen disruptions in the supply chain, whether due to a missed payday, severe weather, or other factor. Escaping requires doing more for yourself, taking over more of the services the System provides.

This is the time to start paying attention to from-scratch cooking. Dry beans and rice are much more economical than canned products, they can be prepared in many ways, they store well, and you can prepare them as easily as a giant commercial enterprise can. Pasta is also an excellent keeper. If you enjoy the more exotic legumes such as lentils, go for it.

Soup is a popular basic food, world-wide, and is well-adapted to dried grains and vegetables. Bouillon cubes have little nutrition and most are insanely salty, but one can transform a handful of ordinary ingredients into a delicious soup or stew. Bouillon cubes and pastes are available in many flavors and despite their shortcomings, they're very useful in perking up homestead cooking.

Dried mushrooms make excellent soup, and other mixes are available commercially. However, don't neglect the very best and cheapest soup of all: that which you make from yesterday's leftovers!

This is another art lost to the consumer society, perhaps thanks to convenient trash collection and garbage disposals. There is no recipe for hearty homemade soup made from whatever's in the refrigerator — garbage soup, if you will. A dab of leftover mashed potatoes with a bit of onion and some diced celery and carrots, even if slightly wilted, is not only economical and nutritious, but delicious. If you have some leftover meat — ham, chicken, beef, it makes no difference — all the better. Or use bouillon.

You can keep it simple — chicken and rice — or get fancy — avgolemono (Greek lemon soup) — which is actually quite simple too, once you get into home cooking. It's just chicken broth, eggs, rice, lemon and salt and pepper. French onion, another classic, is even simpler.

A homesteader *never* discards chicken bones without first simmering them for stock. Soup stock, meat or vegetable, is easily made from scraps most people toss. It's obviously better than the salt-laden nutrition-deficient bouillon in every way, but most people caught up in the consumer society can't "afford" it: they're too busy. "Poor" people with more time than money can actually eat better, if they so choose.

Unemployed, but not idle
It can take a little time, but that's one of the important points of this lesson: if a person is un- or under-employed and has more time than money, it makes perfectly good sense to put that time to good use, and save money, by working at self-sufficiency, starting with cooking from scratch. Spending the day moping or watching tv, then scrounging for dinner or going hungry, is insanity, yet many Americans follow that routine, oblivious to any alternatives. They have become like kept animals, unable to fend for themselves.

Earning your daily bread
Bread, the staff of life in nearly every human culture, is only slightly more complicated; and yes, it takes a little more time, but it's even more worthwhile. Bread baking is a surprisingly popular hobby with men, who can brag as pridefully about their crusty peasant or zesty sourdough bread as they do about their four-alarm chili and barbeque.

Most bakers use commercial flour, of course, the stuff bleached with either chlorine gas (which is deadly to humans) or benzoyl peroxide (an ingredient in acne medicine), treated with potassium bromate (a carcinogenic banned in most of the world but not the U.S.) to strengthen the dough, and other additives. Again, anyone who wants to make the effort can enjoy a superior product at a reduced cost, by grinding whole wheat kernels (called berries) in a hand-operated flour mill. Obviously this results in a fresh product that has no need for preservatives to keep it saleable for months after processing.

The huge advantage for a survival pantry is that properly stored wheat berries will keep for years. They also have many uses. Besides providing flour for muffins, biscuits, pancakes and other bread-type products, flour is used as a thickener for soups and stews and a coating for fried foods, and the berries can be cooked (whole or cracked) as a cereal, or sprouted for greens. Play with it some more and create bulgur, or Turkish Delight (made with wheat starch, which incidentally has many interesting uses including faux meat products).

There are entire books on "rules" for making bread. Many of them contradict each other, proof that there are no rules. Kneading methods, yeast amounts and temperatures, ingredients, rising times, oven temperatures — all are infinitely variable and subject to personal preferences. I have baked bread in a wood-fired brick oven at more than 500° and in a solar oven that only reached 250°. The results were different of course, but both were entirely acceptable.

My mother made terrific bread, but it took me many years to match hers. It's odd, but once I got the knack it became almost impossible to botch a batch!

The only "secret" is to start with a recipe that appeals to you, and then experiment. Try other recipes, and tinker until you create something you like. Eventually, you'll become an expert.

However, the experimenting seldom ends, which is part of the fun. Bread can be made from many grains beside wheat and rye; it will become a different product with the addition of beer, milk, eggs or honey; and baking with sourdough is another experience altogether. No wonder baking offers so much satisfaction.

Two important points

We have now touched on two additional very important points. First, just as with stocking up even a small supply of canned goods, acquiring a hand grain mill and other tools will require some cash: yes, an investment in capital goods, meaning a durable (such as a tool) used in the production of other goods. This means you can't wait until the lights go out or until you're flat broke to begin your quest for self-sufficiency: you need to get a running start. Now.

The second point is that we're obviously getting a tad more technical: don't plan on making perfect bread, or a garden, or anything else, on the first try. Some products and activities require more knowledge and skill than others, but all will improve with experience. Again, you can't wait until the lights go out to start acquiring knowledge and experience.

Most people in the consumer society feel superior to their primitive peasant ancestors who were merely "dumb farmers." No doubt those ancestors could quickly learn to flip a light switch, appreciate running water, and probably even learn to use a computer or drive a car.

But how long would it take their supposedly superior college-educated descendents to learn how to butcher a hog, cure the meat and make sausage; milk a cow, make butter and cheese and yogurt; make bread, sauerkraut, pickles, jam, and the dozens of other goods people used to provide for themselves?

Our forebears didn't have college educations, but they learned the dozens of skills and trades required for the times they lived in from childhood on, by watching and working with their elders. They had knowledge most moderns can't even imagine, and will never acquire. (And they weren't nearly as miserable as today's small-screen addicts and couch potatoes like to suppose... or as advertisers of conveniences would like you to suppose.)

The Garden of Eden, revisited

No doubt most urbanites today, including the unemployed, are familiar with couponing and dumpster diving, two ways the freakishly frugal can survive on severely limited incomes. There's another route many will consider even more freakish, although it's perfectly logical, and has a much longer history, like 10,000 years. It's called foraging.

The first humans were foragers. Adam and Eve didn't plant the Garden of Eden: they merely gathered what grew there, naturally. Most people remained heavily dependent on wild foods until fairly recently, including in the United States. Even today, large numbers engage in berry picking, nut gathering, mushroom hunting and more, for both fun and fantastic flavors.

As crops became cultivated and improved, only a few were favored. No doubt you can count the varieties of vegetables you consume in a year on your fingers, but experienced foragers say there are probably 75 different varieties within walking distance of your home, even in the city.

Here knowledge is not only king, but essential, because some edible plants are very similar to poisonous ones, another branch of wisdom children used to absorb from their parents and grandparents and therefore knew "naturally."

In addition, every plant has its peak season. Many people who have eaten dandelions, for example, perhaps the most commonly foraged herb, recoiled at the bitter taste and swore off wild foods for good. They would have reacted the same to any over-mature vegetable from the garden. You have to know what you're harvesting, and when to harvest it.

If you weren't raised by an Earth Mother who taught you how to recognize and use the wild plants within your reach, you need a few field guides, and a mentor. Today, almost every area has at least one enthusiastic forager who is an expert on local flora and is eager to share knowledge and experience.

Our area is fortunate to have Sam Thayer, who says he lives on wild foods year-round thanks to drying, freezing and canning. Tagging behind him on an outing along an abandoned railroad right-of-way is an amazing experience. When you see a fellow plunge into what looks like a mass of brush and emerge with a basketful of dinner, it's difficult to comprehend the statistics that claim millions of Americans go to bed hungry!

Sam has written two field guides, lectures, and not long ago was featured on NPR, where he foraged for greens around the network's Washington D.C. headquarters. Within an hour he found chickweed, mallow, dandelion, prickly lettuce, shepherd's purse ("absolutely gourmet") sow thistle, and Siberian elm samaras (the small green seeds, which can amount to thousands of pounds per tree).

The same radio program contacted John Kallas, a wild food expert, Ph.D. nutritionist, teacher and author. One reason the Mediterranean diet is so healthful, he said, is the inclusion of so many wild greens. Greeks were among the healthiest people in the world, he said: "No heart disease, less dementia with old age, almost no cancers, period!"

His research into the nutritional value of wild greens shows they are generally more nutritious than supermarket spinach — and certainly more than iceberg lettuce which is California's way of exporting water. Mustard garlic has the highest levels of nutrients of any leafy green analyzed, being high in vitamin A, beta carotene, zinc, manganese and fiber.

Dandelions are just as good, providing much more iron and calcium than even spinach. One wag said that if the FDA knew what was in dandelions, they'd ban them.

Speaking of which, herbal tonics and remedies are yet another field of study with great potential for an uncertain future. Here of course, an experienced and trusted guide is even more important.

Hunting and fishing can be considered foraging. However, during the Great Depression, such game was virtually wiped out in many areas, even though most game wardens had little sympathy for hungry poachers.

Gardening is more basic and the absolute foundation of self-sufficient living, although not a sure thing either, especially with climate change. Equipment requirements are minimal, but good organic soil — and experience — are essential. Look back through the sections on gardening in this book for ideas on what to look for in your library or on the web. If you haven't already started gardening, do it now, even if only in containers on the patio.

After the garden, as we have seen in *The War Garden Victorious,* comes preserving the harvest, perhaps by freezing but probably canning and certainly drying. Here again, an investment in equipment will be required, although it's common for some people to share expensive canning kettles and dehydrators without considering it socialism.

The bottom line

This only scratches the surface: independent, self-sufficient, sustainable living can encompass much more. In fact, it can replace much of the entire capitalist democracy System, including those elements that are most destructive of our environment, and our psyches.

But please note this: for some people, everything we have mentioned here and more that we have not is considered a *hobby.* It's not onerous, it's not a job, it's not done on a schedule for a boss, it's not done to accumulate wealth. It's practical, economical, useful and *fun!*

What's more, it's intellectually and morally satisfying and personally fulfilling, providing a sense of purpose and accomplishment.

How many people chained to their workstations can make that claim?

Seen in that light, could this become the New Normal?

Anything is possible.

Small Stock Magazine was founded in 1917; *Countryside* was founded by Jerome D. Belanger in 1969; the two were combined as *Countryside & Small Stock Journal* in 1973.

The Homestead Philosophy, which appears in every issue, is the driving force behind *"ENOUGH!"*

THE HOMESTEAD PHILOSOPHY

IT'S NOT A SINGLE IDEA, BUT MANY IDEAS AND ATTITUDES, INCLUDING A REVERENCE FOR NATURE AND A PREFERENCE FOR COUNTRY LIFE; A DESIRE FOR MAXIMUM PERSONAL SELF-RELIANCE AND CREATIVE LEISURE; A CONCERN FOR FAMILY NURTURE AND COMMUNITY COHESION; A CERTAIN HOSTILITY TOWARD LUXURY; A BELIEF THAT THE PRIMARY REWARD OF WORK SHOULD BE WELL-BEING RATHER THAN MONEY; A CERTAIN NOSTALGIA FOR THE SUPPOSED SIMPLICITIES OF THE PAST AND AN ANXIETY ABOUT THE TECHNOLOGICAL AND BUREAUCRATIC COMPLEXITIES OF THE PRESENT AND THE FUTURE; AND A TASTE FOR THE PLAIN AND FUNCTIONAL.

COUNTRYSIDE REFLECTS AND SUPPORTS THE SIMPLE LIFE, AND CALLS ITS PRACTITIONERS *HOMESTEADERS.*

To learn more about *Countryside* visit
www.countryside.com.

For more ideas on what's involved in
sustainable self-sufficient living and how to get
started, see *The Complete Idiot's Guide to Self-
Sufficient Living,* by Jerome D. Belanger.

About the author:

In 1961 Jerome D. Belanger launched *The Wisconsinite* magazine, which evolved into the Countryside Print Shop, which became Countryside Publications, Ltd., publishing six back-to-the-land magazines and operating the Countryside General Store, which offered tools and supplies for sustainable, self-reliant living.

Now run by the second generation, the family-owned company publishes *Countryside & Small Stock Journal; Backyard Poultry; sheep!* and *Dairy Goat Journal* in Medford, Wisconsin.

Jerry and Diane are avid gardeners on their homestead in northern Wisconsin.